D1610551

*My Life with Boris*

# My Life with Boris

## Naina Yeltsina

ALMA BOOKS

ALMA BOOKS LTD
3 Castle Yard
Richmond
Surrey TW10 6TF
United Kingdom
www.almabooks.com

*My Life with Boris* first published in Russian in 2017
This translation first published by Alma Books Ltd in 2020

Text © Naina Yeltsina, 2017, 2020

Translation © Alma Books Ltd

The illustrations in this volume, sourced from the Yeltsin family archive
and the collections of Dmitry Donskoy and Yuri Feklistov, are reproduced
courtesy of the B.N. Yeltsin Presidential Center. All rights reserved.

Cover: nathanburtondesign.com

Printed in Great Britain by CPI Group (UK) Ltd, Croydon CR0 4YY

ISBN: 978-1-84688-466-5

*My Life with Boris*

# Author's Note

I don't like publicity. I try to avoid doing interviews. I only began to agree to them after Boris died. Now it is my duty to my husband. In the years since his death, a generation has grown up that knows little about the first president of Russia and about 1990s politics. It has become fashionable to tell horror stories about that era, and not everyone can distinguish between truth and lies. I see quite young people at the Boris Yeltsin Museum in Yekaterinburg, and I can see that they are discovering the recent history of their country right before my eyes. This history turns out not to be as hopeless as they have been told. I have observed how they are simply glued to screens showing interviews taped for the museum with eyewitnesses and people who took part in the events of the 1990s.

When we speak honestly of the hope with which we lived in the 1990s and don't hide the problems and pains that accompanied it, we are believed. What I saw in the museum of Russia's first president became an important moment for me. Before, I was certain I was recording my memoirs only for my grandchildren and great-grandchildren. My daughters tried to talk me into turning my stories into a book, but I didn't agree. Only after the opening of the museum did I understand – they were right. And although at the time I never felt like the wife of a president, I realize that for almost ten years I stood by the side of a person who was responsible for an enormous and very complex country at a defining moment in its history. I saw a lot that had huge significance for the new Russia from very close by, and that is how it turned out – my personal life became part of Russia's history.

This book is not a historical essay, and I do not claim to portray a full picture of events. These are not the memoirs of a politician – I am not attempting to analyse societal problems. This is not literary prose – I wrote in the language I speak. To be honest, as an author, I have only two virtues: I cannot bear a lack of accuracy – I try to be precise in details – and I am unable to embellish facts.

– Naina Yeltsina

# Editor's Note

While Naina Iosifovna was preparing this manuscript for publication, we spoke at length, of course, and I could not stop myself asking questions. I recorded her answers on a tape recorder in the hope that we could transcribe them together later, but this turned out to be impossible. There are certain things about which, for various reasons, a person will not talk – unless they are asked about it specifically. I asked – and I really wanted our conversations to be part of the book. I'm glad that Naina Iosifovna agreed. This is how my "Questions on the Margins" have come to be in her memoirs.

– Ludmila Telen

# NAYA GIRINA

# An Attempt at a Genealogy

My very first memory is from Titovka – a village with which our whole family history is associated:

I am in a cottage. I am probably about four years old; I am lying on a Russian stove and my ear aches badly. A pillow is being warmed for me so I can warm my ear. My grandfather is stroking my leg – he obviously feels very sorry for me. I think it was winter. This is my first memory of Titovka. After that trip, I only went there in the summer – but I went every year, throughout nearly my whole childhood. The last time I went was in 1946, when I was fourteen years old.

According to historical archives, Titovka (which is approximately 150 kilometres from Orenburg) was founded in 1928 by a citizen of the Ryazan and Voronezh Governorates. Peasants from Central Russia began to settle in the area during the time of Catherine II, but were considered state serfs. The neighbouring village was called Khokhly, and Ukrainians lived there. A little farther afield was the Tatar village of Mustafino. There were no mixed marriages between Russians and Tatars, but I don't recall any conflicts.

Both my mother and father had the same last name: Girin. They were probably very distant relatives – there were a lot of Girins in Titovka. There were also a lot of Zhdanovs, Podkovyrovs and Samorukovs – people referred to one another by nicknames rather than their last names. Children, on the other hand, were known by their father's or mother's name. If the mother was Alexandra – or "Lyoksa", as they would say in Titovka – her children were called Lyoksiny, or "Lyoka's". If the father was called Konstantin, the children would be called "Kostiny". There were Maksimkiny, Anyutkiny… The children of my grandmother Domashi were called "Domashkiny".

Apparently, the founder of our village was called Tit Podkovyrov. The maiden name of my great-grandmother, Vassa Nikitichna Girina, was Podkovyrova. Birth certificates state that her son, my grandfather Alyosha, was married in 1908 to Matryona Timofeyevna when he was twenty-two years old, and in 1910 their son Iosif, my papa, was born in Titovka. Later, they had two daughters: Vassa was born in 1917 and Yekaterina was born in 1923.

My mama's parents, Fyodor Fomich Girin and Domna Gavrilovna Samorukova, were married on 5th November 1899. In 1912 – there is a note on the birth certificate – my mama Mariya was born, and three years later her sister Anna was born.

*Questions on the Margins*

"Why did you begin searching for information about your family's past? Was it fashionable to do so?"

"My grandchildren began asking me questions, and I suddenly realized that I didn't know anything, really, about my grandparents. It's strange, but while they were alive it never occurred to me to ask them anything – the same with my parents: we never spoke of the past. It was somehow not right – or rather, we just weren't keen on it. I don't even know exactly where I was born…"

"According to the documents, it was in Titovka."

"Yes, I know that – and soon after my parents married, they moved to Orenburg (known as 'Chkalov' back then). Did my mama return to Titovka when she was about to give birth? Or did they go to Orenburg only after I was brought into the world? While my parents were alive, I wasn't interested in this, and now there is no one to ask."

Mama and Papa had known each other since childhood – you could almost say since birth. Their homes were near each other. They studied in the same school – there was no other in the village. Mama's mother told me that at first they didn't want Papa as their son-in-law. They had in mind some other young man, from a more well-to-do family – who, as my grandmother said, "was very good with his hands". But Mama loved Papa very much and insisted on having her way. Papa served his stint in the army, and in 1930 they were married. In 1932 I was born.

My name also has an interesting history. The name I was given at birth was Anastasiya, but for short I was always called Naya. This isn't just true of me, though – I have some acquaintances in Orenburg called Anastasiya whose names are shortened to "Naya" by their families to this day. So, at home, I was called Naya from birth. "Naya" turned into "Naina" when I was about ten years old.

Papa liked how I watched over younger children, and said that I should be a teacher. But it seemed to him that the children wouldn't be able to pronounce "Anastasiya Iosifovna" – "Naina Iosifovna" was easier. When my friends came over, they heard how my parents addressed me. Igor Bogdanov, a boy in our friendship group, would greet me at social gatherings with a paraphrase of Pushkin's line from *Ruslan and Lyudmila*: "O knight! Here comes Naina!" And that's how it was – to my family and friends I was Naya or Naina, and Anastasiya according to my documents. I liked both names. A school friend from the Institute told me only recently that Boris, when he heard my name, told his classmates, "Let's call her 'Nastya'…" But it didn't work – I was already "Naya" to everyone.

Mix-ups with my name began at work. I would go on a business trip with ID saying "Anastasiya", but my colleagues called me "Naina" – and the questions would begin. Or the chief engineer of the Institute would come into the office and address me as "Anastasiya Iosifovna" and I wouldn't react. Eventually, I grew so sick of this that one day, on my way home from a trip with a colleague, I went into the register office (which just so happens to be the very same one where Boris and I would register our marriage in 1956) and asked, "Can I change the name on my passport?" The CRO official said "Of course" – and then she asked why. "I've been called 'Naina' since childhood, and I can't get used to

'Anastasiya'." She was surprised. "Such a pretty name – everybody is called 'Nastya' nowadays…" Nevertheless, it turned out to be easy to change – I wrote a statement and brought in my documents. Boris was away on a business trip, and only when I received my new passport did I show it to my husband. He didn't react at all, and didn't say a word. But he called me "girl" for a rather long time after that – he didn't call me "Naya" or "Naina". If he had asked me then to put my name back to "Anastasiya", I would have done so, without a doubt. But he didn't ask.

## Questions on the Margins

"Did Boris Nikolayevich really like the name 'Anastasiya' better than 'Naina'?"

"He didn't say so at the time, but in later years he spoke with regret of my changing my name. He really did like the name 'Anastasiya' a lot. 'Why did you stay quiet when I changed the name on my passport, then?' I asked him. He replied: 'That was how you decided it.' That was, in general, his nature – he was a very tactful person. We returned to this topic a number of times. One day, out of the blue, Boris proposed to the children: 'Let's call Mama "Nastya"!' Of course, everyone decided against it – the whole world already called me 'Naina'… But for some reason the topic kept coming up again and again.

"Once, when we were holidaying in the South with the Chernomyrdins, Boris and Viktor Stepanovich (Chernomyrdin) called me 'Nastya' for an entire evening. Another time, Galina Pavlovna Vishnevskaya proposed calling me by a double-barrelled name. We laughed."

"And you never regretted changing your name?"

"It's not an issue that ever bothered me. Although I do remember I once said to Galina Pavlovna Vishnevskaya, 'When I die, let them put "Naina-Anastasiya" on the headstone'… But even though my life has been lived with two names, both lived peacefully within me."

# Childhood Memories

Papa worked in the militarized security at the Orenburg Railway. I think it was due to his service in the army that he ended up in the railway troops – after he completed his service, he decided to move to the city, and he found a job where his army experience came in handy. He almost always wore a railway uniform – a tunic and breeches. Papa only got as far as eighth grade at school – but completed the last two years as an adult in evening classes, and loved studying for the rest of his life. He joined the Party early. He graduated from the Party school – the evening university of Marxism-Leninism – and travelled to some course or other in Kharkiv. He wrote very correctly.

In 1934, he was transferred to the city of Chelkar in Kazakhstan – something to do with the running of the Orenburg Railway. My recollections of that time are rather fragmented. That is understandable: we went to Chelkar when I was seven years old. Even so, some memories of our life in that city are preserved clearly.

I remember endless sands stretching to the horizon, the heavy frost in the winter and the dry heat in the summer. The sand would get so hot that we children could poach eggs in it. We would sprinkle hot sand on a raw egg and, when the sand cooled, roll the egg to a new place and once again sprinkle hot sand on it. We would do that several times, and as a result the egg could be eaten, although the egg white was a little runny. Sometimes we would hide the eggs from one another, and then try to find them – so they were a food and a game at the same time.

Another recollection: one year, on 1st May, Mama and Papa went to visit someone. Mama wore a long chiffon scarf, which blew in the wind. The scarf was bright and semi-transparent – I had never seen it before. Mama would rarely dress up – there was never really an occasion for it. Another time, when my parents were getting ready to go out, I asked Mama if I could have that scarf – but of course I couldn't tie it the way she had. I simply wrapped myself in it. I didn't wear it for long – it was so hot I had to take it off. Later, when I went to study in Sverdlovsk, Mama gave that scarf to me. I wore it for many years.

Here is an episode that has stuck in my memory – I understood its meaning only years later. One day Papa, returning home from work, took down a portrait from the wall that had apparently been cut out of a magazine. He folded it four times, took the photograph of his parents down from the wall and hid the portrait behind the backing. Mama asked what had happened. "Now Marshall Vasily Blyukher is an enemy of the people," said Papa. And he added a phrase – I don't remember it word for word, but the sense of it was: "Time will tell." For some reason, he didn't tear up the portrait of Blyukher – he didn't burn it, he didn't throw it away: he hid it. Decades later, I tried to find that portrait; I asked my brother to look through the old photographs. He found the picture of Papa's relatives in a frame, but nothing behind it.

\* \* \*

In 1939, Papa was transferred to the Emba Station – this was also in Kazakhstan, but closer to Orenburg. We moved into a three-storey building: there were several such buildings at the station. The railway workers' families lived in our building. We occupied two rooms of a three-room apartment. Our neighbour had also once worked at the railway, but when we moved to Emba she was already retired. To me, my sister Roza and my brother Lyonya, she was simply "babushka", or "grandmother". In fact, she took the place of our grandmother – she looked after us when Mama was out, she fed us… Her help was really needed when in 1944 a fourth child – Tolya – was born.

In Emba, I started school. In 1941 I was in second grade.

Papa wanted to go to the front, but he was left in the rearguard, "in defence". The railway was a strategic component, and work there equated to military service. Papa was often away on various trips, accompanying freight. He was usually only away for a day or two, but due to unforeseen complications or inspections he could often be delayed. Sometimes, when he returned, he would say: "They opened up a train carriage." Although the culprits were severely punished, there were even robberies during the war years. I remember that Papa would often say, "How could they not be afraid?"

Of course, we did not understand the full horror of the war, but we saw the constant fear in the eyes of the adults. The words "once again a city surrendered" rang in our ears… Everyone was afraid that the Germans would take Moscow. In fifth grade, we began to learn the German language. Our teacher, I now realize, was a Volga German. We definitely didn't want to study German – why did we need to speak the language spoken by our enemy?

For some reason, I don't have detailed recollections of school, although I attended it from first to fifth grade. All I remember is the faces of almost all of my classmates – but I have forgotten their names, except for my first school friend, Ali Kulagina. Her parents had been evacuated from the Baltics. Amazingly, I remember the name of the place where they lived: Zasulauks. Many years later, I learnt that this was a suburb of Riga, but at that time I only knew that Alya had come to us from somewhere far away – from a territory occupied by the Germans.

I also remember Valya Korostylyov, who lived in the house across the street. Sometimes I saw him in the window, and I always hoped I would meet him when I went over to visit Alya. This was the first time I fell in love – from a distance.

During most of the war years, there was a shortage of regular notebooks, so instead we wrote on notebooks sewn together from cut-up newspapers. In order to see our writing more clearly, we made the ink thicker by chipping lead into it from a pencil.

Later, Boris told me about the terrible famine in the Urals, which his family endured during the war. A piece of half-baked bread mixed in part with bran was shared between everyone – and then there was no more food for the entire day. We lived more comfortably, of course. We had our own kitchen garden during the war years, where we grew potatoes, watermelons, melons and pumpkins. Mama would bake the pumpkins in the winter. I can still remember their sweet taste – which was most probably made all the better because we were always hungry. Later, at our dacha near Moscow, I began to grow pumpkins myself. Of course, they were nothing like the ones I ate in my childhood. In Emba, the pumpkins grew huge – as big as a wheel – and were white on the outside, with juicy, yellow pulp inside – a special sort that I have never come across anywhere else.

What saved us from starving was not only our kitchen garden, but also help from our relatives from Titovka. Both Mama's and Papa's parents had their own farms – with cows, sheep and chickens. And, of course, kitchen gardens where they grew not only vegetables but wheat, rye and millet. In Titovka, on the whole, everyone lived fairly well. Although the farmers turned in a large portion of the produce to the State, something remained for their families. When we returned to Emba after the summer holidays, we were given grain and flour – just as much as we could carry.

In the summer of 1943, Grandfather Alyosha gave us money to buy a cow. The cow lived with us for a year, or perhaps a little longer – thanks to her, there was always milk at home for the children. But one day, as Mama told us, the cow was "led away". We kept her in a dilapidated barn not far from our house, and it was not particularly hard to open the door. We don't know who "led her away". There was talk of some exiled Chechens in the area – perhaps it was them who did it. There weren't many Chechens in Emba, so they stood out – they wore big fur hats called "Chechenki". They were a sorry sight – thin, eternally hungry, living in temporary huts made out of any materials they had to hand. The locals would give them something to eat occasionally – especially when the watermelons, melons and pumpkins were ripe. I remember Papa was sorting through the potatoes near our cellar one day when a Chechen came up to him and asked for help – Papa dumped some potatoes into a large cloth sack for him. People were afraid of the Chechens in Emba – even the children were afraid of them, but they pitied them more, and they didn't mistreat them. Of course, I didn't understand how they had ended up in Kazakhstan. Chechens were simply part of our lives. I learnt of their deportation in 1944 only later, when I was quite grown up.

Really the only delicacy for us in those years was dried milk, which came in a sort of large white pancake. The dried milk could be crumbled and chewed for a very long time, and it had a slightly sweet taste. Kazakh women sold it at the railway station. When we didn't have any money, they would break off a piece and give it to us for free. We ran every day to the railway station to get it; like all children, I loved sweets. To this day, I remember the taste of Mama's "rooster" candies and sugar boiled in milk. In those years, there was no granulated sugar: there was only a lump of sugar that Papa would very neatly cut with a knife to make exact little cubes. In my native Titovka there was only one type of candy sold in the local shop – colourful "little pillows": there were no other sweets there.

No matter how hard everyday life was during the war years, there are also joyful scenes preserved in my memory. Tulips bloomed along the River Emba in the spring. The terrain there was rugged – hills interspersed with meadows – but the tulips covered them with colourful carpets: at first white, then yellow, and later red. They said there were black tulips growing somewhere, but I never saw them. It's strange – the colours never mixed. We gathered armfuls of these steppe flowers (for some reason we called them "field flowers") and brought them home to give to our neighbours. We didn't have vases – we put them in jars, pots and cans.

They lasted a long time before wilting – perhaps because we changed the water often, and maybe because it was ice-cold: the water was from the pump. Once, I talked about these childhood memories at a meeting of the heads of the Commonwealth of Independent States which took place in our presidential residence.

After that, the Kazakh President Nursultan Nazarbayev and the Ukrainian President Leonid Kuchma would wish me a happy birthday by sending huge baskets of tulips.

In early 1945, Papa was transferred to Orenburg. My parents went with the younger children – Roza and Tolya – and left Lyonya and me in the care of our neighbour until the end of the school year. I remember, during the move, Mama wanted to take the house plants with her – two roses and a ficus plant. The roses were so huge that they had to be left in Emba, but they managed to squeeze the ficus into the freight carriage.

I lived with Lyonya, who was nine years old at the time, in two half-empty rooms without curtains, without Mama and Papa. Our neighbour, the "babushka", made us meals and washed and ironed our clothes. She had long since become an honorary member of the family, and my parents left Lyonya and me with her with no qualms.

On 9th May 1945, Emba celebrated Victory Day – quite differently to how it was marked in Moscow: there were no fireworks, no evening festivities, but it still felt like a holiday. Not far from our home were several big reservoirs. In order to prevent the water from overheating in the summer or freezing in the winter, they were covered with earth, and they looked like little hills. During the Victory Day celebrations, boards were put over them, creating a podium for speakers. There were lots of people around, hugging each other, making noise and rejoicing. I think there were also loudspeakers, from which music could be heard. I remember well the feeling, which was like that of a festival.

The days went by, and the school year came to an end. Lyonya and I waited for the day when our parents would come to collect us. To this day, I get upset remembering what happened during those days in May, although it was more than seventy years ago.

The little boys in Emba collected animal bones – big ones – and drilled holes in them, into which they poured lead to make heavy balls called *asychki*. They used them to play a game that had its own rules. The lead could be melted only on hot coals; parents didn't give coal to their children, of course – the boys collected it at a railway siding, where engines were shunted off the main tracks.

One day Lyonya went along with his older friends to collect coal. As I understood later from the grown-ups' stories, he saw some lumps of coal on the tracks behind a train, and made towards them. Just at that moment, the engine driver pulled the whistle – my brother probably thought the train was going to move forwards, and it seems he quickly lay down on the tracks, so he could be the first to reach the coal. But the engine driver, who hadn't seen him, moved in the reverse direction... Lyonya was killed instantly.

I learnt about what had happened from our neighbours. This was a huge tragedy for everyone. The engine driver lived in a nearby house – our families were friends. Mama, who was summoned from Orenburg, was in a terrible state, of course. Papa came a little later, and tried to support her as much as he could. On the same hill where the victory had just been celebrated, they placed the little coffin on stools. Mama threw her arms around it and sobbed convulsively. For many years, Mama and Papa went to visit Lyonya's grave in Emba. Sometimes Papa went on his own.

Time went by, but Mama could not recover from the tragedy. She would cry quietly all the time. I noticed that she had tears streaming down her cheeks, no matter what she did – whether cooking dinner or washing or sewing. She only began to recover when Volodya was born, in 1947. She had to pull herself together – our younger brother was born, and Tolya hadn't even turned three yet. Once again, we had four children in the family.

\* \* \*

1947 was the first year in which I didn't go to Titovka for the summer. Mama didn't let me go: my brothers were still quite small; she needed my help – I was already fifteen, after all.

Even before that, as I recall, Mama hadn't joined me in spending the summer with our relatives – in 1945 and 1946, Mama brought me to Titovka and then returned to the city. I remained there all summer. The village was very beautiful – it had a kind of soft beauty – and was rather large, divided into five kolkhoz brigades, or "collective farms". My grandparents were in the second brigade.

I would wake up in the morning and the shutters would still be closed – it was dark, but through the cracks bright sunrays shone through. It was still early – I could hear the roosters crowing. I heard the voice of one of my grandmothers, Motya or Domasha, calling, "Have you woken up yet, Granddaughter?" I would take it in turns staying with my mother's parents and my father's parents – my grandmothers would be very cross if this routine was broken.

When they made blini for breakfast, I would run to the cellar, which was covered over with animal skins in order to preserve the ice collected earlier in the spring. Cellars were not locked in Titovka. Milk, cream and farmer's cheese were kept on a block of ice; sometimes meat was kept there as well: all our relatives slaughtered their lambs in turn and shared them between several homes. In the cellar, I would stick my finger into every pot and take a taste of the cream. Then I would return home with a pot. We always had farmer's cheese, sour cream and heavy cream on the table. All the food was cooked on a Russian stove, in what were called "skulls" – brown clay pots. If we didn't eat all the blini, Grandmother would pour cream on them and leave them soaking on the stove. Then they would be cut up with a knife, like a pie. I still do this today – and my daughters, although they try not to eat fattening things, can't turn down this delicious rustic food.

*Questions on the Margins*

"Do you really still do your own cooking?"

"Yes, I often do. Boris and I had a tradition of family dinners on Sundays. After he passed away, I continued to gather everybody together; when the weather allows it, we eat by the large Russian stove near the house."

"The stove is outside? Why?"

"The food cooked on a Russian stove always turns out very special. I always wanted such a stove, but there was no space for it in the house. I decided that we would put it outside, next to a big table, under an awning – when the children and grandchildren visit, we have dinner here, as a rule. If the weather is good, of course. The stove was installed in the traditional way – I even phoned people in Titovka to find out what size a Russian stove should be. No one remembers any more – they all have hobs and ovens nowadays. Then I found a heritage stove craftsman, who was from the Volga – he is a young man, but his great-grandfather and grandfather installed stoves. It was all done very professionally. My grandchildren love to climb up on the stove. In the summer, we dry apples from our garden on top of it."

My grandmothers baked *chinyonki* – sweet pies with sorrel – which are a speciality in Titovka, and have a bittersweet taste. We also made them with wild strawberries, or sometimes with *poznika*, which is what we called nightshade. There were two types of nightshade in our garden: black and green. When Grandma took me to weed the garden, she'd let me eat the nightshade right from the bushes. Although it was wild, it was not weeded out – it was left between the rows of potatoes and millet.

We made *shchi* (cabbage soup) and *kulyosh* – a soup seasoned with millet. In the summer, very often we would have *okroshka*. A hard-boiled egg would be crumbled into kvas, a drink made from fermented rye bread. Chopped onion, dill and cucumbers would be added. I don't think it even had potatoes in it. No meat. We made the kvas ourselves, of course, and it was – as they said in Titovka – "invigorating". You definitely also had to add grated radish and sour cream.

For supper, we would have either potatoes with meat or *pelmeni*, a kind of dumpling, with potatoes, but in the summer we would not usually cook meat. We would chop the potato with a *sechka* – a short hatchet with a round blade – into a special wooden trough (not so long ago I was given an almost identical *sechka* and trough, and I use them to this day). In Titovka, we made the *pelmeni* larger, like *vareniki*, another sort of stuffed dumpling, and not small, as they do in the Middle Urals, where Boris grew up.

We baked bread ourselves twice a week. It was wrapped in hand towels so it wouldn't get stale, and it was called "pie". My childhood pleasure was to cut off a piece and dip it into heavy cream or sour cream – to this day, nothing seems more tasty to me.

Even now I can see all the details of this village life – I can describe them quite precisely; I remember not only where the houses were, but also the flowers and their scents.

My paternal grandparents' *izba*, or cottage, was smaller than my maternal grandparents' home. The house was at the end of the street. The front door led through wooden vestibules to a long plank table and a rough-hewn bed, where Granddad loved to rest in the summer when it was hot. Beyond the vestibules was a room where a large iron-framed bed stood. Then there was a room with homespun rugs. In that room was Papa's sister Katya's bed. It had a coverlet, from under which peeped a crocheted lace runner. And from this room you could enter the kitchen with the Russian stove.

Mama's sister Anna also crocheted lace, and there was a lot of it in the house. I can still remember a crocheted tablecloth, throws on a hill of pillows with a *dumka*, or little cushion, on top and lace stitching on the pillowcases. The lace and the bedlinen were light, and the blankets were bright. They were sewn from multicoloured scraps, which were usually square in shape, but sometimes a square was sewn from four different triangles – the finished thing was very pretty.

The bedlinen was made from hemp, which everyone grew in their kitchen garden (the grandmothers had looms, but I never saw them working on them, for some reason). After washing the sheets, in order to make them softer, they were beaten with a rolling pin, village-style: they would be wrapped around the rolling pin and then beaten with a *valyok* – a long wooden stick – or a *rubel* – a board which was corrugated on one side. There were also irons, which were heated with coal – they were only used to iron blouses and skirts.

My maternal grandparents' large, bright house stretched out along the street. There was a front garden where mallow and white roses grew – this is probably why, to this day, I love to plant them wherever I live; I even planted them at the presidential residence in Barvikha – where, of course, these village flowers were not grown before I arrived. I remember how we once drove up to the residence and I saw from the car window mallow bushes on the side of the road. A day or two later, I returned there on the commuter train with one of my grandsons. We dug up the bush and returned to the residence and planted it there. The guards reprimanded me later for travelling without an escort. Those mallow bushes took very well. Later I replanted them – now they are growing around the gazebo at my house. As well as the mallow, there were lilacs in my grandmother's front garden, although I never saw them bloom – the summer holidays began when the lilacs were already past blooming.

For fuel, people in Titovka used *kizyak*, or pressed dung, which was made during the summer. I happily took part in this. The process was very simple. We collected dung, mixed with straw, from the stables. The straw served as bedding for the cattle, which were kept in a cold building. The straw was changed every day, so a lot of dried dung accumulated over the winter. In the summer, we added water to it. A horse was made to walk around in a circle to crush this mass of straw. Then, with the help of a special wooden mould (called a *stanok*), we would put the crushed straw on the grass. The mould made two *kizyaks*. I was given a lighter *stanok* to hold, and made just one *kizyak*. The *kizyaks* were shaped like bricks, although they were about one and a half times larger. They were dried in the sun – first on one side, then on the other. All the smells were thus aired out. We didn't know of any other type of fuel in Titovka. What firewood could you get when all that was around was the steppe? The *kizyaks* were stacked up, sometimes under the roof and sometimes simply under the open sky, covered over with straw to protect them from the rain. You could get a lot of heat from a *kizyak* – and in the winter, I was told, it was warm in the cottages.

A nameless creek – now called Klyuch – ran through the village. Each home on that side of the road had little kitchen gardens out front, where cucumbers, tomatoes, onions and dill were grown – these gardens ran down towards the river. And the "big kitchen gardens", as they were called, were at the back, where the livestock was kept. Potatoes, carrots and peas were planted there, as well as wheat, rye and millet. Many people had barns in front of their vegetable gardens, where they kept the grain – although by the summer they were already empty. In order not to disturb those in the house, young people would often spend the night in the barn. Sometimes they would party all night, dancing to an accordion or singing folk songs to a Gypsy balalaika. Sometimes they played cards until dawn. Even so, I never saw the young people in the village drink alcohol.

In front of the barns grew a soft grass which we called *murokh*. I learnt the correct name only recently: *sporysh*. In the morning, you would walk barefoot over the grass, and it would be covered with dew. The water in the creek at that time of day was pure and cold. Then – before carts went across the river or the livestock was driven over it – people got their drinking water from this river, too.

Several years ago a film was made about me, in which I was surprised to discover a sequence claiming that my parents were Old Believers. The film toured an abandoned village where they supposedly lived. I don't know where the journalists got that idea from. The village did not look at all like Titovka, and there were never any Old Believers in our village. There weren't any in Boris's family either – although, for some reason, there was a rumour there were. My grandparents were religious, but as far as I remember they did not go to church, which closed in Titovka in the 1920s. Icons hung in the front room of both sets of grandparents' houses. From an early age I knew that you had to be careful with icons, which were kept under glass. I would very carefully wipe this glass with a dry cloth – not a homespun towel, but a waffle towel bought in a shop.

Both of my grandmothers always prayed before they went to bed. Thanks to them, I learnt the Lord's Prayer and the Hail Mary very early on. Now I myself go up to the icon to pray before bed. In our village, no one prevented you from praying; children were baptized and funeral services were held for relatives. I was baptized, of course – just like everyone else in Titovka.

The so-called feast days were always celebrated widely. Obviously, I could only witness one of them first hand: Holy Trinity Day, or Pentecost, was celebrated in June. The day before, children and adults alike went into the steppe to collect thyme. In the village, it was called *chubur*. The grass was collected in the hems of long skirts or in aprons – whatever people could manage. They returned home and covered the floor and the window sills with thyme. The fragrance in the air was so strong that it made you dizzy.

## Questions on the Margins

"Are you a believer?"

"Yes, I am a believer, but not a churchgoer. I have lived my whole life with God in my soul. And I go on living like this. I remember that I, along with the local children, would climb into the kitchen gardens at night and dig up carrots, cucumbers and peas – then we would go down to the creek and wash and eat them. Not because we were hungry – it was just an adventure. Once we got into our garden. Grandmother noticed the mess and asked me if it was our doing. "No," I replied. Grandmother kept silent, and then, after a little while, she said, "You know, we have an icon in the corner, and God is on it. He sees everything, and always punishes people for lying, for betraying and for being mean. If not you, then your family." These words had a great effect on me, and have remained impressed on my mind ever since – especially the part about our family. I can't stand lying. If I realize that someone is lying, I feel something churning inside me. I tried to imbue my daughters with the same attitude towards lying."

"How did belief coexist with a Soviet atheistic upbringing?"

"It coexisted quite well. At Easter, we always had an atheists' evening, in which we all took part, and then we all went to church to bless the Easter bread, *kulich*. At home, we celebrated both Easter and Christmas. I always knew that we were atheists. And that God existed."

"Were you married in church?"

"No. In later years we intended to do that. Patriarch Alexy II of Moscow encouraged us to do so – but it was too late."

After Holy Trinity Day, the harvest of hay began. The haymaking and harvesting, I soon realized, were the most important events of the summer in the village. My parents' sisters always took me along to the harvest. We dressed for the fields in the same way as for evening festivities, except that we put on bast shoes – other than that, we wore the same clothes: long skirts, blouses with peplums and kerchiefs tied behind "*chik*-style", as we said in Titovka.

The way people spoke in Titovka was different than in the city, and not just in terms of local idioms and expressions – it was a proper dialect. During the first days of my summer holiday, I would become accustomed to speaking like one of the villagers so I wouldn't stick out. It was enough that I dressed like a city girl: my knee-length dresses by village standards were short and very different to those of my Titovka peers. Their clothes were very similar to those worn by the adults – the same long skirts and kerchiefs. I looked like a peewit next to them in my short dresses. My mother sewed dresses for me, usually adorned with small flowers – she loved such a pattern. They were in short supply, so any dress seemed elegant to me.

On our way to the fields, we would all sing together. We would go by cart, standing up, leaning on the high sides where the scythes, rakes and pitchforks were stowed. We would leave very early in the morning and returned at sunset. The work was very hard, but I had the lightest load – I raked the bevelled and dried rows. Then the rows of hay were gathered into mounds and dragged to the place where haystacks were made. A stack was about four metres high – no less. We worked all day, with a short break for lunch – everyone brought food with them from home. We got very tired. On the way back, we didn't sing.

Harvesting the wheat was even more difficult – the wheat had to be cut by hand and tied into bundles; harvesters turned up only later. Then about ten bundles were combined into stacks to dry, with the ears upwards. Only after this was the wheat taken to the *tok* – a special platform under the roof of a barn – where it was threshed with a flail. During the harvest, all I was allowed to do was turn the milled grain so that it would dry better. The dried grain was poured into sacks and hauled away to the grain silo.

During harvest time, we sometimes worked at night – in Titovka, in the moonlight, nights were amazingly bright. Unlike during the hay harvest, we didn't bring food with us to the wheat harvest, as there were camps in the field where food was prepared.

War, of course, changed life in Titovka, but my mama still came with us every summer – she missed her parents a lot. To be sure, getting to the village and back to Emba became more and more difficult.

Once we were returning home from Titovka. We travelled to Orenburg in a pickup truck loaded with grain. Grandfather Alyosha stopped the car on the Big Road (that's what they called the highway to the city in Titovka). The driver didn't want to take us: he refused to put children on the flatbed with grain sacks – it was dangerous.

But there were no other options: there were no empty trucks going from Titovka to the city, and only one other person could sit in the cabin. Grandfather practically begged the driver, promising to give him a bag of grain. The road was hard, and we were jerked from side to side – we had to hang on either to each other or to the sacks. Then, when we reached a hill, something happened to the truck. The pickup rolled downhill, gathering speed. Grabbing us, Mama shouted: "Hang on tight!" It was very frightening. The driver tried to control the vehicle with the steering wheel. When the speed fell a little, he turned the wheel and brought the truck to sit across the road – it rocked and came to a stop, and by a miracle it didn't turn over. Ever since, I've been afraid of any form of transport except trams.

*Questions on the Margins*

"Are you also afraid of planes?"

"Of course."

"And yet you flew so many times in the years of Boris Nikolayevich's presidency. How did you cope?"

"What could I do? But I was very afraid. Boris would say, 'Why are you shaking? You're with me.' 'And how will that help?' I'd ask him. 'If we crash, we'll be together,' he said. He never even fastened his seat belt."

"And you're afraid even now?"

"Not so much for myself. But I'm always worried about my children and grandchildren."

When the truck came to a halt, the driver jumped out of the cabin and came straight over to us and said: "Are you alive?"

Somehow the truck was repaired and we safely reached the city. As for the sack of grain that had been promised to him by Grandfather, the driver would have none of it. That was very generous of him – to refuse grain during a time of hunger was not easy.

During the war years, there were almost no men left in Titovka – there was just the chairman of the kolkhoz, who had returned home from the front wounded. There were also old men (in my view, of course) – above fifty years of age. There were teenagers – boys who were not yet old enough to be drafted. The old men, the teenagers and the women worked in the fields. That constituted the entire work force. And in the evenings, when the work in the fields was done, the women knitted socks and mittens for their men at the front.

Whenever the postman brought a death notice, half the village would gather around the home in question. There was desperate wailing. The bereaved would cry for a while – and then go back to work.

Even so, in comparison to our life in Emba, life in the village seemed to me to be calmer and more comfortable. Therefore, even during the war years, the trips there were a joy to me. It so happened that, after 1946, I stopped going to Titovka. I returned there only five decades later, in 1996.

I had, for a long time, wanted to return to my native village, but for some reason it never worked out. But one day I was in Orenburg – I was visiting my papa's grave. All the relatives had gathered, and someone had come from Titovka, so Papa's sister Katya said, "Naya, come to Titovka right now and have a look around!" To be honest, I hadn't intended to go there – Boris was already President, and I was travelling with security; if I had been alone, I would have agreed without hesitation. But after wavering for a bit I decided: "I'll go." I spoke with my security guards, and asked them to organize the trip, although there was very little time – we would have to return within a day. We travelled for a fairly long time. Finally, the van stopped in front of a club that had recently opened. And there was a crowd. The entire village had turned out.

"Why all this?" I asked. I became completely flustered. The priest came out to meet me, with an icon he gave to me as a present. The head of the district came. So I asked: "And are all the lads and lasses here?" In Titovka, they didn't say "boys and girls", but rather "lads and lasses". They thought I wouldn't recognize anyone – so many years had passed... they were no longer lads and lasses, but granddads and grannies. I myself was already nearly sixty-five. I began to look closer, and I realized that I recognized almost all of them, and called each one of them by name. Each one! They were amazed. Then we all went to the school. Suddenly, I smelt chicken noodles. It turned out that lunch had been prepared in the school cafeteria – "Just like when I was a girl!" I said. Chickens

27

and lambs had been slaughtered for my arrival by the family of Papa's sister Katya, I learnt. The chickens went into noodle soup, and the lambs became shish kebab – something they didn't use to make in Titovka. I looked at the tables: there was every sort of thing you could imagine laid out. But most astonishing of all were the soaked pancakes from the Russian stove. We forgot our age and joined together in remembering our childhood – how we had cut the hay, what we had used to thresh it, the location of a rye field, of a wheat field, the place where the potatoes grew – and I don't think anyone was left feeling awkward.

All of my grandparents had died by this time, but it turned out that our neighbour and distant relative Aunt Fekla was still alive. Of course, I wanted to visit her! But suddenly it started raining, which it had not done in Titovka since the spring. Everyone was happy – except me: I was wearing white shoes. At least I was wearing low heels! I was told, "You can't get through the mud there." But they couldn't talk me out of it. Of course, my feet got very muddy. But even so, I felt such peace of mind talking to the old woman who remembered both me and my grandmother so well. It was just a shame that we couldn't reach the cemetery where my relatives were buried, as the rain got in the way.

When our van was about to drive off, one of my childhood friends came running up with a jar of wild-strawberry jam and knocked on the window. "Naya, take this... Take this – I always loved you," he said.

# One of Five

When we moved back to Orenburg in 1945, we didn't have our own home. At first we lived with a distant relative of ours, who worked in the Party Executive Committee from morning until night – during the day there were only her two children in the large three-bedroom apartment. We occupied one of the rooms – it was quite cramped, of course. After a while, we moved in with other relatives, who had built a large house. They didn't have any children and could give us two rooms. Life became more comfortable, but Mama and Papa were very aware that we were crowding other people's houses, and they tried to find other accommodation.

My parents, following someone's recommendation, found a place on Komsomolskaya Street. The owner of the house, Vasily Isayevich, was single and, as it seemed to me at the time, an old man.

We had the whole house to ourselves, except for one small room. Vasily Isayevich worked a lot and returned home late. He came in quietly, poured himself some tea and went straight to his room by the front door. We didn't get in each other's way. We had a common room, which also acted as my parents' bedroom, and two smaller rooms, where the children slept. In this house, my brother Vova was born.

In January 1947, Grandfather Alyosha came to visit, and he said firmly: "It is time for you to have your own house." It turned out that he had kept some extra calves and lambs, which he sold in order to raise money for our home. He found us a log house, and a year later we moved in. Later, Papa bought some used railway sleepers and added a large kitchen extension, in which he placed a Dutch stove – Mama loved to bake pies on it.

Around the house was a small plot of land, and Mama used every inch of it as a kitchen garden. There she grew cucumbers, tomatoes, cabbages and aubergines. We also had a second plot of land – a melon field, just beyond the River Sakmara – where we planted watermelons, melons and potatoes. In preparation for the winter, Mama made pickles in two oak barrels. She had a special recipe: tomatoes, small watermelons and the "collective farmer" sort of melon, with layers of cabbage. All winter long, all the way through to the next harvest, we had this food on the table.

After the war, almost all produce was obtained with ration cards – you had to wait for hours in long queues with these cards. Usually that task fell to me, since Mama was busy with the younger children. Sometimes we went to the local market, which was called the Green Market. I remember huge rows of meat. Papa usually bought meat from fellow villagers from Titovka, so it was always good.

Mama earned some money on the side knitting kerchiefs. She bought goatskin down at the market, removed the black hair from it and then combed it with a special tool made of steel needles, which turned it into a uniform fluffy mass – almost weightless. Roza and I helped her with this. After the down was combed, Mama spun the thread on a spindle. The kerchiefs turned out beautifully, and always sold quickly. But she never knitted herself one. She always wanted the down to be of the finest quality – soft and long, so that the kerchief would turn out fluffy. It happened sometimes that she bought the down and thought it was what she needed, but when she started knitting it she became dissatisfied: "I see other people have fluffier kerchiefs – I'm not happy."

Once Mama sewed some bedlinen for us – from maps. A neighbour came back from the market and told her that large maps made of batiste were on sale. The local women had quickly figured out that, if the maps were soaked properly and boiled, the dye would melt away and only the fabric would remain. In fact, Mama was able to convert the maps into snow-white batiste, and she sewed coverlets and pillowcases out of them. We used them for a very long time – I even took them with me to the Institute. Ever since, I have tried to sew exactly this kind of batiste bedlinen – stuff like that is not sold in shops.

I never saw Mama sitting or lying down – she always kept herself busy. As far as I remember, she was always at work – knitting, cooking, cleaning, washing, sewing. She cooked fresh meals every day. I often thought about this on days when I left my daughters a lunch cooked the night before which they had to heat up. Mama sewed a lot. Not because she loved it, but because she had to. There were no clothes in the shops – or if there were, we couldn't afford them. The Singer sewing machine with the foot pedal – part of Mama's dowry – was constantly spinning.

Watching her made me want to learn how to sew, so I was pleased to take some lessons – I made patterns myself, and mastered all the forms of sewing – by hand as well as on the machine. Mama also taught me how to crochet with a hook. I crocheted collars and cuffs for my school uniform – they turned out nicely. I decided to sew my graduation-ceremony gown myself. Mama helped me, of course. She bought some fabric, which was chequered with small blue and white squares, and we came up with the design ourselves: short sleeves, white trim on the pockets and a white belt. I really liked my graduation gown. We didn't have graduation ceremonies of the kind they have today, however, nor formal floor-length gowns: we were just handed our diplomas in school. I don't believe there was even any dancing.

There was a comfortable atmosphere in our home. This probably came from Papa: he was a bright, open and generous person. Mama loved him very much. He called her "Marusya", and she called him "Osya". In about tenth grade, I realized that Mama was very jealous – when my parents returned from visits, Mama was often angry; Papa always tried to distract her somehow, but she would sharply interrupt him. It would become clear, listening to their conversation, that she was unhappy because Papa had looked at someone "the wrong way", talked with someone too much or danced with them. Papa always answered very calmly: "Marusya, I don't reproach you for spending the whole evening singing without me." (Mama would often sing with her sister – she had a lovely voice.) It must be said, by the next morning Mama had usually already forgotten about the upset, and everything went back to normal. I think women liked Papa. He was stocky, he had blue eyes and a thicket of dark hair, and he always had a smile on his face. But Mama was pretty too – even after giving birth to several children she still had an excellent figure and a straight back. Mama kept that posture until the end of her life.

Mama was easily irritated – we sometimes got it in the neck from her. Papa, on the contrary, was very calm. I never heard him raise his voice. He travelled on business a lot, and had friends everywhere. When he was sent to the Caspian region or to Astrakhan, he always brought back fish. "Where are you going with that fish?" Mama would say. "Marusya, I was given it as a treat – how could I refuse?" Papa would say, to justify himself.

We would often have visitors at our house – mainly relatives – many of whom came all the way from Titovka. Although food was sold by ration cards and there wasn't always enough money, the table was always groaning – Mama's famous pickles, *pelmeni*, *pirogi*… People would have a drink and sing songs in chorus before they were seen off at the coach station. On their way home, they would also sing quietly. To be honest, I didn't like having guests. After they left, there was a mountain of dirty dishes, which I had to wash up!

When I grew older, many aspects of my mother's character became clearer to me. She was a temperamental person by nature. She had grown up in comfort and plenty, and had to cope with the difficult everyday life of the war and post-war periods. Had it not been for Papa with his kind soul, I don't know how she could have endured it. He was a very mild man. Mama would get mad at him at times. "Why should I always be the hellhound in the family, while you only stroke the children's heads?" But Papa couldn't help himself. He never raised a hand to my brothers, as far as they can remember – let alone my sister and me. A scene from my childhood comes to my mind: it was early in the morning, still dark outside, and it was time to get ready for school. Papa was making breakfast. I heard his quiet voice: "You stay in bed,

Marusya, I'll do everything…" I got up, went into the kitchen and saw that he was heating something up for us. Papa set the dishes on the table and went, just as quietly, to wake the other children.

*Questions on the Margins*

"Did you want to have the same kind of atmosphere as in your parents' home in your own family's house?"

"Somehow I never thought of that."

"Were you close to your parents?"

"Yes, although we never talked about certain things. Perhaps because we didn't have time – we had a big family and lots of concerns."

"What is it that you didn't talk about, exactly?"

"Well, things to do with relationships. I didn't like discussing that with anyone, in fact. To this day I don't like it. And not just about my own relationships, but other people's personal matters, too. Mama would often joke: "You are so tight-lipped." I always tried to avoid conversations of that sort – who, what, with whom – both at work and with friends. It was good that Boris and I were very similar in that sense. He thought it was unacceptable to talk about someone else's private life. It was that way in our family, too. Even now, if Lena says something about Tanya, I never pass it on to Tanya. Or the other way round. Not to mention about other people."

"Are you more like your mama or your papa?"

"More like Papa. I am generally a balanced person. I never raise my voice. When Mama used to yell at me about a floor that hadn't been washed, I'd say to myself: 'When I grow up, I'll never force my children to mop the floor.'"

"And you didn't force them?"

"I just reminded them that they had to wash the dishes or the floor. On the whole, both my daughters – Tanya and Lena – have always been very independent. Once, when she was in third grade, I asked Lena whether she had done her homework, and she told me: "Mama, that's not something for you to worry about." "All right," I would say. "I won't ask you about that again."

"And did you really never ask her again?"

"Never. They were very good students."

"Boris Nikolayevich was, apparently, more temperamental?"

"He never raised his voice either. Sure, he could say something very quietly but in such a way that it would be remembered for a long time. He was supportive of our daughters' independence. And he told me: 'Let them do as they think they should.' I couldn't always reconcile myself to that."

I went to an all-girls' school. Of all of the subjects, maths was the one I liked best, but the teacher I liked the most was the Russian literature and language teacher. All the girls liked her. Her name was Alexandra Yefimovna Bezmagarychnaya. She seemed unusually pretty to me, despite the fact that she was fairly full-figured. I so loved how she would pull a small, lacy, perfumed handkerchief from her sleeve, and I kept trying to repeat the gesture. It didn't work. But I made myself batiste handkerchiefs and fringed them with coloured threads.

I always wore my hair in tight braids, wound about with a ribbon – brown on regular days and white on holidays. There could be no tail or loose hair – that was unacceptable. I always liked my hair, especially its dark-chestnut colour. People sometimes asked me what I dyed my hair with. But on the whole I did not pay much attention to my appearance.

I loved the theatre. My friends and I belonged to two drama clubs – one in school and the other at the Oktyabr Cinema near our house. When we got home from school, we would often turn on the radio and listen to the programme *Theatre on the Mike*. There were plays by Alexander Ostrovsky, Alexander Griboyedov, Anton Chekhov, Molière and Oscar Wilde… But by ninth grade I no longer had time for clubs – being the eldest, I had to give Mama more and more help at home. We didn't have hot water on tap – to give the younger children a bath in the evenings, we had to heat a whole water urn on the stove. Papa was often away on business, and Mama could not cope with this on her own – and of course there were a lot of other chores around the house: cleaning, babysitting my brothers and going to the shop.

Even with all of that, I can't say that my studies and duties at home completely deprived me of free time. There was time for books (true – I mainly read at night), films (very rarely) and talk with friends (also not very often). I loved novels. I read Charles Dickens, Maxim Gorky, Guy de Maupassant, George Sand… but for some reason I particularly loved *Tess of the D'Urbervilles* by Thomas Hardy. The first time I read *Tess* I was rather young – I don't remember where I got it from, but it made a deep impression on me. We didn't have a library at home – it wasn't easy to get hold of books. I remember someone in my class brought in *The Count of Monte Cristo*. We weren't patient enough to take turns reading it, so the thick tome was cut into sections and read in separate parts, which we passed on to each other when we were done with them. After we finished reading the whole book, we carefully glued all the sections back together – but it didn't survive for very long. But what could we do when there weren't enough good books about? There were long queues for books at the public library – you would have to wait weeks, if not months, for a book. And it wasn't very convenient to walk to the library, either – we lived outside the city centre, near the outskirts, in the private-housing area.

*Questions on the Margins*

"When you read these novels, did you dream of another life for yourself?"

"I knew perfectly well that I couldn't have another life. There was only the one I had. After all, we lived behind the Iron Curtain. We were told that in Europe, and even more so in America, people lived in total darkness – in utter poverty and brutality – and the rich oppressed the poor. We, on the other hand, had a bright future:

everyone was equal, everyone lived for the sake of their country. I didn't want that other life."

"Did you believe all that?"

"It never entered our heads to doubt what the teachers told us, or what was written in the newspapers. After the war, we lived in constant fear of spies and saboteurs. We were terrified that they would seek revenge against the Soviet Union for having won the war – and that they were sending enemies. In Orenburg there was Factory No. 47 – we didn't know what it produced, but we had no doubt that spies were very interested in it. And we believed that we must be vigilant. We would walk around town and peek into lower-ground-floor windows – was there anybody suspicious living there? It's funny to remember it now, but at the time we lived in fear, and took conversations about spies and saboteurs quite seriously."

The cinema was closer to my house than the library – it showed very few films then, and we saw them all several times. There were Soviet films – *Springtime*, *They Met in Moscow*, *Jolly Fellows*, *Seven Brave Men*, *Volga-Volga* and *Six p.m.* – and, as they called them then, the "trophy films" (seized by the Red Army in Germany during the war): *The Great Waltz*, for example.

In seventh grade I began collecting photographs of actors – Marina Ladynina, Lyubov Orlova, Sofya Pilyavskaya, Yanina Zheymo, Vladimir Zeldin, Pyotr Aleynikov, Yevgeny Samoylov and Vladimir Druzhnikov... These postcards were sold in every newspaper kiosk, and cost just a few copecks. Many people collected them at the time – some of my friends would stick them on their walls, others filled special albums. I found an old, battered suitcase of Mama's and put my collection in it. Little did I know that many years later I would meet and even become friends with some of the people whose portraits I kept in that old suitcase. Unfortunately, my collection was lost – when my mama moved to Sverdlovsk with my brother, he decided that these postcards were no longer needed, and left the suitcase in our old home.

We weren't able to go to the cinema very often, although we really wanted to… Once, my friends and I ran away from our lessons to see *The Ballad of Siberia*. We went past the garden at the Oktyabr Cinema, and one of us suggested that we leave our school bags in the snow and pick them up on our way back. So that is what we did. But when we came back to the garden after the show, the school bags were no longer there. The following morning we learnt that a policeman had seen us bury our school bags and had brought them back to the school.

They summoned our parents. Mama said to Papa: "I can't go! You go…" Papa came back from school upset, and gave me the only telling-off I ever received from him. It was brief: "I'm ashamed of you. Promise me that this will never happen again."

I was prepared for this, and answered him defiantly: "What if I really want to see a movie?"

"Well, you can see it later – after school," Papa replied calmly. Nothing like that ever happened again, and my parents were not summoned to school again.

I was very happy to join the "Pioneers". I remember really liking the tie (and the button through which you had to push its ends even more so – because in those days it was not tied in a knot). The Pioneer activities were very interesting, but in time I grew tired of them. We had to stay within bounds at all times; this weighed heavily on me – perhaps because I am a person who loves freedom in general. I thought: that's it – I won't join the Komsomol! But at that time, it was almost impossible to avoid doing so: I had to join.

I had four close friends at School No. 17: Sonya Sveshnikova, Lyusya Semyonova, Valya Pigareva and Lyuba Bobyleva. We were referred to as the "school activists": one was head of the class, another was in a Komsomol committee. We were nearly inseparable – both in school and after lessons – and we remained friends our whole lives

Although we went to an all-girls' school, there were boys in our friendship group. Most of them lived near me, in the neighbouring streets. Zhora Shchurovsky, Igor Bogdanov, Yura Kononov, Boris Pryakhin, Volodya Kovalyov – only Boris Dementyev lived farther away. Zhora's parents had a large house, and that was where we usually gathered.

In senior school, we organized parties to which we would invite the students from School No. 7, the all-boys' school where the boys in our friendship group went. We always had a set list of activities for these parties: we would do magic tricks, play charades, quiz one another, read poetry and dance. We were delighted to learn to dance the pas d'Espagne, pas de quatre and the polka at the school dance club, but our favourites were the tango and the waltz.

Sometimes romantic attachments would develop, which meant that you spent more time with the person you liked – not alone, but with the others. It didn't matter whether you went sledding or to school parties or simply for a walk – the attraction was expressed in a childlike fashion. Once Yura Kononov gave me a curved glass tube, which he had clearly nicked from a chemistry lab. I thought it was very pretty.

If I was ever held up after school, Mama got very anxious – in the post-war years all sorts of rumours went around: someone had been robbed, someone else had been raped… I wasn't particularly scared by the stories Mama told me, but she did communicate her anxiety to me. We always tried to go around in big groups – and I was usually walked home by not just one, but two or three boys. I was haunted by a fear of the dark for a fairly long time – even when I was an adult.

When Boris came to Orenburg to ask my parents for my hand in marriage, I saw him off on the train, and on the way back home I dropped by a friend's house and we sat up late. As a result, it was already dark when I returned home. Suddenly I had the feeling that a man was walking behind me; wherever I went, he would follow. My legs were trembling. What was I to do? I turned around and said sharply, "Excuse me, would you walk me home? It's late, and I'm afraid." And I saw before me a decent-looking young man who was simply walking along, minding his own business, in the same direction as me. We reached my house together; he didn't try to speak to me – he just asked where to go a few times. At the gate he politely proposed continuing our acquaintance, but I ran away.

When I was in senior school, I wanted to try to get into the Medical Institute. One of my neighbours, Rita Usovich – who was older than me, but a friend nonetheless – studied at the Medical Institute and tried to interest me in her profession. I helped her revise for her exams by testing her, and thanks to this I learnt a lot about anatomy – I even knew the names of all the bones in the human body. It was Rita who taught me not to be afraid of blood, and she explained to me that it was only the liquid that circulated in our bodies. This knowledge seemed to banish any fears, and I calmly treated my brothers' grazed knees and elbows when necessary. Rita said that she wanted to be a therapist – and of course I wanted to be one too. My parents were happy with my decision. Although he had dreamt of my becoming a teacher, my father said, "It's not such a bad thing to have a doctor in the family." Up until then, there had only been one medical person in the family – Papa's sister Vassa, who worked as a nurse.

Once my final exams were over, I put together my application for the Institute and took it to the admission office – we had a medical institute in Orenburg. On the way, I ran into some friends who had left school the year before and were now studying in Sverdlovsk (now Yekaterinburg). "Where are you going?" they asked. I said, "I'm submitting my application to the Medical Institute." And they said in chorus: "Are you mad? To cut up corpses?" And they began to tell me about their "polytechnic". I remember them saying that what they loved the most was the student life. Well, they also liked the classes – and the city. Without paying too much attention to what I was doing, I wrote another application and posted it.

The Urals Polytechnic Institute. I didn't tell my family straight away. Papa was on a business trip, and I decided to wait until he returned to tell them. The prospect of living far away from home didn't frighten me – I was fairly independent. After all, I was the eldest, and my parents often left my brothers and sisters with me and I managed. When I finally told my parents about my decision, they were not happy. They really didn't want me to leave. "How can you live on your own in an unfamiliar city?" Mama also said it would be hard for her to cope with three-year-old Vova and five-year-old Tolya. Roza was also very upset: now she would have to wash the floors. But I didn't want to change my mind. And my parents didn't press me to do so.

Papa saw me off to Sverdlovsk. We were both a bit tense. To calm my nerves, Papa got on the train and went several stops with me. Thanks to him, I began to relax. As we approached Sverdlovsk, the steppe landscape I was used to changed – to the right and left of the railway track there was dense forest. I really didn't like this wall of trees – I had grown up on the steppe and loved the open spaces. I still do.

At first Sverdlovsk seemed a bit gloomy – the buildings were grey, unlike those in Orenburg, which were mostly bright. But I immediately liked the Institute – UPI, as it was known – with its spacious buildings, columns, high ceilings and enormous stairways. It was very beautiful, as though it was in a film set.

I applied to the Department of Energy, where my classmate Rita Tambovtseva and some other friends were studying. While we sat the entrance exams, we lodged in large auditoriums: in one building there were more than a dozen beds (the dormitories were being renovated). I wasn't at all fazed by this: I made new acquaintances, and a lot of my friends from Orenburg had gone to UPI too, so I wasn't lonely.

I passed the first two exams. A fifth-year student of the Department of Energy heard that we were seeking admission and tried to talk us out of it. "Work at a power station? It's bad for your health – and you haven't had children yet…" I thought about it – and then I saw a notice about vacancies for a new profession called "Engineer Instructor" at the Department of Construction. That's just what I want, I thought.

I tried to retrieve my papers from the Department of Energy, but they wouldn't give them back to me. They said: "Take the exams, then we'll see." Someone suggested I should simply not turn up at the next exam, which was physics. So I didn't go. As a result, I had to make up the necessary exams at the Department of Construction. I remember I was very afraid of the drawing exam. But I was lucky: the problems were simple, and I got a high four. I was accepted.

The students on this course were mainly female: there was one boy in the whole class. When I went home for the summer, Papa was very happy – he had always wanted me to be a teacher. Unfortunately, this specialist course was curtailed after only a year, since they were unable to find teachers of psychology and pedagogy. We were offered any other specialization in the same department, so I chose "Water Supply and Sanitation". And I have to say I never regretted it.

NAINA GIRINA

# Before Boris

I return to our Institute every year – UPI has become a university, the UrFU (Urals Federal University), and the Institute is now named after Boris Yeltsin. Before the Yeltsin Center opened in Yekaterinburg, it was here that first Boris, then later I, handed the Yeltsin bursaries out to UrFU's best students. For us, this was always a joyful occasion. Even now, when I go to hand out the bursaries, I'm filled with a special feeling. I know how difficult life can be for students today, and I am pleased that the Yeltsin Foundation can help the best of them.

In the post-war years, a lot changed, both inside the Institute and around it. Today, the grounds are well kept – everything is clean and well looked after. A beautiful square with flowers has been installed in front of the entrance. Back when I was young, the main drive to the entrance (from the Lenin Street side) passed between two half-ruined buildings. For some reason, we never took any interest in the story behind these ruins, although we helped to dismantle them as part of our volunteer programme.

We loved our Institute very much, and it always felt very comfortable. There was a huge auditorium, a mezzanine built around a large foyer and spacious, bright classrooms. Our favourite areas were the "Roman" rooms (marked with Roman numerals), where the seating was arranged like an amphitheatre, so that the teacher could see the students and vice versa. Lectures were held here – for two or three groups at a time.

I can't say that I found my studies very difficult – nor were they too easy. Some of the subjects were easier, some harder – I had some problems with English, for example, possibly because I had studied German. But I didn't find drawing too difficult – I always had a good eye, and I loved to sketch. I just about managed to cope with descriptive geometry – which many people found tough – but not half so brilliantly as my eldest daughter Lena did many years later in the same institute. I wasn't able to take notes quickly; at first I found it hard to separate what was important, and I didn't manage to write down everything in the right sequence. Sometimes I had to copy notes from my classmates. But the most difficult thing was sitting the exams. I always worried that my mind would go blank – that I would forget things I knew perfectly well. I only managed to get things under control in the third year. What I didn't like was "Foundations of Marxism and Leninism", which was one of our subjects. Reading the works of Lenin was simply torture. It wasn't that I was critical of what I read – rather that I didn't understand why we had to study it.

I was in the third year when Stalin died; his death filled us all with great sorrow. We had grown up with Stalin, and everyone saw him as the reason for our successes. I remember the day when his death was announced: we were gathered in the auditorium, where a huge portrait of him hung, and the lights were dimmed. Everyone cried. My classmates Zina Shabalina and Raya Akhtyamova went to Moscow for the funeral – thank God they weren't crushed in the crowd there.

We didn't talk about Stalin or who would take his place – such things weren't of interest. The cult of personality, the mass repressions, the Gulags… we only learnt about all that many years later.

In 1953, we were ordinary Soviet students who believed what the newspapers said – although for some reason we were not taken in by the ideology. Yes, like everyone else, we sat through Komsomol meetings – but then we returned to our lives, in which there was no place for politics: there were friends, dances, outings, sports competitions… no politics.

46

*Questions on the Margins*

"When did you learn the whole truth about the Stalin repressions?"

"The details only emerged in the late 1980s. It turned out that we lived the greater part of our lives without knowing the truth about the history of our country. You could say that we lived a lie. I hope it will be different for my great-grandchildren when they study the history of the 1990s."

"We can only hope so. There are already many legends about the 1990s."

"Yes, today it seems more and more the case that people talk about the 1990s as if it were some sort of horror film. But, after all, the time of reform was difficult and wonderful at the same time: difficult because it brought many trials; wonderful because we lived in hope. I would very much like for those who do not remember the 1990s to learn the truth about that era."

When the school year ended, we all went our separate ways, into various internships. In my first internship I mastered surveying – I learnt to use the instruments, do site plans and build elevation profiles.

My next internship was in construction. My friend Lyusya and I went to Zlatoust, her home town. We worked on a construction site in quite an important role: we had to draft budgets, do estimates – and even give orders. It is not hard to imagine how we were viewed by the workers, whose earnings depended directly on our estimates. That was probably the first time we felt like real engineers.

Three years into my training, I completed an internship at the Rublyovsky Water Treatment Plant in Moscow. Ten years later, when Boris was President, I visited the plant again – the government's dacha in Barvikha, where we lived for many years, was right next to it.

To be honest, my memories of the Institute years are mainly connected to student life rather than to my studies or work experience.

We had a wonderful time – so many years have passed, but I still keep in touch with my friends from the Institute. This has always been the case, wherever I have been.

In the first year, there were eight of us to a room. It was a typical dormitory room: beds, bedside tables and a simple table covered with an oilcloth. There was also a crammed wardrobe. Most of our things were kept in suitcases under our beds. I immersed myself in student life with gusto: I wasn't too bothered about having to share a dormitory. Sure, at first I would often soak my batiste coverlet in boiling water in a bucket in the communal kitchen, but that didn't last very long. Soon I relented and used the bedlinen they handed out in the dormitory, even though it was yellow and smelt of chlorine.

In the second year, I was moved to a room for five people, and I lived with the same four girls until I graduated. This room was near the one where Boris lodged – his was on the other side of the communal kitchen. Boris and I were already on speaking terms, but in the second year we grew closer – sometimes the other girls and I invited the guys over for tea or supper in our room, or we ran over to their room for some trifle, and I often crossed paths with Boris in the corridor.

# In Boris's Field of Vision

Almost all my student memories are connected to Borya in one way or another. For a long time we were just friends. I was very cautious around him because he was popular with the girls in our class – and perhaps because he didn't single anyone out.

## Questions on the Margins

"Do you remember when you saw Boris Nikolayevich for the first time?"

"No, I can't. It was probably during our first lecture. He was very tall – there were no more than five people as tall as him in our class – it was hard not to notice him. But I can't say 'I saw him and – ah!' There was nothing like that."

"But when did he start paying attention to you – do you remember?"

"Our relationship developed gradually. We talked, and we saw one another at parties… but nothing special happened between us until the second year."

Boris stood out among his classmates – not just because of his bright appearance and great stature, but also because of his personality. Even in his youth he possessed the qualities that make a good leader. He was very energetic, and was forever thinking and organizing. He was always at the centre of attention. He was a year older than us – although he enrolled in 1949, he fell ill (he had strep throat, with a heart complication) and had to take sick leave – that was how he ended up in our year.

Boris played volleyball, and we sometimes went to watch and cheer him on. In those days, volleyball was the number-one sport – like football is today. But it wasn't just volleyball he was interested in – for example, as a member of the Student Sports Association, he helped to organize a relay race, which usually took place in early May – the winners of which would take part in city-wide competitions. The students of the Faculty of Construction, of which we were of course part, made up the majority of the competitors. I ran in the race several times – I really liked it.

Another classmate of ours, Pasha Bogdashin, was fairly successful as an amateur race-car driver. He won a little KVN-49 television set and some leather trousers at the All-Union races. Television broadcasting had only just begun in the Urals, and half the class gathered in the hall where Pasha had put his television. The picture was tiny, was only enlarged a little, and was distorted by a lens – it was absolutely impossible to make out any faces, but to us it was a miracle.

Another form of entertainment was hiking to Kamennye Palatki – the granite cliffs by Lake Shartash. In the winter, we would bring our skis with us and fly downhill, always ending up sprawled in the snow. It was usually Boris who organized these hikes.

In the spring, we loved going to listen to nightingales in the evening. We always went in groups – I usually went with some of my friends, and often Misha Karasik, too, who was older than us. Boris would sometimes join us. One night, on a dare, he went to the Mikhailovskoye Cemetery, which was closed at night. "I was building character," he joked – but it was really a way of hardening himself. I remember how he spoke of wanting to travel around the country on the roof of a train during the summer holidays. "That's dangerous!" people told him. He would reply: "You have to train yourself."

Our salary was 230 roubles per year (in 1953, a loaf of white bread cost one rouble 45 copecks – the starting salary of an engineer was 80 roubles a month). Sometimes our relatives helped us out with cash. The 100 roubles that Papa or Auntie sent me from time to time – not every month – came in very handy. Borya, who was also helped a little by his parents, parted with his cash easily. They would send him 100 roubles, and he would immediately spend it on books, which he kept under his bed. These piles of books, tied with twine, followed us when we moved to our first family room in a communal apartment. He loved books – he valued them highly, and would buy them at every opportunity. There were even books in the sports bag he took with him to competitions. In those days, he knew the Russian classics very well – and Chekhov remained his favourite author all his life. Boris was a binge-reader – he would *devour* books. He had learnt to speed-read at some point, and his eyes whizzed along the centre of the page – and he could always remember what he had read, too. He had a fantastic memory. Later, at work, he could make calculations without even glancing at his papers – and he never mixed up people's names, even though there were always a lot of people working under him. Either because he was naturally gifted, or because of some form of effort or training, Boris was blessed with a brilliant memory for the whole of his life.

Once, after Boris had retired, our youngest daughter Tanya and her husband, Valentin Yumashev, came to visit us. Valya was reading Haruki Murakami's latest book. Boris said he had already read it – Valya said he doubted that this was possible, as the novel had only just been published. But Boris recounted a section in detail – he even remembered whereabouts it was in the book. "Open the book and check it," Boris challenged Valya. He was not mistaken.

Surprisingly, Borya never got involved in the Komsomol meetings. But he was behind everything else we did – whether it was a student wedding, a prank or a hike. He was always a good organizer, and had the wisdom not to pressure anybody – he knew how to persuade them. But if he set his mind on something, it was not easy to dissuade him – even if it created problems for him. When he came to take the exam on the Theory of Elasticity, which was a very difficult subject (and the only exam where you were allowed to consult notes and reference books), it just so happened that some sort of commissioner came to oversee the exam. Wanting to show off, the dean, Rogitsky, called his best student first.

Boris didn't even manage to glance at his notes – Rogitsky hurried him, saying, "You don't need to prepare – you know everything, anyway." Boris gave his answers from memory, and got a four. The dean apologized to Borya, and proposed that he retake the exam so he would have a five on his diploma, but he refused: "I got what I got."

We usually had lunch at the Institute – if we didn't manage to get to the Institute cafeteria, the buffet at the construction faculty would save us, and on our way home, we would almost always stop at the pastry store, where hot marzipan puffs and jam rolls were sold. We ate them while they were fresh, on the street on the way to the dorm. The cafeteria was on the student campus – and there was one for all seven dormitory buildings. There was even a supermarket on campus. For some reason, we went there mainly for canned food – courgette caviar, beans and sprats… There was wine on sale in the shop as well, but we rarely bought it – usually only on holidays. Borya loved Riesling – there was no other dry wine at that time.

A journalist recently wrote that our classmates drank a lot of beer, and that Borya carried it into the dormitory in buckets on a yoke. That's total nonsense. Borya didn't drink beer at all, like most of his friends, as they were involved in sports. Now, Misha Karasik really did love beer. Once, on Misha's birthday, Borya and his friends gave him a bucket of beer. But as for the yoke, although I've since learnt from some classmates that it was a real story, it had absolutely nothing to do with Borya: two or three times, some students who weren't in our group brought beer on a yoke into the dormitory – and it was ascribed to Boris. There are a lot of myths that have sprung up around his name in recent years.

The boys weren't saints – but they really did only drink a little. I remember that once, after the Institute days, when we were married, we spent New Year's Eve at Misha Karasik's house. The only alcohol on the table was vodka. I said to the guys, "Borya's not allowed – he has a competition tomorrow!" Well, he wouldn't be drinking… but they all chorused, "Then you drink it – for you and for him!" They gave me water in one hand and vodka in the other. I drank it.

I had never tried it before. At first I didn't feel anything, but then I realized something was wrong – my head was spinning. I took myself off and found myself in Misha's mother's bedroom. Meanwhile, downstairs, Boris stretched out an arm to me – only to discover I wasn't there. He came upstairs and found me – and, taking a good look at me, said, "You can't stand up?" I replied, "I'll get up now." And then I fell fast asleep. All I can remember after that is the guys putting their ear to me in turn and saying, "She's breathing." Boris was afraid for me. His friends didn't have a telephone, but somebody ran out to a phone booth and called their relatives to ask for advice. They advised drinking a raw egg. There were no eggs in the house. I missed the New Year – I slept through it. My classmates often reminded me of that story later... with gales of laughter, of course.

From the outset, Boris and I spent a lot of time together – we were in the same friendship group, and it always seemed to me that I could understand what made him tick. Our friendship group had a rich student life – theatre, sport, dances and many other traditions were gradually established. Even the city itself left its mark. Sverdlovsk in the 1950s was not only an industrial city, but a theatrical city. Our favourite theatre in those years was Muzkomediya (Musical Comedy Theatre). We saw the whole repertoire, over and over again: *Tobacco Captain*, *The Violet of Montmartre*, *Circus Princess*, *Silva*, with brilliant performances by actors famous throughout the country – Anatoly Marenich, Nikolai Badyev, Ludmila Satosova, Yury Chernov. And although we went to the theatre fairly often, the novelty factor never wore off. We didn't usually have time to change before we went, so we went in the clothes we had worn all day – for me, normally a skirt and jacket. But when we had the opportunity, we dressed up for the occasion. What exactly did "dressing up" entail? Wearing a dress. I had two wool dresses, both of which were sewn by my mama's friend in Orenburg, who was a seamstress – one was dark blue with a white lace collar, and the other was maroon. My favourite summer dress was made from fabric brought over from Germany by my relatives – a green silk with bright flowers scattered over it. I still have a photograph of me wearing that dress, which was taken at the Institute.

There were often concerts in the UPI auditorium, starring such people as Alexander Vertinsky, who had not long before returned to the USSR. If we weren't able to get tickets, our friends on the architecture course could draw well, and would forge tickets for their friends. We all used them.

Borya had just been a friend until the second year – but then one day everything changed.

Besides the usual Saturday dances at the Faculty of Construction, there were also parties in other departments. One weekend Rita Tambovtseva and Yura Zadvornov, friends from home who studied at the Faculty of Energy, invited me to a party – and I was surprised to find Borya there as well (his volleyball friends had invited him, and they came to the party after training). The volleyball training sessions took up a lot of his time, so Borya didn't usually go to dances – and when he did find time to go, he didn't single me out, so we rarely danced together. But this day was different – as soon as he saw me, he came over and asked me why I wasn't with my room-mates, and we stayed side by side for the rest of the evening. We only danced with each other. Borya was a good dancer; he especially loved the Boston Waltz (although I don't think we danced the Boston Waltz that evening). At one point, he led me away from my friends to the mezzanine on the first floor, and there, behind a column, we kissed for the first time. "Behind which column?" people always ask. I have no idea – they were all identical! Borya could never remember, either, so we decided that it was the column in the corner. Maybe that was the right one, after all – and anyway, what difference does it make now?… What's important is that it was as if there was a spark between us that evening. After that, it was impossible to stay and dance and chat with friends, and we ran away from everyone.

It was a warm autumn, and it was raining, but we didn't notice. We walked through the streets until late at night, kissed and chatted about whatever came to mind. I felt warm and comfortable with him. When we got back to the dormitory, I went straight to bed – I didn't want to speak about what had happened between Borya and me. I didn't even tell any of my friends about that night until much later. In the morning, I suddenly felt very afraid of meeting Borya. The feeling of being in love frightened me, for some reason. I was utterly unprepared for the transformation of our relationship from friends to something else. As I later understood, he felt much the same way. Why? Most probably it was a realization that a serious relationship would require changes in our lives – perhaps even some hard decisions. We wanted to live as we always had, without losing our freedom. For several days, we didn't see each other – Borya was busy training, and when I ran into him in the hallway, we greeted each other as if nothing had happened. We sighed with relief: it was clear that neither of us wanted anything to change – so nothing did, and wouldn't for another four years.

Above my bed hung a photograph of a young man – my girlfriend's brother, whom I had met during the summer holidays between ninth and tenth grade, when we had gone to the cinema, walked and chatted. He went to the Suvorov Academy, and I found his stories fascinating. There was nothing serious between us, but for some reason I took his photo to Sverdlovsk. Whenever he came to my room, Boris would always take the picture down and joke, "I don't want to see that photo here again!" When he left, I would hang it back up. That happened many times – he'd come, he'd take it down, I'd put it back up... Only after that night did I remove the photograph for good.

But other than that, our relationship remained much as before. Before graduation, we didn't even go out together once. Nonetheless, we were very close emotionally throughout those five years, and we seemed to sense each other. It's hard to explain why it all turned out that way. "I always kept you in my field of vision," Boris told me later, and it was quite the same for me.

We quickly formed a common friendship group. From my room there was me, Lyusya Vedeneyeva and Rita Batsulova; from Boris's room, there was Nolik (Arnold) Lavochkin and Volodya Anisimov. We spent a lot of time together, and the boys came over for dinner. In the second year, Boris said, "That's enough feeding us," and proposed organizing a kolkhoz, pooling our money. We called our kolkhoz *Shkodnik* ("Troublemaker"). Why – no one can recall. Because we liked the word. Thanks to Shkodnik, our everyday lives were much easier, and we were all part of something – something that fills us with enormous pleasure to remember now we're no longer young. Borya was chosen as chairman, and it fell to him to draft a charter for the kolkhoz, including an assignment of duties to the members. It was like this:

1. *The kolkhoz is created voluntarily and on the basis of friendship and fondness. The total number of members is six.*
2. *Assignment of duties:*
   *Chairman – Borya*
   *R. Treasurer – Lyusya*
   *Hygienist – Naya*
   *Secretary – Rita*
   *Foreman – Nolik*
   *Plunderer of Kolkhoz Goods – Vova*
3. *The members of the kolkhoz are obliged to: attend lectures without absences; go to the cinema, the theatre and to sports events at least once a week, and go to the sauna once a week – money to be allocated for this purpose; celebrate holidays and birthdays of the kolkhoz members, close friends, and so on.*
   *Approved at the first annual general meeting of the kolkhoz.*
   *November 1952*

"R. Treasurer" meant "ruthless treasurer", which was a reference to the fact that Lyusya should keep a stern eye on our expenses. I think I was appointed "hygienist" because I always asked: "Did you wash your hands?"

We took it in turns to make meals – and on Sundays we always tried to make something special. Once, when it was my turn, a large pan of compote disappeared from the kitchen. We found it on another floor – empty, of course. Years later, a classmate – Vitaly Sismekov, who by that time had become Dean of the Faculty of Construction – ran into me at the Institute and said unexpectedly, "Oh, Naya, that compote was very tasty!"

We loved playing pranks. One night we moved a sleeping student, along with his bed, into the women's bathroom, and left him in the far corner. In the morning, the girls ran in to wash, and they didn't notice him straight away. The poor boy was horrified when the screaming woke him up.

My relationship with Boris didn't change. We each had our own lives. It seemed to me that Borya liked my room-mate, Lyusya. I started going out with Nolik Lavochkin in the third year. We went for walks, we kissed... Once Borya took me by the shoulders in the hallway and asked, "Did you kiss him?" "Ask him," I replied. My relationship with Nolik couldn't be called serious. From the very beginning, I understood that it wouldn't go anywhere – and that's essentially how it turned out. After a while, everything fizzled out. But Borya remembered this for a very long time. Even when we were married, he would half-jokingly remind me about my dating Nolik. It seemed that on these rare occasions he was jealous – but this didn't prevent us from preserving our friendship with Nolik for our whole lives. In the 1990s, he and his family left for Israel, but we still speak to each other on the phone.

Borya also had other girlfriends from time to time. He was the centre of attention, as before, and many of our classmates were in love with him. Sometimes, knowing he was my friend, they would share their suffering with me. I would honestly do my best to help them, trying to turn Borya's attention to them. He always laughed it off. Just as I would laugh off any mention of my admirers.

In the third year, Boris gave me a photo and wrote on the back: "To my beloved Naya." I didn't attribute any meaning to this, but my room-mate was very troubled by this and kept asking me what it meant. As usual, I laughed it off: "He wrote that he loves me – that must mean he loves me." Boris kept up this game, and even asked me from time to time in front of everyone, "When are we going to get married?" "Sometime," I would reply. That became our long-standing joke. Only now do I realize that this game helped us both to preserve our special relationship whilst keeping our distance.

Later, Boris's mother, Klavdiya Vasilyevna, told me about a conversation she had once had with her son. "Do you have a girl at the Institute?" she had asked him. "Yes," he had answered, "but she's busy." "So why don't you show some initiative?" she asked. "She knows I love her," Boris said. "How does she know?" she asked. "She knows…" Klavdiya told me that, from that moment, she was sure that Borya and I would one day be together. But I didn't think about marriage at all during my student years.

Our student life – with its amiable, jocular atmosphere and constant teasing and prank-playing – didn't go very well together with a grown-up relationship. Of course, some of us fell in love, went on dates, kissed at the dormitory window… but no more than that. In a sense, we were very naive. At that point, to us, "grown-up relationships" meant the ZAGS (Russian Register Office), marriage and family. And all of that – according to public opinion – could get in the way of your studies. And that meant "grown-up relationships" had to wait until after graduation – that was so accepted that any exception to the rule was quite shocking.

In the third year, one night, when we were lying in our beds almost asleep, Rita Yerina told us that she was getting married to our classmate, Misha Ustinov. We tried to talk her out of it: "What's the rush? We still have two years of study left…" She suddenly spurted out: "I'm pregnant." We were stunned – and we even suspected that she was having us on at first.

Rita and Misha were married in the third year, and were the first among us to tie the knot. Borya organized their wedding, of course. Unfortunately, their relationship didn't last, and after the

Institute they divorced. It must be said that this was a rare case in our friendship circles. Almost all our classmates who got married young lived together for the rest of their lives, just as Boris and I did. After the Institute, only one more couple, the Bogdashins, divorced – but they married a second time, and their families turned out to be all the stronger for it.

While it was common not to get married during one's student years, I remember Papa cautiously trying to talk to me about it when I left Orenburg. I immediately interrupted him: "While I'm studying at the Institute, I will not get married."

But I never spoke about such things with Mama. I remember the only time she broached the subject – she mentioned a distant relative who had had a child while she was still at school. I wouldn't get into a discussion about it with her. I just said: "Don't worry about me."

I only later understood that Borya and I hadn't really let each other out of each other's sight. I remember well that I wasn't remotely interested in any of my friends' vivas – apart from Borya's.

I went to the auditorium, where the viva was taking place, to meet him. He came out and announced: "I got an excellent grade!" We hugged, and he suddenly said, very seriously: "Listen, you and I have to get married." And I was serious, for the first time, and said: "I don't understand – how can you talk about marriage? I'm going back to Orenburg and you'll stay in Sverdlovsk." The conversation didn't go very well. Borya was hurrying off to catch a train to Tbilisi for his next tournament. I was hurt that he had spoken of marriage at such an unsuitable moment.

"All right, let's go our separate ways for a year – it'll test our feelings, and then we can meet again on neutral ground," he said in parting. I agreed. We said goodbye. It was clear that it would be for a long time – perhaps for ever.

# Getting Together with Boris

In 1954, when I came home at the end of the summer, I was surprised to discover that Mama was pregnant again – she was forty-two years old. Today it's not an unusual age to be pregnant, but in those days it was unthinkable. "Mama, you already have four – why more?" She was hurt. I later learnt that she had health problems, and the doctor had advised her to have a baby, so, for her, this was a forced decision – although Papa was simply delighted. I first met Vitalik when I went home to Orenburg after my viva. He was already six months old, and he was wonderful – a joy for the whole family.

I was taken on at the Vodokanal Trust as an engineer in the Technical Department. My main duties related to the operation of the filtration station. I worked with pleasure – the year went by without my even noticing it.

I corresponded with many of my Institute friends. Borya wrote to me from the very beginning – about business, about his feelings, about how he missed me. I didn't think he was writing to me alone – I even asked a couple of classmates about it, but it turned out that, apart from me, he didn't write to anyone.

I once received a letter from a friend we had in common, Galya Dvoryanchik – she had gone to the same school as Borya, but she was his junior by two years, and at the request of her parents he had, touchingly, watched over her. Galya sent me a photograph from a picnic at Shartash of a happy Borya in the company of girls from her friendship group. He had a plate in his hand that he was banging like a drum, and he was grinning from ear to ear. The picture somehow didn't sit well with what he wrote about himself, and I stopped replying to him completely. He summoned me by telegram to a telephone call centre – that's how we communicated in those days. "Why aren't you writing to me any more?" he asked. I tried to explain, but he just laughed. "Isn't it good that you're jealous of me?…" he said. After that, we carried on writing to one another – although, to be honest, I didn't like writing letters.

## Questions on the Margins

"Did you keep his letters?"

"Every one. But I destroyed mine – Boris was very upset when he found out. I didn't show his letters to anyone, even to my daughters. And I never used to reread them."

"Why?"

"While he was still around, it just didn't occur to me."

"And once he was gone?"

"I reread them now. Often. He comforts me with his warmth. But I never discuss this with anyone."

In June 1956, I received a telegram from Kuybyshev (as Samara was called then) from Seryozha Palgov – a friend of Boris's from his volleyball team.

The telegram read: "Boris has heart trouble – come immediately." I didn't hesitate for a minute. I took leave from work for three days, at my own expense. Without that, in those days, it would have been impossible to go. There were no flights from Orenburg to Kuybyshev, so I asked Papa to buy me a train ticket – thankfully, my parents didn't ask too many questions. Rita Usovich had a sister in Kuybyshev, and she called her and asked her to put me up. Rita's sister and I called all the hospitals and hotels, but we couldn't track down Borya. Finally, I managed to find out which hotel the volleyball players were staying in.

I reached the hotel by bus, but couldn't get in because the entrance was controlled by a turnstile. I had no choice but to wait until someone from his volleyball team came so I could ask after Borya. Suddenly, I saw him walking through the lobby. "Borya!" I shouted. He ran out of the hotel and stood there – alive and well. "What's wrong with your heart?" I asked. "It hurts. A lot," he replied, grinning from ear to ear. "From love for you." I yelled at him – what a thing to joke about! "You wouldn't have come otherwise," he said. He was right – I wouldn't.

My hotel was right on the banks of the river Volga, and had a large park in front of it. It was an amazingly beautiful place. We strolled around for several hours. When we got tired, we sat down on a bench and embraced, and we sat that way until morning. We talked endlessly – we hadn't seen each other for a year.

"You know, now we'll definitely get married," Boris said. Or perhaps I said that to him. In my mind, it almost seems that we burst out with this at the same time.

Everything was decided. Early in the morning, Borya put me on the first bus and went to the hotel alone: that day, he had an important game, and there was no time even to sleep. I promised I'd go to see him play. To this day, I don't understand why I suddenly changed my mind and returned to Orenburg – but that's what I did. I got all flustered – how could I go alone to Borya's game, in some unfamiliar stadium, without friends?

Borya was surprised – offended, even. But a few days later he sent a telegram to Orenburg – "Meet me at the exit of the railway station" – and gave me the date and time of his train. I took my sister Roza with me – she only knew Borya from his photograph. She waited for him at the exit, and I went to the platform and met him as he came out of the carriage. He hugged and kissed me, and I think we both felt as though we hadn't seen each other for an eternity. Interrupting one another, we shared our news. We went to my house – Borya wanted to talk to my parents about our wedding immediately, but Papa was at work, and only returned late at night when we were already sleeping.

As a result, Borya asked for my hand in marriage early in the morning. To my surprise, I became very excited, and I ran about in the yard. Then we sat down with the whole family at the table. Mama and Papa were happy with our decision, although Papa said, "It's too bad you're going away. Maybe you'll stay with us in

Orenburg? You could find work here, too…" Mama kept silent. She was happy for me and upset at the same time – once again I was going away from home. Now, possibly, for ever.

Then Borya, Roza and I went for a walk along the Ural river. We decided to go for a swim; I'm not a very good swimmer, and don't go in where I can't feel the bottom under my feet, but Roza swam a bit better and started showing off to Borya. The Ural is a very fast-flowing river, with whirlpools, and Roza was carried away by the current and began to drown. Borya rushed to the rescue – he grabbed Roza by her bathing suit, which remained in his hand when he dragged her to shore. I didn't even notice at first that the upper part of her bathing suit was gone. We never found it. We laughed for a long time. I saw him off on his train that night.

A month later, I took leave and went to see him in Sverdlovsk. We went with our friends Seryozha Palgov, Kolya Glebov and his wife, Nina, to the ZAGS in 1905 Square and scheduled our marriage registration for 28th September.

At that time, Boris was living in the men's dormitory at the Verkh-Isetsky Metallurgy factory (or "VIZ" – an enormous factory which is still in operation today). He had his own room, but there was no way I could stay in a men's dormitory – women were not allowed there. He did, however, suggest I stayed: "Lock the door! What will they do – break it down?" I categorically refused, so he suggested I go to Berezniki and live for a while at his parents' house, but he couldn't accompany me – he had to work.

I have to say that it didn't seem like a strange suggestion – perhaps because I was well acquainted with Boris's mother. She had sometimes visited Boris in Sverdlovsk and spent the night in my bed – it was comfortable for her there, as my bed was blocked off from the rest by a wardrobe. I knew that she felt very warmly towards me. She had once dared to ask about my relationship with Borya, and was very surprised when I said that we were just friends.

I wasn't only acquainted with Borya's mother, but also with his younger brother, Misha. "And I still have a sister, and a grandmother and grandfather… and the house is on the shore of a lake," said Borya. I was immediately filled with a desire to see that house on the lake, so I agreed to go.

Borya phoned his father at work to warn him of my arrival – there was no telephone at the house. His parents met me at the railway station in Berezniki, along with his brother and his sister Valya. Grandmother Afanasiya and Grandfather Vasily, Borya's mother's parents, were waiting for us at home. All of them were so glad to meet me that I didn't feel the slightest awkwardness.

They had four rooms. Borya's grandmother and grandfather were in one room, his mother and father in another; Misha slept on the couch in the living room, and I slept in Valya's room. She was still a schoolgirl.

Valya offered to give me the room, and said she would sleep on the living-room floor. But I was opposed to this, as we could fit together quite comfortably. So that's what we did, and no one objected.

Borya had slightly exaggerated in his description of the house. It wasn't on the shore of a lake, but rather across the road from a lake – but it was none the worse for this. It was white, clean and very beautiful. The Yeltsins had their own boat and a banya (sauna) on the shore, and there was a small kitchen garden by the house.

Boris's family had a kind of natural intelligence, even though none of them had had a higher education. Later I realized that all of them, including Boris's uncles Ivan and Dmitry, whom we met later, were people with a strong character. (The youngest of these brothers, Adrian Yeltsin, was killed in the war.)

During my first trip to Berezniki, I learnt that Borya's grandfathers, Ignaty Yeltsin and Vasily Starygin, were accused of being "kulaks" (prosperous farmers) in the 1930s, and faced much persecution. Vasily Starygin was accused of exploiting his workers. Of course, he didn't hire any hands – they were young men, usually relatives, who learnt the building trade from him. They would often build another relative's home, and that was how they learnt. Grandfather Vasily was a carpenter until his death.

Boris's grandmother Afanasiya was also very skilled. Not only did she do the whole family's sewing, but she also took orders. Before the revolution, she was a milliner. In her youth, she was very beautiful, and she preserved her beauty despite all her trials. She had fluffy, curly hair that was carefully coiffed, bright eyes and a straight back.

It was the same story for the Yeltsins. In the 1920s, four brothers had built a mill. For that reason, their property was seized, and they were accused of being kulaks. The family was not wealthy, but everything was seized – not just the mill and the house, but the axes, sheepskins, *valenki* (felt boots), and even a mattress filled with hay. The family was banished to the north, near the city of Serov, stripped of their belongings and property. It quickly transpired, however, that their village could not survive without their skills, and they were called back to fix some machinery that needed repairing. When they returned, they saw people wearing their clothes. Their house was quickly claimed by someone from the kolkhoz management.

Klavdiya Vasilyevna never spoke about the arrest of Boris's father. She didn't say a word to me – neither did she speak of it to Boris, his brother or his sister, and none of them ever knew about it: their parents didn't want to make their lives difficult.

Borya only learnt later – when he was given his father's file from the KGB's archives in 1992 – that Nikolai Ignatyevich had been arrested and sentenced to three years' hard labour on the construction of the Moscow-Volga canal. He learnt that his father had been sentenced under Article 58 – "Counter-Revolutionary Activity"; someone had informed on him – he had reportedly forbidden workers to read newspapers during work hours, and was supposed to have complained about bad food in the cafeteria. I think they needed experienced workmen for their construction projects of that time, and used these underhand methods to assemble a skilled workforce for free.

From the very beginning, I felt as if I was among my own relatives in this family. They didn't overburden me with work, and I was a very willing student in the kitchen, and learnt Borya's mother's recipes. We talked a lot about her life and about Borya's childhood.

I went back home to Orenburg – I had to choose the fabric for my wedding gown, and, try as we might, Klavdiya Vasilyevna and I couldn't find anything suitable in Berezniki. I asked Mama to hunt about in Orenburg, and she found some peach-coloured crêpe de Chine which I loved. A young seamstress made the dress, and one of her relatives guided her – and it seemed to me that it turned out better than if we had ordered it at some atelier. It was ready in just three days. It had a round collar, pin tucks along the shoulders, lantern sleeves and a thin belt with a ring covered by the same fabric.

Amazingly, the dress has been preserved to this day, against all odds. I wasn't aiming to look after it so well; Tanya and Lena loved to dress up in it when they were young, pretending to be princesses. When the skirt was pulled up under the belt, a train would appear behind. They grew up, and the dress was lost and forgotten. When we moved to Moscow, my sister had to pack our things, and we unpacked them as needed. My wedding dress turned up in one of the boxes – even the belt was still there. I was surprised to see the waist size again, which was just 65 centimetres. The hem was torn, the elastic in the sleeves had been lost with age and it had not been washed once – but it turned out that the dress could be restored: we had it cleaned, sewn up and the elastic replaced, and it looked like new. Now it is in the museum of the first president of Russia. Meanwhile, Boris bought a suit – he chose a dark-blue one, which was his favourite colour. He wore it to work for many years afterwards, until it was worn out.

NAINA YELTSINA

# Room with a Groom

Three days before the wedding, I returned to Sverdlovsk, where Borya had managed to get permission for me to live with him at the dormitory. Apparently the fact that we were to marry in three days held some sway. On 25th September we became man and wife – that's the day I consider to be the date of our union, even though our wedding wasn't until the 28th.

*Questions on the Margins*

"What day did you celebrate with Boris Nikolayevich – the 25th or the 28th?"

"We didn't celebrate either date. The first time we marked the occasion was on our 40th wedding anniversary – my daughters remembered about it. And for our 50th, we were sitting at the table, planning. We couldn't do the 28th – it was a work day, or we already had something in the diary, or something like that. 'Well, we'll just have to celebrate it on the 25th, when we became man and wife,' I said. 'Why didn't we know until now that you sinned before your wedding day?' my girls asked. We laughed so hard. But really, although that day – 25th September – was of great importance to me, Boris was the only man in my life. There were no others."

"Did you ever ask your husband about other women in his life?"

"Never. Why? For me seeing how he looked at me was enough to reassure me. He didn't speak about his feelings very often at all. When I was still quite young, I would sometimes be hurt, and he'd simply say, 'Well, you know everything anyway…' It was true – I did. Once, when he was no longer President, we were visiting Sergei Pavlovich Mironov, the head of the Presidential Medical Centre. I had to step out of the room for a moment, and Boris, nodding in my direction, said to Juliya, Mironov's wife, 'That is the woman I love – I have loved her my whole life.' Juliya only told me about this once Boris was gone."

We didn't think of having a fancy ceremony with a flowing veil and an exchange of rings – that just wasn't done in those days. At the Institute, Borya had organized our classmates' weddings, and now he started to make arrangements for our own festivities. Of course, we couldn't call it a "student wedding" any more – although the guests were mainly Institute graduates. Borya had his grandfather's copper wedding ring, but I don't think he ever wore it – I believe he returned it straight after the wedding. I didn't have a ring.

The ZAGS was quite small, and there was no special procedure, music or champagne. We simply registered our marriage. We drank champagne later in the dormitory. Everything that we could break – bottles, glasses – we broke for good luck.

Some friends created a planning committee, which included Misha Karasik, Yura Serdyukov, Kolya Glebov and Seryozha Palgov – about five or six of them in total. They booked a restaurant, came up with a programme and drew up the guest list. The whole evening – toasts, jokes, songs, conversations – was recorded on a tape recorder. Earlier on the same cassette an interview with our classmates had been taped. Unfortunately the reel was lost – we only listened to it once. The photographs were lost, too – the film turned out to be exposed. Only one picture remains – of my school friend Lyuba Bobylyova at the dormitory before we went to the restaurant. I was already in my wedding dress with a crêpe-de-Chine flower on my breast, which Lyuba had brought with her. At first I didn't think it really matched the colour of my dress, and it took us ages to pin it on – it never seemed to be in the right place. But our trouble wasn't in vain – it really livened up the dress.

There were a lot of guests gathered in the restaurant – we counted them later: there were 140 people – but only Borya's parents came to the wedding. Mine couldn't come – my youngest brother, who was only eighteen months old then, was ill.

When we entered the restaurant, we found that our friends had arranged themselves into two long rows – with boys on one side, girls on the other. We had to walk between them, but my legs were wobbling. I was wearing high heels – about three inches tall. Borya said to me quietly, "Don't shake! God, you're like an autumn leaf…" That was the first time I experienced something like that. It happened again many years later, when Boris had just become President, the first time I accompanied him as First Lady into the St George Hall at the Kremlin: once again, my knees were shaking – I couldn't walk. He sensed this, and took me firmly by the hand, and walked more slowly. Back then, on 28th September 1956, I only just reached the table at the end of the hall – I grabbed the corner, and then calmed down.

Yury Serdyukov was standing in front of us, holding a scroll about a metre and a half in length – our nuptial agreement. We had to dip our fingers in finely ground lead and leave an impression on the document to confirm that we promised to adhere to it – which would not be an easy task! I remember it required us to have enough children "for two volleyball teams – women's and men's" – that is, twenty. We read the agreement aloud, and it caused much merriment. Sadly, like the recording, it was lost – apparently it was used at someone else's wedding. I'm still hoping that I might find it at someone's house, and from time to time I torment our classmates – perhaps somebody will remember to whom it was given!

After reading out the nuptial agreement, we sat at table, and our friends raised toasts to us and cried "*gorko!*" – a Russian word that means "bitter". The custom is for the bride and groom to kiss to counter this and make it sweet. So we kissed. A lot. Even when, instead of "*gorko!*", our friends began to shout "Borka!", which was Boris's nickname.

For our wedding present, our friends chipped in to give us a little Saratov refrigerator – we had never dreamt of such a present. Neither my family nor Borya's had a refrigerator – there was only the cellar. It served us – and then my sister – for a long time.

*Questions on the Margins*

"What did Boris Nikolayevich give you as a wedding present?"

"Oh, nothing. He didn't give me anything, and I didn't give him anything. It didn't even enter our heads. And, to be honest, we didn't have the money."

"But did you regret not having a wedding ring?"

"Back then, I didn't think about having a ring. It was only a few years later that I suddenly wanted to have one. I bought a thin one myself, for 120 roubles. I remember the price – I had received my salary that day. I still have the ring. Boris saw it on my finger, and was surprised – and on my birthday gave me another one with a little diamond in it; before that he hadn't given me any jewellery. I don't even know how he guessed the size – but he did guess it right, and I really liked the ring and almost never took it off. My daughters liked it too – especially Tanya. At some point I gave it to her to wear. Unfortunately, the stone fell out. Tanya took the ring to a jeweller, and after a while I noticed that the gem was dull – she had been duped, and instead of a diamond they had put in a piece of glass. But what can you do – we didn't have the money for a new gem, and no one was wearing the ring… Much later, Tanya bought a new gem, and I began to wear it again, almost never taking it off."

"You said that your husband had not given you jewellery before that. Why?"

"Because I didn't wear it. Now, my Mama loved baubles, although she didn't have very many – only what her parents had given her in her youth: two pairs of earrings – one larger, one smaller – and some rings. She also had a wedding ring – a wide one. I don't think it was gold – I couldn't say what metal it was made from. In my parents' families there was no money for jewellery. For that reason, most probably, I wasn't attracted to it. The second and last time I bought jewellery for myself was also in Sverdlovsk. I really wanted some earrings and a ring with alexandrite, which changes colour – one of my colleagues bought herself some. Well, I went into the jewellery store and bought them. Apart from these two occasions, only Boris or my daughters bought me ornaments or trinkets."

After the wedding, we went to my parents' in Orenburg. We wanted them to share in our joy as well. We got our relatives around the table – there were a lot of people, but the party was not noisy: it was warm, homely. We returned in a train compartment – Papa bought us tickets, which was not easy then. My dowry – a metal bed with tubular mesh and a feather mattress sewn at one time either by Mama or Grandma – went in the baggage car. That bed served us many years, until we bought our first bedroom suite.

After that, of course, we went to Berezniki. I wanted to celebrate with Borya's grandmother and grandfather, and his father's brothers, for whom it was hard to travel to Sverdlovsk.

I remember these days as being amazingly bright and joyful. Borya and I felt very happy.

I resigned from my job – marriage was considered a good reason for not working off the three years required on assignment. Without a marriage certificate, my resignation would not have been signed. That was the procedure.

# By My Husband's Side

Soon after our wedding, Borya was transferred to a construction site building homes for workers at a chemical machine-building plant, Khimmash. We were given our first family home – a room in a two-room apartment. We moved in with the bed we had brought from Orenburg and the table and stools from Borya's dormitory. We didn't have any other furniture, but there were a lot of books that remained in piles on the floor.

Our neighbours in the apartment were the same kind of young specialists as we were – Yury and Zina from Voronezh. We lived together very amicably.

I immediately found a job as an engineer at the Soyuz-vodokanalproyekt (Union Hydro Canal Design) Institute. The work turned out to be interesting, and the group I was working with was simply marvellous. There was only one inconvenience: the Institute was in the centre of the city, so I had to commute in on the trolleybus. This wasn't the usual sort of trolleybus, but a single-track line. In order for oncoming trolleybuses to pass, the drivers had to get out of the cabin and move the rods by hand. Meanwhile, the passengers waited – and in the winter, this was especially torturous, as the trolleybuses weren't heated. As a result, the trip took two hours in each direction. Boris, unlike me, worked right next door, and he was usually home by the time I was back – at least, at first.

One day, when I was coming home from work, I met a classmate at the bus stop. "Did you know Borka Yeltsin got married?" she asked. "To whom?" I asked. She gave the name of the girl from the photograph which had been sent to me that time in Orenburg. "I'm very happy for her!" I said. Well, what should I have said – "No, he married me"? It was stupid. I told Borya about this, of course, and he had a good laugh.

It was a happy time. I positively swam in his attention and concern. To be honest, I would often pinch myself and think, "It can't be that one person could be so happy!" But I was.

## Questions on the Margins

"Was it hard getting used to one another?"

"No – it seemed as if we had known each other from birth. I think it's because of Klavdiya Vasilyevna's stories. During my first visit to Berezniki, she told me many stories about Borya's childhood. Well, and then we were together throughout school. So we didn't have to get used to each other. Our tastes and habits – everything seemed familiar. There was the sense that we had always lived together."

"Do you remember your first quarrel?"

"No – we never seriously quarrelled."

"That can't be!"

"Well, it can. Of course, there was the occasional tiff, but it never reached the point of having an argument – much less hurling insults or not speaking to each other. Even if I suddenly took offence at something, Borya would react with humour, and everything would go back to normal immediately."

"You both worked, and got tired… and you never snapped at each other?"

"We were accustomed to leaving work troubles at the door. Of course, sometimes Boris would come home upset – especially when he was working for the Party. I could see it, but I never badgered him with questions. If he wanted to, he would tell me himself, I reasoned. Sometimes he would go into his office and pull himself together. Neither I nor my daughters ever bothered him."

Gradually, Boris had more and more work, and he had to stay late, and I had to wait about at home in the evenings. I had to get used to this – I knew there was a lot of work at the construction site.

Lena was born eleven months after the wedding. When I told Borya we were going to have a child, he was delighted. He really wanted a son. It was a difficult pregnancy: I had morning sickness almost all the time; I couldn't eat – even the smell of food made me nauseous. When my colleagues had lunch at work, I had to leave the room.

I went to Borya's parents' to give birth – my youngest brother was three years old, so Mama couldn't take care of me. I didn't want to go to Berezniki – it was hard to leave Borya, but he was worried that if I stayed at home on my own all day something might happen, and we didn't have a telephone at home. So, about ten days before my due date, I got on a train with my big belly. Boris accompanied me to the car. His parents met me in Berezniki.

From the very beginning, I felt calm at Klavdiya Vasilyevna's house. Ever since our wedding, I called her "Mama" and used the familiar form of "you". It somehow came about naturally – perhaps because it was the custom of my family.

The birth was a difficult one – the contractions began in the evening, and I gave birth to Lena at 10.20 the following morning, on 21st August 1957. She weighed seven pounds, two and a half ounces, and was 52 centimetres long. We had expected a son – there was no ultrasound back then, so the sex of the baby was guessed by the shape of your belly. Boris always referred to the baby as "he" – in his letters he would ask, "Well, how is he doing in there?" Even in the telegram Boris's parents sent him after the birth, they had written, for some reason, that we had had a son – I've kept that telegram to this day, just as I have the note that Borya sent me while I was at the birth centre. Borya's brother Misha brought it to me. It turned out later that Boris had sent the note to him in a letter before he knew the sex of the baby – but the fact that we had a girl didn't bother him at all. He was happy, and he only said: "The next one will definitely be a son."

After giving birth I stayed in the hospital for a week. Borya couldn't come to visit because of work. Every day – sometimes more than once – Klavdiya Vasilyevna visited me, and she brought warm pirozhki. She made very tasty dough. I was terribly hungry. I remember that when they brought my daughter to me to nurse, I couldn't tear myself away from the warm pirozhok, which had cheese on it and raisins that tasted like fresh grapes.

We didn't pick a name right away. At first we had thought that if we had a girl we would call her Sveta. Then we wavered between Sveta and Lena. We agonized, and asked our friends. In the end, we decided that "Yelena Yeltsina" sounded pretty, and the choice was made. We registered Lena's birth in Sverdlovsk.

After Lena's birth, I remained in Berezniki for almost a month, staying in Valya's room. Borya was working, and it was hard for him to get away, as it was the end of the third phase – the submission of construction plans – but at some point he managed to take leave. I couldn't meet him off the train, of course, and when he came into the house, Lena was asleep on Valya's desk. Boris really wanted to wake her up to see what kind of eyes she had – I had told him in a letter that our Lena was a beauty with green eyes.

As soon as she woke up and started crying, he immediately took her into his arms with the utmost calm.

We discussed the possibility of moving to Berezniki – in Sverdlovsk we had a room in a communal apartment, but how could that compare to his parents' home, after all? Boris tried to arrange a transfer to a potash-plant construction site more locally, but it didn't work out. He was instead offered a new job in Sverdlovsk. In mid-September, a telegram arrived from him: "Tell me when to meet you." I understood: it was time to go home. But my return had to be postponed again – Lena fell ill, and I returned with her only in late September. Klavdiya Vasilyevna went with me.

It was a Sunday, and Boris met us at the railway station. I remember he had a smile plastered across his face the whole time. He was wearing a new ivory-coloured tussore-silk suit. It was a summer suit, and it wasn't the right season for it, but he evidently wanted to be dressed up for the occasion. Klavdiya Vasilyevna later said, "A happier father I have never seen in my life!"

We came home to find a warm kitchen with a heated stove, and I could unwrap Lena. There was no gas in our first apartment – we had to heat the stove with coal or firewood. Later on, Borya left the room and asked us to wait for a little while. A few minutes later he called us, and we went in; on the table was his present: an orange crystal punchbowl with cups and a ladle. Why a punchbowl? I imagine because it was such a pretty thing, and it caught his eye. We didn't drink any punch, of course, but when guests came, we could pour wine, beer or compote into it. Now Lena has the punchbowl – she didn't want to give it to the museum; she only gave them two of the cups for their collection, which are now in the same window as my wedding gown and the note my husband sent to the birth centre.

Boris wasn't at all afraid of taking little Lena into his arms. He helped me to bathe her – which, without hot water in the house, wasn't easy. Klavdiya Vasilyevna stayed with us for a week – she cooked and did the laundry, so all I had to do was take care of the baby. When she went back to Berezniki, everything fell onto my shoulders – but if I got too tired, Klavdiya Vasilyevna would drop everything and come again. After Lena was born, I took maternity leave for three months. With great difficulty, I managed to come to an arrangement with my employers so that I could take an additional two months' leave without pay. When I returned after maternity leave, Lena was still breastfeeding. I had to pump milk at the Institute and feed her later from a bottle. She liked that, and a month later she refused the breast.

Klavdiya Vasilyevna arranged for a friend of hers to work for us as a nanny. I always think of Aunt Shura with gratitude; she was a very kind and conscientious woman, and I had no trouble trusting her with Lena. Aunt Shura became like family to us. She cared for Lena until I next took maternity leave, when I was expecting Tanya.

Zina, my neighbour from the other room in our apartment, also helped me out – and I helped her too: it just so happened that our daughters were born at almost the same time. First came Lena, and then she had Lyuda. If Zina had to go out somewhere, I would look after Lyuda; if I had to go out, she would take care of Lena. Lena was about three months old when we were offered a two-room apartment – with hot water and a gas oven. It was in a new building, but on the same street, Griboyedov Street, as our communal apartment. I was very glad – but I couldn't think how I would get along without Zina.

I do still remember a few trivial details of everyday life, which provide a fuller picture of how we lived. The building had many flats, and the empty lot behind it was divided into allotments for the tenants: each family was given about 160 square metres of land. Our friends persuaded us to take the land, and we planted potatoes – which we immediately forgot about. My papa, when he visited us that autumn, remembered about the plot. He could hardly see it for the weeds, but when he pulled out a bush, he found some decent, large tubers. As a result, we dug up even more potatoes than friends who had spent the summer tending to their allotments. We kept them in the cellar – each family in the building had a spot there.

Our door was always open to our friends. When Klavdiya Vasilyevna came to visit, she was always surprised to find that some classmate or other was living with us – our old classmates would always stay with us when they were in Sverdlovsk on business. Sometimes they stayed for a long time – Nina and Kolya Glebov spent six months with us while they waited for their own housing. We liked this life. It was never an inconvenience – even when our daughters were born.

We had to move quite often – and each time we got closer to Boris's work. We gave up one apartment and were assigned another by the authorities. Sometimes the new one would be worse than the previous one, but we didn't have much choice. This happened, for instance, when Boris was transferred to a development site building housing for workers at a nearby rubber plant. In order to get there, he had to get up at six in the morning and walk ten kilometres, whatever the weather – there was no direct transport from Khimmash to his new workplace. Therefore, when we were offered a three-room apartment next to the construction site, we moved without hesitation. The apartment was bigger, but it turned out that the plumbing didn't work, as the builders had made a mistake. The toilet was in the street. This is how we spent the winter.

But one day we decided we couldn't stand it any more, and we moved again to a two-room apartment which was significantly closer to the city centre – this was now our fourth apartment. There were two entrances to the building: one was for residents, and the other was the entrance to Yuzhgorstroi (South City Construction) – the trust for which Boris worked.

In 1960, Tanya was born. She was 52 centimetres long, just like Lena. But she was two hundred grams heavier. Boris had once again hoped for a boy – everyone said that this time we would have a son. And, for some reason, we had believed these predictions.

*Questions on the Margins*

"Was your second child planned?"

"No – neither Lena nor Tanya were planned. It was God's will, so it seems."

"Did you discuss whether you wanted children or not?"

"We never talked about it. We were glad to have them."

"You weren't afraid that your second pregnancy would be as difficult as the first?"

"I don't think I thought about that."

"And was it difficult?"

"Not as difficult as with Lena – but when she was born it was harder, because I had to carry her in my arms, and Lena was still small. I would go to the shop, and in one hand was my bag and in the other a baby."

I remember the doctor's face when Tanya was born – huge dark eyes looked out over a white mask.

"What is it?" I asked. "A daughter," she said. I cried out: "We want a boy!" "Be glad that you're still alive," she answered. I don't remember anything after that – they put a mask on me and I passed out. I can still see in my mind's eye the scene before I fainted – the doctor was waving her hand and shouting, "Hurry! Anaesthetic, quick!" And then all was dark…

A little later Borya came to the birth centre with our old classmate Misha Karasik. I saw them standing under the window – I knocked on the window and held up a note saying "Too bad, it's a girl!" They found a piece of paper somewhere and answered straight away: "Thrilled to hear it!" As a present for the birth of our second daughter, Boris gave me a little gold watch – which, like the punchbowl, I kept for many years, until I passed it on to Tanya, who gave it to the museum.

It turned out that the doctor who delivered Tanya lived next door. After a while I ran into her while I was out for a walk with a perambulator. "Are you crying?" she asked. "No, I'm just happy," I said – and I really was very glad that I had had another daughter.

Maternity leave was by now extended to a year. Tanya was luckier than Lena – I could breastfeed her for a year. I only stopped because I fell ill with pneumonia.

When I was ill, Boris took the year-old Tanya to Berezniki. He had to travel at night. Unfortunately Tanya started crying, and Boris wasn't able to soothe her.

Later on, he described how his fellow passengers had advised him to wrap bread in a rag and give it to the baby to suck – but even that didn't help. Eventually, he unbuttoned his shirt and hugged Tanya to his chest, where she suckled for a while, and then calmed down and fell asleep. I can't quite picture this happening, but Borya insisted that it was true.

*Questions on the Margins*

"Did you want more children?"
  "Boris wanted a son."
  "And you?"
  "I didn't."
  "Why?"
  "Both pregnancies and births were very difficult. And after that it was hard, too – there wasn't a great difference in age between my daughters, and I worked… All in all, I realized I couldn't risk having a third. Now I regret it."
  "Only now?"
  "I've regretted it for a long time… But it was already too late to have a child by the time I began to regret it."

We had both Lena and Tanya baptized in Orenburg. There was no question of baptizing them, as far as I was concerned. There was only one church in town, however – but I didn't want to have the girls baptized there, so we went instead to a prayer house where my godmother, Mama's sister, went. It was she who baptized both of my daughters. Even though they were baptized, however, neither ever wore a cross.

*Questions on the Margins*

"Did Boris Nikolayevich know that you had your daughters baptized?"
  "Of course!"
  "He didn't object?"
  "No."
  "Did you ever talk about faith?"
  "Never. But at Easter I always baked kuliches, as my Mama had done – although I didn't go to church before, and I didn't bless the kuliches. But whether or not they observed church holidays in Boris's family, I don't know."

"When did Boris Nikolayevich start to go to church?"

"When he became President. We had never been churchgoing people."

When I went back to work, Aunt Shura wasn't able to babysit Tanya, so I had to look for a new nanny. Someone recommended an old lady, who was deaf – but I taught Tanya to touch her hand when she needed something. After a while, Aunt Shura returned. Lena initially reacted well to having a new sister, but she did at times get cross with me, as she thought that I loved Tanya more – she was jealous. I tried to explain to her that Tanya was small and required more attention, but after that I began to be more careful, so that both daughters got equal attention.

In April 1964, I was appointed chief project engineer – a role I had not sought. On the contrary, in fact: I had turned it down, realizing that it would be very hard to juggle my career as well as the family. For a year, however, I was acting chief project engineer – and then I could not longer say no: my colleagues insisted that I should take on the position on a more permanent basis. I worked more than twenty years in that job, until we left for Moscow. I always loved my work – although, of course, it demanded much time and effort, and I sometimes had to stay late and go on business trips, since our projects were scattered across the Urals. But it was an interesting role nonetheless.

# By a Builder's Side

Boris worked so well that he rapidly moved up the professional ladder. Foreman, section head, department head, chief engineer at the Home-Building Plant (DSK), director...

And this was despite the fact that he was regarded as a difficult character. He got into arguments with his bosses, was issued reprimands – and then again was noted for his successes.

Again and again he was assigned new projects – he always delivered the desired results.

He constantly thought about construction, and was always searching for something new. His first idea was installing panels with wheels. The panels were brought from a reinforced-concrete factory – enough for an entire floor – and installation would begin at once. In this way, the construction process was greatly accelerated. The homes that were built in this fashion later came to be called "Khrushyovki", after the then Soviet leader Nikita Khrushchev – they were the first affordable housing we had in the country. Today they are criticized, but back then they gave people the chance to move out of barracks and shared accommodation into modern apartments with plumbing and central heating – and there were millions of people living like that. Another innovation was the no-less-famous "team contract", where members of a team mastered all the technical specializations necessary and took on a whole construction job.

Whether Boris headed a section, department, whole development or, finally, the whole Sverdlovsk region, no matter what his responsibility was, it always became the best of the bunch.

He was also very punctual. I don't think he was ever late during his whole life – and he demanded this of others, too. His discipline amazed even me sometimes. I was quite capable of being late for work – when I took my daughters to nursery, they would start crying – all sorts of things would happen. As a result, I never scolded those who reported to me for being late. But Boris simply could not bear it.

I never saw such tidiness on anyone else's desk, either. It was always that way – both at home and at the Regional Party Committee, and even in his Kremlin office. If a piece of paper lay on the desk, it was perfectly smooth. At home, stacks of documents were piled on the desk. Once I went looking for a piece of paper, and I accidentally moved something – Boris, of course, noticed and asked who had been there.

If we ever returned late from visiting friends, I could carelessly toss my things onto the floor. He would never do that – he would always hang up his clothes neatly. When he came back home after work, if he saw that there were some scraps of paper lying around on the shelf where the telephone sat, he would get rid of them as he passed. He taught our daughters tidiness, too – and both of them grew up to be as organized and neat as Boris.

The greatest threat for Lena and Tanya when they were misbehaving was "I'll tell Papa". Now *that* was what they feared! Boris didn't even have to raise his voice – he would just look at them, that's all. But, at the same time, if they were trying to defend their opinion in an argument with me, they would run to him, and he would allow everything. He would say to me: "They'll make mistakes, they'll get some bumps – they'll learn on their own." That was his principle.

We had no great problems with either Lena or Tanya. Our daughters were always very responsible and independent. As I said, I never interfered in their school affairs. In the lower grades, they walked to school with a girl living nearby, who was usually accompanied by her grandmother. They always stayed for the after-school programme, from which the lady picked them up again. When they got home, they heated up supper themselves and did their homework. If it was the day for it, they went to sports training. All I could do was call from work – which I did, constantly. My colleagues would often laugh at me: "You don't even let them walk across the street without calling them!"

Of course, we never laid a finger on the girls. Tanya claims that I once hit her with the belt from a dress. Perhaps that happened – to be honest, I don't remember. But it was important to both me and Boris that family relations should be peaceful.

Work did not leave us much free time. Boris later admitted that he couldn't remember details from our daughters' childhood well – when they began to walk, what their first word was. I understood, and I wasn't offended.

On work nights, Boris didn't get home until late, and the girls and I waited for him so that we could chat a bit while he sat down to supper – of course, that was only on the days when he got home before midnight. On Sundays, we always tried to have family dinners. These evenings – when the whole family would sit down at table together – became our tradition. Even now that Boris is gone, we still get the whole family together on Sundays at my house.

One day, the old women who always sat in the courtyard on a bench saw Boris and me together for the first time. He was holding Lena and Tanya by the hand. We were, in fact, on our way to a restaurant for our Sunday dinner. When I saw them the next day, they said, "What a man you've landed yourself!" "What man?" I said. "He was so affectionate when he took your daughters through the courtyard yesterday," they said. "But that's their papa! You can't have seen him before – he goes to work when you're still asleep and returns when you're asleep again."

On his days off, Boris would play with Lena and Tanya – which, for him, was a joy. On Sundays he would usually go around the house with a hammer, looking for something useful to do. Then he would think up something for the whole family to do – for example, he would announce: "Today we're having *pelmeni*!" In Moscow, they don't make *pelmeni* the way we do in the Urals. In Moscow, they first roll out the dough – then, with shot glasses, cut out circles and spoon in the filling. In the Urals, they don't roll out the dough, but instead roll it into a sausage, then cut it into even pieces, and only then do they roll it out – one piece of dough for each *pelmen*. So Boris would roll the dough. He would do this with amazing deftness, and always managed to make pieces for the rest of us to get on with. Then we dolloped on the filling and shaped the *pelmeni*. Boris prepared the ground meat himself – he carefully checked the thickness and seasoning. We would usually cook far too many, which we would store during winter on the balcony.

One Sunday the head of the DSK Planning Department came over – some documents needed to be signed immediately. I opened the front door to her and pointed her towards the room in which Boris and the girls were, and I returned to the kitchen. Before too long, I realized that I hadn't heard any conversation, so I went out once again into the hallway and saw our guest still standing in front of the door, not going into the room. "Is that him?" she asked, pointing. Boris was sitting underneath the table with Tanya and Lena. I led her into the room, and she said, stunned, "I didn't expect to see that – he's a completely different person at work."

*Questions on the Margins*

"Did Boris Nikolayevich notice how you dressed?"

"Of course. He had good taste; sometimes he would even say to me, 'Don't put on that dress – put on that other one.' This wouldn't happen very often, but it did happen, nonetheless. Lena and Tanya would always ask his advice."

"But not yours?"

"Of course, I would give them my opinion, but they would run to Papa for advice. Even before their graduation party."

"You once mentioned you bought clothes for Boris Nikolayevich. Was he hard to please?"

"He didn't really buy himself anything. But he was always happy with what my daughters and I bought for him."

Boris never had the time to take care of his health. And it seems to me that he didn't think about it, even though he had problems with his heart – even when he was young, when he suffered complications after severe strep throat during the first year. He seemed not to think about it, but I always remembered it. The first time I saw him clutch his heart was when he was talking to someone on the telephone at home – he was only about thirty-five years old. Suddenly he clapped a hand to his heart and sat down on a chair (he would usually talk on the phone standing up). "I don't feel well," he said. I called a doctor. When he felt better I said, "You shouldn't work so much. Think about me and the children – what will become of us if something happens to you?" "I love you all very much, but work still comes first," he said. Since this conversation, I lived with the understanding that the family and I always came second, after his work, until 31st December 1999, when he resigned from the post of President.

"A Gypsy told my fortune," Boris went on. "She told me that I would live until the age of forty – I have to fit everything in." I felt bad, but I laughed and said, "I don't want to hear that nonsense!" I didn't believe in fortune-telling, of course, and I still don't – nonetheless I subconsciously waited for his fortieth birthday in fear, and when it passed, I thanked God.

In 1962 he was offered a trip to the health spa in Kislovodsk. I was glad – it seemed like a good idea to me. The offer was only for one person. "Don't worry," I said, "the girls and I will be happy spending the holidays in Berezniki." I really wanted him to rest properly. He left.

Two days went by. Then I received a summons to the post office, to the call centre. I was frightened – what had happened?

"Come here immediately," said Boris. "I can't get along here without you. Otherwise I will drop everything and fly straight back to Sverdlovsk."

I tried to talk him out of it. "But it's good for you! There's volleyball, good company…" I tried to convince him as best I could. People around me in the post office listened as I described the charms of resort life, and started to laugh at me – it was a small space, and there were no booths. The men in particular were amused. It must have seemed very funny from the outside: a wife trying to talk her husband into having a holiday without her. I went home from the post office and told Klavdiya Vasilyevna everything. She immediately decided I had to go – she persuaded me, too: "You also have to take a rest!" She took care of the children.

Boris was happy, of course – as was I. He rented me a room in a nearby hotel – I couldn't get a room at the health spa. He met me off the train and took me straight to the park. Kislovodsk was beautiful in the spring – there were raised and sunken terraces filled with roses – their scent was so strong your head spun. Ever since then, I've grown roses wherever I can. Here, in Kislovodsk, was the first time I saw flowering chestnut trees.

We strolled together until late at night – although, before my arrival, Boris had formed a friendship group. We forgot about the treatments. "Oh, the heck with them," said Boris, waving his hand dismissively. This was happiness. Ever since, Kislovodsk became our favourite place. We went fairly often, and holidayed there almost every year. We would usually visit in spring. Even after Boris retired, when we could travel the whole world, we were still drawn there.

That first time, we returned from holiday a bit early so we could spend a few days with our daughters. We flew to Sverdlovsk, and, without stopping at home, went straight to the railway station so we could go on to Berezniki. We brought a huge bouquet of peonies from Kislovodsk. I had never seen those flowers before. The bouquet survived both the plane and the train, and we gave it to Klavdiya Vasilyevna, who was pleased.

Boris immersed himself in work again. He always pushed himself so hard that it was frightening – he never spared himself, as if there was always a safety margin. Since I realized that this wasn't really the case, I constantly worried about him. But it was useless to try to talk to him about it.

According to his colleagues, Boris was strict with his subordinates – but he never indulged in rudeness. If the work required it, he would be firm. If there was no other way, he would fire someone, and for several days afterwards, he would be uncomfortable. And, generally speaking, he would find a new job for the person he fired. He never got into settling scores with anyone.

People think that it is impossible to get by on a construction site without drinking. But over thirteen years of work at various construction organizations, Boris came home sober every single day. He never drank at work – he didn't celebrate the completion of a project with his comrades, as was the custom in those days. Once my colleague, whose husband worked with Boris, came up to me and said, "My husband lost a crate of cognac. He bet that Boris Nikolayevich would join the rest of them at the restaurant to celebrate the completion of the wool plant. But he didn't come." I wasn't surprised.

Boris had notions about how a boss should behave, and he always heeded them. For example, he never swore – even at the construction site, not to mention when he worked at the Regional Party Committee or at the Kremlin.

\* \* \*

When Boris became chief engineer at DSK, we moved to a two-room apartment on Lenin Street, in the same building as the Sporttovary (Sporting Goods) shop. When people asked where we lived, we would say, "At the Sporting Goods." I even say that now, when I speak about that home. Sporting Goods was probably our most comfortable apartment: we had two large rooms, a long hallway… Our daughters remember that apartment as their childhood home – they started school here. It was very convenient for me – fifteen minutes' walk from work, and the shops nearby. I tried not to ride on public transport. Especially after work.

It was in this apartment that we got our first furniture set. Before that, we lived with the things we had brought from Orenburg – the metal bed, the table and stools, the crudely knocked-together bookshelves… These are now at my sister's dacha.

Once, my friend Tamara Golubyova and I went back to my apartment after work. She was quite shocked by my metal bed with its unsightly knobs. She kindly ventured: "There's a set of furniture made from Karelian birch in our furniture store – would you like me to buy it? It costs 600 roubles." "But I only have 300," I said.

"Get a loan from the mutual-aid fund."

We had these funds in every department at work. Everyone put in their contributions, and could take a loan if they needed one. Two or three days later, we bought the furniture: beds, a three-door wardrobe, night stands and a dressing table. We arranged them in the apartment – by the time Borya came home, I even managed to buy fabric for the curtains in the colour of the Karelian birch. They didn't actually fit, but I pinned them up – I hung them on the windows, and they looked nice. I wanted to give him a nice surprise.

Borya came into the bedroom and said, "Where did all this wood come from?" I was almost hurt. "You don't like it?" I asked. He laughed. "Of course I like it!" This furniture went with us from apartment to apartment. Then we gave it away to my brother, and it served him a long time, too.

We bought our first dinner service while travelling through the Carpathian Mountains. We couldn't find any services freely available in Sverdlovsk. The service we bought was of coarse white porcelain with a blue stripe, and suitable for twelve people. There was also an enormous soup tureen – before that, I didn't realize that soup was served in a special dish. From then on, when guests came, I put the borsch or *shchi* into it. I also used it to serve compote. Ever since then, we stopped using the punchbowl – we kept that as a souvenir. The dinner service went with us to Moscow, and we still have some of the plates.

Boris was never interested in material things: he only once proposed making a major purchase – a colour television. The telly, just like the furniture, cost 600 roubles – and again, we didn't have enough money for it. It wasn't that we were poor – Boris made a good living, and I also worked, but just as the money came in, out it went again. Borya said, "Let's borrow money for the TV from Misha." Misha, his brother, worked at the construction site with him, and he had no family. We borrowed some money from Misha, and added what we could, and it was just enough.

We never saved money. We didn't even have a savings account. Both my salary and Borya's sat in a box by the mirror, and we took money out when we needed it. That was how it was in my parents' family – cash was in an unlocked trunk. It never occurred to anyone to lock it.

*Questions on the Margins*

"Did Boris Nikolayevich turn over his salary to you?"

"Borya almost always held managerial positions, so his salary was put in an envelope and brought directly to him in his office. He would carry that envelope in his jacket, and in the evening, when I ironed his suit, I would take the envelope out and put the money into the box by the mirror."

"You left him without money?"

"No, of course not. I always checked to make sure he had ten or twenty roubles in his pocket – he just didn't pay any attention to money. Once, before I turned over a coat to the dry cleaner, I checked his pockets and found a big sum – about two months' worth of my salary. I asked Boris about it. He thought long and hard, and then, after a time, he remembered that he had been given a bonus, and he had put it in his pocket and forgotten about it. Another time, an envelope accidentally ended up in a box of toys that we gave away to our neighbours – luckily, they brought the money back to us. Borya never once asked what I spent money on.

1. Naya Girina. Sverdlovsk, 1953.

2. (above, clockwise from the top) With her fellow "school activists",
Chkalov, 1949: Lyuba Bobyleva, Valya Pigareva, Lyusya Semyonova,
Sonya Sveshnikova; 3. (below) With four fellow students at the
Urals Polytechnic Institute, Sverdlovsk, 1950.

4. (above left) With her school friend Sonya Sveshnikova and her sister Galya, 1954; 5 (above right) In the woods near Chkalov, 1956.
6. (below) Student life, Sverdlovsk, first half of the 1950s

7. and 8. (above) Naya and Boris at the time when they met at the Urals
Polytechnic Institute, Sverdlovsk, 1951;
9. (below, from left to right) The kolkhoz "Troublemaker": Lyusya Vedeneyeva,
Rita Batsulova, Borya, Nolik Lavochkin and Volodya Anisimov.

10. (above) Naina's parents Iosif and Maria, and her younger
brother Vitalik, near their house in Chkalov, 1956;
11. (below) On vacation with Boris in Kislovodsk, 1962.

12. (above) With her daughters Tanya (left) and Lena (right), 1962.
13. (below) Working as Chief Project Engineer at the Hydro Canal Design Institute, Sverdlovsk, 1970s.

14. (above) Boris and Naina holidaying with friends in Abkhazia, 1966;
15. (below) With Boris and her daughter Lena, Sverdlovsk, 1971;

16. Boris and Naina on the day of her birthday, Sverdlovsk, 1971.

Our student friendship group stayed in touch over the years, and we spent as much time together as we could. We celebrated holidays together, even though we had young children. Once, our friends descended upon us to celebrate our new home – we hadn't even managed to set out the furniture – we had to sit on the floor. They bought lots of watermelons, and we put a sheet on the floor instead of a tablecloth.

Another time, our group of friends got together one Friday evening, and we decided that we'd go to Perm for the weekend to visit some of our classmates (there were seven of them there), whom we hadn't seen in a long time. We had to catch the train – there was only one, and it left late at night. In the morning, we reached Perm.

Another time we were sitting at someone's birthday party, and found out that one of our friends wasn't able to come, so we quickly packed up and brought food and wine to him. This happened a few times, and we didn't usually call beforehand.

We loved songs, and many of us had good voices. Boris had a great ear; he would usually sing the harmony part. We always asked Yasha Olkov and Roza Klimova to sing a duet. Yasha also wrote poetry (and even published several collections). Andrei Mogilnikov and Volodya Sakharov wrote comic epic poems, which were really funny.

\* \* \*

In 1966, Borya's papa Nikolai Ignatyevich started getting his pension. He and Klavdiya Vasilyevna went together to Basmanovo to visit relatives. In the neighbouring village of Butka, at that time, there was a house for sale. They sold their house in Berezniki and returned to their homeland, from which their family had been deported during the collectivization thirty years before. That summer, they bought a farm, with a cow, pigs and chickens, and they built a banya.

Borya and I were thrilled – Butka was much closer to Sverdlovsk for taking the girls to see their grandparents than Berezniki was. From then on, we sent them to Butka for the whole summer. They loved their grandparents very much. Klavdiya Vasilyevna sewed them dresses and went with them into the forest to pick berries. Sometimes their grandfather took them on his motorcycle in search of strawberries. They also picked mushrooms, which were amazing in Butka, and Klavdiya Vasilyevna pickled them beautifully.

Grandma bought the girls identical blue tracksuits at a local shop, and white kerchiefs, which they tied behind their heads, village-style. They looked exactly like their Butka friends, who they spent a lot of time with.

Klavdiya Vasilyevna gave Tanya and Lena fresh milk to drink, believing it to be very healthy – but they couldn't stand it. Grandma, however, would call them after every milking: "Tanya, Lena – milk!" She'd give them brown kalach with the milk, which she baked herself – even to this day, my daughters don't think there is a tastier bread. Lena and Tanya eagerly helped Grandma with the housework, and they worked with her in the kitchen garden, learnt to milk the cow and to churn butter. First, they divided the cream from the milk in the separator, then they churned the cream into butter using a special sort of plunger. Grandma also made them wash the wooden bridges that led from the house to the road with sand. Essentially, Klavdiya Vasilyevna taught Lena and Tanya everything she could – and the girls couldn't get enough of it.

Nikolai Ignatyevich continued to work after retiring – he had a natural talent for building, although he had had no special education. He had always dreamt of inventing a bricklaying machine – he never created one, but he submitted so many proposals for streamlining work that the bonuses he received for them added up to more than his salary. Under his direction, a hospital, school, post office and shop were built in Butka. Even today, the whole village remembers him with great affection.

One day we decided to organize an adventure for the girls and go camping. We chose a patch near a dam on the Belyakovka River near Butka. We put up tents – we stuck birch branches into the four corners on the outside. It looked very nice.

At night, however, I woke up because I heard some loud breathing right next to the tent – and then, a little later, there was a heavy thumping. The day before, people in the village had spoken of a bear being spotted in the area, so I woke up Boris. "I think it's a bear," I said. He listened. "Somebody seems to be snuffling," he said. As he was going out of the tent, I said, "Take a knife!" He went out, and I heard him laughing. I crawled out of the tent to see a cow with black and white splodges standing in the morning twilight, nibbling at the birch branches. As hard as we tried, we couldn't chase her away – it seems she had wanted to drink some water from the creek and had then wandered into our camp.

*Questions on the Margins*

"What does the word 'love' mean to you?"

"It's hard to sum up in one word the feeling that connected us. They often say a connection is made of more than love. That's how it was with us – it's not a question of words, but it's about the feeling that you simply can't live without a person. He never let me go, and I didn't let him go."

"What words did you use between yourselves to talk about your feelings?"

"He was spare with words – he didn't keep telling me 'I love you'. He would simply come up to me, put his hand on my shoulder, and it would seem as though he had said everything he needed to say."

"So there was never any strong display of feelings?"

"Of course – but I won't speak of it. That belongs just to him and me."

Later in that same year, 1966, Papa tragically died. He and Mama were standing near a neighbour's home and chatting with the owner. It was already dark. Mama said that she heard the sound of a motorcycle, but she didn't see it. Other witnesses said the motorcycle was racing at a great speed, weaving from side to side. Mama landed in hospital with a fractured cervical vertebra – Papa was killed on the spot.

Boris and I were on holiday at the time. We had gone to Adler – it was my first trip to the seaside. We stayed in a private apartment near a fish plant. We didn't like it very much there – the smell of fish followed us everywhere – so we decided to change our plans and go to my sister Roza's house in Leningrad. She was supposed to come back from holiday in Germany, where she was visiting her husband, a military man, who served there (although his parents lived in Leningrad). When we arrived, Roza had not yet returned, so we strolled happily around town together.

Meanwhile, our relatives were looking for us in Sverdlovsk, in Berezniki – no one knew that we were already in Leningrad. They sent a telegram to Roza, but we received it instead. It was Navy Day, and we returned from watching a parade of Navy ships, happy and gay, to this terrible news.

With great difficulty, we managed to buy plane tickets – the telegram wasn't certified by a doctor, and it was the holidays. There were no direct flights, and we had to fly via Moscow. We only managed to get to Orenburg on the day of the funeral – we took a taxi from the airport to my parents' home, but it was empty: everyone had already gone to the cemetery. We didn't manage to get there until the last minute – the coffin was at the edge of the grave. My sister only got there after the funeral… When I saw Papa, my eyes glazed and my legs gave way – Boris was only just able to catch me.

Papa died in the fullness of his health and vigour, at just fifty-six years of age. There was a huge number of people at his funeral – many knew and loved him.

We returned to Sverdlovsk, but I was in a real state – it felt as though I was slowly going mad: I kept having strange feelings.

Boris and I would come out of the cinema, and I wouldn't be able to understand where the crowd was going. Boris started to come home earlier, and often suggested we visited friends or went to see a film – he was afraid of leaving me alone. In short, he understood that there was something wrong with me. I went to see a doctor in our building – where else could I go? There were no psychotherapists at that time. The doctor, who I knew quite well, listened to me patiently, and I asked her to give me some kind of sedative. I don't recall how long we talked for that day – what I do remember, almost word for word, is what she said to me at the end of our conversation: "It's easy to give you medication, but no good will come of it if you don't understand that you have to pull yourself together, for the sake of your children and husband." This conversation had more of an effect on me than I could have imagined. When I left, I saw the world in a different way – the sun was shining again, and it was a beautiful day… I had long since stopped noticing such things. I ran home, quickly climbed to the third floor, went into our apartment and began to mop the floor.

Of course, the stress that I had been suffering from had left its mark. I noticed that my face had become terribly bloated; my eyelids were swollen and almost transparent. It turned out that the nerves had brought on an allergic reaction. I was given tablets that made me fall asleep at my desk at work. This made me worry even more – after all, I was the Chief Project Engineer, and my colleagues relied on me. The doctors changed my treatment to injections of calcium chloride, and to keep the allergy under control I had to run over to the surgery on the way to work – but I was never able to overcome the allergy completely: it has remained with me for the rest of my life. As soon as I get nervous, I swell up – I'm often told now that I look better than in the years Boris was President. It's quite likely – there were too many worries then.

\* \* \*

My first pleasant memory after Papa's death is of a trip to the South in the summer of 1967. A group of our old classmates took a road trip in two cars – three families, with our children. Zhenya Bespalov's car was a Volga, while Yura Poluzadov had a Moskvich (he and his wife worked in Indonesia and earned enough money for such a car). All in all we were six adults and six children – three boys and three girls. Borya and I didn't have a car, so our family was split between the two cars.

We consulted a map and chose a route. At first we decided to go to the Caspian – where there were sandy beaches, unspoilt nature and fewer people. We reached Uralsk and then realized that we couldn't go any farther – the harvest had begun, the roads were packed and there was an endless procession of trucks filled with grain. What could we do?

We decided to go back and change our route, and travel along the Azov Sea – despite the fact that we had been on the road for two days already. We reached Orenburg and spent the night at my parents' home – we parked the cars in Mama's yard. There were lots of us, so some had to sleep on the floor in sleeping bags. The next day, we packed Mama's cucumbers and tomatoes for the road, and once again were on our way.

Finally, we reached the Azov Sea. We stayed at Berdyansk, which was a quiet, sparsely populated resort. The Azov Sea charmed us. It was very shallow – you could walk half a mile and the water would only be up to your waist – and there were no waves… Then we decided to go on to the Black Sea.

On the Moscow-Simferopol motorway, Boris offered to take the wheel of the Volga – and Zhenya immediately agreed. "You can't let him drive," I protested, "he doesn't even have a driving licence!" I knew that Boris had driven a dump truck a long time ago, in his younger years, at the beginning of his construction career, but I had never seem him at the wheel myself. At first he drove slowly, but we gradually picked up speed – I think at one point he was going a hundred kilometres an hour… Thank God, there were few cars around, and it was an open road. He spent about five or six hours behind the wheel. Since I'm quite scared of going fast, I could barely contain my fear. At one point my right leg began to hurt – it turned out that I was back-seat driving, stepping on an imaginary brake.

Finally we made it to the Black Sea, and we drove along the coast looking for a clear spot without too many people. We enjoyed the fresh, salty air. In the evenings, we sat at the campfire, singing songs and just listening to the waves breaking on the shore. Boris really loved the sound of the sea – he could sit on the beach by himself for a long time.

The children quickly became a tight-knit group, but their fathers spent a lot of time with them, too – taking them fishing and organizing games for them. Everyone had fun.

We spent about ten days on the Black Sea. In the South, it was still warm and sunny, but on the way back, the temperature dropped. Somewhere outside Kazan, when we woke up in the morning, we found frost on the grass. Boris proposed sending the women and children home on the train – we bought tickets with difficulty: everyone was returning home, and the start of the school year was just around the corner.

This was one of the best trips of my life – we changed the route on the fly, and we didn't know where we would be spending each night; we saw two seas, drove through many cities, and saw mountains, rivers and amazing landscapes.

We didn't go on any more road trips – perhaps because we only got our own car, a Moskvich, when we were in Moscow.

# By a Party Worker's Side

In 1968, Boris was invited to work for the Regional Party Committee. He didn't want to accept the offer; he never loved Party work – he always believed that doing work was more interesting than supervising those who did it. Those who derive pleasure from power probably love controlling others, but Boris wasn't that sort of person, and Party work seemed dull to him. I understood him well, and for that reason I didn't want him to be transferred to the Party Committee either. The pay was significantly less than he received as the director of the home-building firm: on top of the basic DSK salary, he was regularly paid bonuses – although, of course, salary wasn't the most important factor in our choice.

The first time the idea was floated was when we were at a birthday party at the home of a former classmate, Ala Chernetsova, whose family was friends with the Ryabovs – Yakov Petrovich was then Secretary of the Regional Party Committee. When Ryabov offered Boris the opportunity of joining the Party Committee, Boris replied evasively: "Thanks – I'll think about it…"

I was there during the conversation, and when we got home, of course, the subject came up again. Boris said firmly, "I'm not leaving construction." Soon after their conversation, Ryabov invited Boris to a talk at the Party Committee. While he was there, the offer was extended again, and it was rather hard to refuse in such a situation, so Boris agreed to become head of the Construction Department. I was not happy.

Of course, I quickly realized that this work was just as interesting for Boris: it turned out that he could still work as he had before – only it was now on a regional scale. His routine didn't change much – he would still leave for work early in the morning, and would only return when our daughters were already asleep.

He did, however, have to go on more business trips – there were a lot of construction projects scattered across the region.

Although, as before, we didn't discuss work problems at home, I did keep up with what he was doing. I was always fascinated by the construction projects he was working on – and I was, of course, involved myself in construction in my job. Boris found his bearings fairly quickly in his new position. Soon he began to be invited to the ministry in Moscow – this became quite usual, but he didn't want to leave Sverdlovsk.

I can't say that our life changed drastically with Boris's transfer to the Party Committee. Everything felt the same – my work, our friends, our everyday problems. Klavdiya Vasilyevna helped me to look after the girls just as she had done before – she would come to us six or seven times a year. My mother wasn't really involved with her granddaughters – my youngest brother, Vitalik, was only two years older than Lena, and that was enough for her to worry about.

Mama took Papa's death very hard. She remained in Orenburg with my two brothers, Tolya and Vitalik – Volodya had by that time left for Sverdlovsk to study, like Boris, Industrial and Civil Construction at our Institute. The whole family was ever so proud of Volodya – he was the only one of us to graduate from school with a gold medal, and from university with honours. Mama, Tolya and Vitalik lived together for several years, until another tragedy struck our family in 1972.

Late one night, Tolya was returning home from a Komsomol meeting. It was raining heavily, and he was walking next to the thick acacia bushes at the side of the road. After a while, he had to cross the road – he stepped out from behind the bushes and went straight under the wheels of a taxi – the rain had apparently drowned out the sound of the vehicle. The driver was a decent person – he took Tolya to the hospital as fast as he could, but it was already too late.

A year later, my younger brother was drafted into the army. He was sent to serve far away from home, in Mongolia – and Mama was left alone. We understood how hard it was for her to stay alone in the house where our large family had once lived – moreover, it was hard to keep up such a house. Despite all this, she didn't want to move – she said she wanted to stay in Orenburg with Papa and Tolya. Even so, we insisted she moved in with Volodya – he wasn't married at the time, but he had been given a nice studio flat – so she sold the house and moved in with Volodya. She ended up living with him until he got married – then she moved in with Roza, who had returned from Germany and also lived in Sverdlovsk. Every summer, Mama went to visit Papa and Tolya in the graveyard, and every time she went, she would stop in Titovka. Her last visit was in 1982 – a year before she died.

In 1972, Boris's papa died. A few years before, he had unexpectedly suffered a severe stroke when he was at our house. He was sitting in front of the television, and suddenly fell over onto his side. Fortunately, the ambulance arrived quickly. After that, he had problems with his speech, and he couldn't move around on his own. To make life easier, he and Klavdiya Vasilyevna moved in with their youngest son, Misha, who also lived in Sverdlovsk, and they spent the summer at the dacha. Misha had a little house on a nice plot of about 550 square metres of land. Klavdiya Vasilyevna worked in the garden with pleasure, and she kept the home beautifully. Nikolai Ignatyevich was much better for a little fresh air.

Klavdiya Vasilyevna would visit us often, of course. She would call us and say, "I made some *pelmeni* for you and froze them – I'll bring them over straight away." Her *pelmeni* were always amazing – so neat, and completely identical. Mine never turned out like that – Papa never got used to them. He would say, "You have to put three in your mouth at a time in order to get any taste!" Klavdiya Vasilyevna tried to help me – she even wanted to wash the windows for us. Of course, I wouldn't let her. At her age, she shouldn't have been washing windows at all, let alone on the third floor. She treated me with more care than even my own mama did. Whenever I go to the cemetery, I always say "thank you" to her – not only for Boris's sake, but for my own, too. I loved her very much.

*Questions on the Margins*

"So your mother didn't want to live with you?"

"No – we did offer her a room a number of times. I think she was a little afraid of Boris, even though they got on brilliantly, and Boris called her 'Mama' from the very beginning of our married life. Also, our lifestyle seemed too hectic to Mama. Once, when she was in our house alone, Borya's assistant went in to get a suit for him. She just couldn't understand it – how a stranger could come in, open the wardrobe and take some clothes away…"

"Did your mama come to visit you in Moscow?"

"No, not once – I went to visit her. Unfortunately, Mama died when I was far away. She died of cancer. During the last month of her life she was rarely conscious, and we took it in turns to sit with her round the clock at the hospital – my sister, my brother, some relatives from Titovka and myself. It came at a time when Boris was expected to fly abroad for official visits – I was torn between sitting with Mama and my duties as First Lady… When I returned, it was just in time for the funeral."

"He wasn't jealous about you and Klavdiya Vasilyevna – he wasn't hurt that you also called her 'Mama'?"

"Not at all – he was happy. He said, 'You're lucky.' You couldn't get jealous about Klavdiya Vasilyevna."

A little time after Boris's transfer to the Regional Party Committee, we moved again into a new apartment: we moved to Plotnika Street, into a three-room apartment – which, although it had more rooms, took up less floor space than our previous one. The building was old, too, which I didn't like, but it did have the virtue of being closer to the Party Committee headquarters, and it was near the polyclinic where Boris was registered. We had our own bedroom, which is where we put the Karelian birch set; the girls had their own room, too, and the third room served as our living room. A huge plus for me was that School No. 9 – one of the best in Sverdlovsk – was just next door. Lena and Tanya moved there straight away. Lena was in seventh grade and Tanya was in fourth grade. It was a school specializing in physics and mathematics, and in order to get in they both had to go for an interview – which they managed to pass.

Lena was very active at school. Back in fifth grade, she had become the head of the Lastochka (Swallow) children's club, which was held in our courtyard. It was a big meeting point for the kids from our courtyard and neighbouring ones, and they all loved to go there after school – but the club was hidden away in the basement. Lena went to the ZHEK (housing office) to demand that a more suitable space be found for them to meet up – and her request was accepted.

Once, Lena was awarded a holiday to Artek (an international children's camp at that time). One of the activities there was writing a letter to a "foreign friend", sealing it in a bottle and throwing it into the sea. Lena's letter resurfaced, and ended up in a magazine called *Vozhaty*. She had included our home address, and she received replies from all over the country. Even soldiers wrote – they didn't know how old the author of the letter was. There were so many letters that she didn't manage to read them all.

Lena was also the chair of the Pioneer Troop Council, and she helped out at the Komsomol... She wasn't a busybody – it was just that her classmates looked upon her with respect. She took on all these civic burdens very seriously, and spent lots of time and effort on them.

When Lena was in charge of organizing Komsomol matters for her class, she didn't get on with her biology teacher, who began to pick on her. My daughter, knowing the attention she would receive, would prepare especially well for biology, so that she could answer impeccably – but it never helped. She would still be given a four – always one off the highest mark. Her classmates believed that the teacher was simply mocking her; one of the other pupils would be answering at the blackboard, and the teacher would interrupt them in the middle of a sentence and say, "Yeltsina, continue." None of the other students were treated like this – but, as ever, I didn't interfere until I was summoned to the school – of course, it was I who had to go, since Boris's time was taken up by then.

When I got there, I put my head into the classroom and introduced myself: "I'm Lena Yeltsina's mother." The teacher came out into the corridor, and told me straight away that she could not give Lena a five – to which I replied, "That's your right. You're the teacher. I don't understand why you summoned me."

To be honest, I was upset by the teacher's treatment of Lena, but I thought that my daughter could take care of it by herself. Unfortunately, that didn't happen, and she graduated with a four in biology on her report card – although her average grade, which was more important for getting into the Institute, was a five.

Usually, for our girls' birthdays, we would create a newspaper and put it on the wall. I brought the special paper from work, and we would write articles and draw the accompanying pictures. I remember one year, for one of Lena's birthdays, Boris wrote one of these articles about her future: "I see a serious, businesslike woman – she holds an important, high-up post…"

*Questions on the Margins*

"Why do you think Boris's prediction didn't come true?"

"After Lena graduated from the Institute, which she did with honours, she got a job at a construction exhibition at the VDNKh (Exhibition of National Economy Achievements) organization. But she didn't make a career out of it."

"Was it a conscious choice, or did it just happen that way?"

"I think it was her choice – she was busy with her family. And I don't think she regrets it at all. She has three remarkable children, and five grandchildren already – and a model home. She's a beautiful housewife."

Tanya was also very independent from an early age. She asked me to sign her up for figure-skating sessions, and she went to train six times a week on her own. Although she was quite small, no one accompanied her, and no one followed her athletic career. She turned out to be very talented – she was one of the best in the club, and if she had not had problems with her back, she would have continued the classes, as she had dreamt of being a figure-skater. But it didn't work out: the doctors said that jumps were doing her no good – especially the hard landing on the ice – so she had to give up figure-skating at the age of eleven. But she immediately found a replacement, and she took up volleyball, like her father, and this time everything worked out for her – she became a good player, and travelled to compete in various tournaments with her team. Later, she played on the Moscow State University team. Boris often invited her to play with his team – she would pass the ball to him, and he would spike the ball powerfully. I would often see them play and watch how they would slyly exchange glances when they made such strikes. It was obvious that Papa was proud of his daughter, and Tanya was proud of Papa.

Like Lena, Tanya did well in school, and she mainly got fives. Even so, she really wasn't a nerdy honours student – she was always the ringleader; everything revolved around her in class, and she was forever at the centre of everything. Like Lena, she was chair of the Pioneer Troop Council. Most of her friends were boys – not only in school, but also at the Institute, and then later, at work, her friends were mainly male. She never had close girl friends. "Where are your girl friends?" I would ask. "It's boring being friends with girls – they gossip, and that's of no interest to me," she would reply. From an early age, Tanya was always help-ing someone. If one of her friends fell ill, she would hurry to help them so that they didn't miss out on their lessons.

Tanya and her friends were always thinking things up – one day it was a "secret language", so that adults couldn't understand them, and the next it was going on all-day hikes along unusual routes. Her fondness for adventure continued well into her Institute years – I remember that during the first year, when she came to Sverdlovsk in the winter, she and her classmates went on a hike. Some of the other girls were afraid of the frost and dropped out at the last minute – but Tanya wasn't afraid, and went on the hike with four boys. The woods were already snowy, and it was cold; one of the lads took his dog, which blazed a trail for them, and they even put up a tent in the snow.

From time to time my daughters would quarrel – sometimes Lena was hurt that we were spoiling Tanya a little, as she was the youngest in the family, and sometimes Tanya would get upset that Lena wouldn't allow her in her "grown-up" group. But, of course, these childhood hurts were not serious. Their friends were often at our house – on Sundays, Boris sometimes joined them, and they drank tea together, and I knew them all by name.

There was always a lot of jokes, laughter and surprise in our family, especially on birthdays or holidays. Boris always tried to go beyond simple presents.

On one of my birthdays, he came home to find me with guests around the table. He unbuttoned his coat and, like a magician, began to pull pieces of silk from his pockets: at first it seemed it was a few pieces for making a dress – but then he had an entire bunch of flowers in his hands.

My birthday is in March – which, in Sverdlovsk, is still mid-winter – but Boris always managed to find fresh flowers, probably from the greenhouses that were sprouting up everywhere then. At some point, Boris began a tradition of giving me enormous potted azaleas, which were nearly as tall as me. It turned out that they were grown in a greenhouse at the Kalinin Factory. Azaleas are capricious flowers, but very beautiful. I put ice in their pots, and they bloomed for a long time. And when their flowers were gone, we gave them back to the greenhouse.

Boris always gave me enormous bouquets, too – he wanted his presents to be "a lot". He always chose big toys for our daughters – and, later, for our grandchildren.

He knew how to make us happy, often in entirely unexpected ways. Once, on 7th March, the evening before International Women's Day, one of our friends brought us perch and whitefish from the North. Boris donned a burgundy-coloured apron – a present I had bought him for Red Army Day on 23rd February, which I had picked up during a trip to Germany – and shooed everyone out of the kitchen. As we later discovered, he had found a recipe in a book called *Tasty and Healthy Food*. He fooled around for two or three hours; I tried to get into the kitchen, but he wouldn't let me – "You'll come in when I'm finished!" he said.

By the time our classmates arrived, he had set the table – he knew how to do it properly, and he would sometimes do it. In the middle stood a plate of stuffed fish, which turned out to be very tasty – but he never made it again.

In choosing gifts for Boris, I did things more simply – I usually bought him books, shirts and ties. Later, the girls and I would give him watches. He would be happy with his gifts, but casually give them away later – he would take off his tie, watch or cufflinks and give them to someone. Lena, Tanya and I would be very upset. "That was our present!" we would say. He'd laugh. "So what? Let the man be pleased."

Boris was invited to the tenth anniversary of the Academy of Architecture and Construction Sciences, which had been one of his initiatives, in 2003. He was given a cloak, and by way of thanks he presented them with his gold watch, which we had given him on his birthday. Several years later, Natasha, the wife of Alexander Shirvindt, the art director of the Moscow Satire Theatre, told me that the watch had been given to her relative – and he was still wearing it.

Our daughters inherited their passion for surprise from Boris. They always arranged our family holidays, and did everything they could to make them memorable.

When Lena was turning eighteen, we decided to give her earrings. Tanya wanted to make a big candle in the shape of a woman's head looking like Lena and wearing the earrings. It was not an easy job – first, the head had to be sculpted from clay, then it had to be covered with plaster. Tanya got the plaster and paraffin from a friend whose mother worked in a hospital. She made the plaster mould, then she poured paraffin into it – but there wasn't enough. She went round the house gathering up all the candles, and melted them. But even that was not enough, so Tanya and her friends went from door to door collecting candles from our neighbours. They filled the bathtub with cold water and put the head in it, and it cooled – and it turned out just as she had hoped. We lit the wick for Lena, but she immediately blew it out. The candle has remained whole up to this day, and she still has it in her home.

At the building on Mamin-Sibiryak Street, we had wonderful neighbours. We grew very close to the Bashilov family. Sergei Vasilyevich was head of Glavsreduralstroi (Main Mid-Urals Construction). I remember his mother made the tastiest *tyanuchki* – toffee sweets made from milk and sugar – which were like the Korovka (Little Cow) sweets you could buy in the shops. She taught me how to make them, and his wife, Alexandra Ivanovna, taught me to knit. There was no wool in the shops, but I bought a blue Japanese lurex sweater, unravelled it and knitted a blouse. That was the first and last time I knitted something – but the blouse lasted even until we were in Moscow.

We would often visit our neighbours, and they would come to our house as well. Sergei Vasilyevich and Boris would return home together from trips to various construction projects, sometimes very late. Alexandra Ivanovna and I would wait for them, and when they returned we all had supper together.

Many Party Committee workers with whom we were friendly also lived in that same building – we were especially close to Fyodor Vasilyevich Vashlayev, head of the Department for Forest Industry, and his family. When Fyodor Vasilyevich went on a business trip to Tavda, he usually brought Tavda carp back to Sverdlovsk, and he always invited us over for dinner – he would bake the fish in sour cream in the oven. I never ate such tasty ones in my life.

In general, Boris had an informal relationship with his colleagues. They would celebrate holidays together, and loved to play pranks on each other. One time the head of the Agricultural Department gave Boris a chick for his birthday. The present was loaded with meaning – they were building a chicken factory in the region. The chick bobbed around the apartment and squawked constantly. We put him in the bathtub for the evening, but he got even louder – there were evidently good acoustics in there. It seemed that the chick didn't like our house: we couldn't sleep at night. We could probably have simply returned him – that wouldn't have provoked anything but laughter, I think – but I was embarrassed to do so.

I called the chicken factory, hoping to place him there, but they refused: "He would have to be quarantined," they said. Boris's driver, Yura, saved the day. He heard us talking on our way to the dacha, and proposed taking the chick to his relatives in a village. So that's what we did. From time to time, Yura would report to us on how the chick was getting on: he soon turned into a huge rooster, and he crowed beautifully. They didn't slaughter him: he guarded the chickens and lived until a ripe old age.

We tried to spend the weekends at the dacha in Istok – that was our first government dacha; before that, we had rented a room in a house with four apartments in Shartash. We really loved the dacha. We thought it likely that there was an estate there at one time – there were unusual plants, and a white pavilion still remained. I still believe there's no more beautiful place in the suburbs. But I haven't been there for a long time – maybe everything has changed…

The Party Committee's dacha was a little bit more spacious, but there we also had a room in a two-storey home – room enough for just two beds, a sofa and a table. Lena and Tanya slept on campbeds. Unlike the home at Shartash, this dacha was winter-ready, so now we could spend weekends outside the city during the winter, as well as in the summer. Sometimes we had to go without Boris, as he was often away on business. We celebrated holidays with our dacha neighbours in a cafeteria – the food was great, and that way I could forget about cooking.

*Questions on the Margins*

"Did the Party crowd bother you? Presumably the atmosphere was quite different from that with your student friends?..."

"No – there was nothing about these people that bothered me. They were great people. But, without a doubt, we weren't as close to them as to our classmates. They were mainly connected to Boris by their job."

"None of your classmates worked with him?"

"No. Boris didn't think it was possible to mix personal relationships and work – and none of our friends ever turned to us asking for a job."

We had agreed back in our Institute days that we would spend our holidays together once every five years. So in 1960 and 1965 we got together in Sverdlovsk, and in 1970 we organized a grand adventure. We bought tickets for a cruise from Perm to Rostov-on-Don. There were seventy of us all together, including the children.

It was a wonderful holiday. We kept thinking of fun things – first we dreamt up KVN (The Club of Happy and Inventive People), then a Neptune Holiday, or a musical evening, and we made a noticeboard every day. Everyone would run to our party room for concerts, and if they couldn't fit in, they would glue themselves to the windows. The children made firm friends with one another, and wanted to spend all of their holidays together.

I remember moments and stories from that trip to this day – especially a performance of the "Dance of the Little Swans" by Boris, Yasha Olkov, Zhenya Chinyakov and Zhenya Bespalov. When they came out onto the improvised stage, everyone rolled about with laughter. The four "swans" were all about six feet tall, barefoot and had parcels of towels strapped onto their hands and feet with bandages – we couldn't find any ribbons in our cabins. People laughed so hard you couldn't hear the music – but the performers never smiled once, and they danced with serious faces until the end.

We sailed to Rostov-on-Don, and from there we all flew to Gelendzhik on the coast. Lyuba Olkova's parents lived there, and we set up camp in their garden. In the midst of the tents, we put out a table with a curtain over it, and pinned on a sign saying "TAVERNA". We took it in turns to cook, and we ate fresh fruit and drank local wine. We walked rather a long way to have a swim – we didn't want to have to push and shove on the crowded beach which was close by. As always, the atmosphere was easy and happy.

One day when we were on the beach, Boris noticed that all the women among us were wearing earrings. "Why don't you pierce your ears?" he asked me. I hadn't ever thought of doing so – but why not? Lyuba Olkova pierced my ears there and then with an ordinary needle – but, to be completely honest, the holes weren't quite symmetrical. Someone lent me some gold earrings so the holes wouldn't close up. When we returned to Sverdlovsk, Boris gave me my first pair of earrings.

We kept up the tradition of spending our holidays together every five years for the rest of our lives – even when Boris became President, nothing changed.

*Questions on the Margins*

"Student friendships normally fizzle out quite quickly. They didn't for you?"

"No – we still meet up, even now. After the 1970 trip, there were other trips together. In 1975, we sailed on the Yenisei River from Krasnoyarsk to Dikson Island. In 1980, we went to Bulgaria. In 1985, we took a ship from Perm back to Moscow. After that, we decided that the years were passing by too fast, and that we should meet up more often – so we tried to meet twice every five years. In 1987, we went to Pushkinskiye Gory (Pushkin Hills). In 1990, we went to Jūrmala. We've met up many times in Moscow and Yekaterinburg. And we marked the 50th anniversary of our graduation in Kislovodsk."

"When a classmate becomes President, don't relationships with old friends change?"

"Not at all."

"No one was shy?"

"No. Yet, after Boris was elected, some people called him 'Boris Nikolayevich' when we met."

"And how did he react?"

"He would say, 'Are you mad?'"

During the years Boris worked at the Party Committee, we often took boat trips on the Ural rivers, which we really liked to do. The group was usually made up of Boris's work friends. One of the first boat trips we went on was on the Chusovaya River.

We drove to Tagil in our government cars, and only reached the city in the afternoon, so we set sail late. It was rather risky – lumber used to be floated down the river, so there was a lot of driftwood, which made it dangerous to sail in the dark. Towards the evening it started raining, and we had to find somewhere to set up camp and spend the night as quickly as we could. That turned out to be quite tricky: both of the riverbanks were very steep, and by the time we found a place to drop anchor, it was already dark – thunder and lightning rent the sky, and it was no longer just raining, but pouring down. Although we were wearing waterproof ponchos, we were still thoroughly soaked. No matter what, we decided we had to moor the boats. We dragged them on shore in the dark, and it was only in the morning that we discovered we had put them on a high ledge – how we managed to do that was a mystery! We had to lower them back down into the water.

We sailed up the Chusovaya a few more times. There were no mobile phones in those days, and since Boris was involved with Party work, we sometimes had to stop and call Sverdlovsk from a rural post office.

Besides the Chusovaya we also loved to sail up the Belaya River, which wasn't as dangerous – although it too has rapids. The Belaya has amazing banks, which were totally covered in flowers – they would be red from fireweed, then turn to purple from willow herb, then white from daisies, then lilac from bluebells.

We mainly ate canned food and fish on our trips – although one of Boris's colleagues once brought along four live chickens, which strolled around our campsites, and were kept tied to pegs. We made "Bishop's Soup" from the chickens – first, we boiled the chicken, then we added various fish – freshly caught, of course. I couldn't watch as they slaughtered the chickens – but the soup was very tasty.

We passed on our love of camping to Tanya and Lena. Lena and her family went to the Kamchatka, to Sakhalin, to the Kuril Islands and Mongolia… Lena's husband was an experienced hiker, and nowadays he sails rafts along the most difficult routes. Tanya is well travelled too – she once went on a catamaran trip along rivers in Karelia and the Kola Peninsula with a group from the Salyut Design Bureau, where she works. She even brought her son, little Borya, with her – even though they had to ford dangerous rapids.

# By the First Secretary's Side

In 1975, Boris was made Secretary of the Regional Party Committee, and, a year later, First Secretary. He worked in that position for nine years – and during those years, the region flourished more than any other.

His immediate promotion to First Secretary was a rare occurrence – but that's what happened. Yakov Petrovich Ryabov recommended Boris for the post when he was transferred to Moscow – Ryabov appreciated Boris very much, and it seemed to me that he was always very happy with his work.

It was only years later that he began to describe working with Boris in Sverdlovsk in negative terms.

*Questions on the Margins*

"It seems that Ryabov changed his attitude towards Boris Nikolayevich after he criticized the course of Perestroika at the October Plenary?"

"Even earlier – when Boris was First Secretary, we often went to Moscow, and we always stopped off to see Ryabov. But when we went to say goodbye to Yakov Petrovich before his departure for France, where he was to serve as ambassador, I sensed that his attitude towards us had changed. I hadn't expected to be met so coldly. I even asked Boris, 'What happened?' He didn't know. I thought it was likely that someone had spread some rumour about Boris, and that Ryabov had believed it. Then Ryabov gave that speech at the October Plenary, where he, like everyone else, attacked Boris. Also, he later wrote a book, in which there are so many lies that I don't want to get into it. It was all very offensive."

"Did you try to talk to Ryabov?"

"I wanted to. Many years after Boris was gone, we met at the funeral of Yury Vladimirovich Petrov, and we sat at the same table at the wake – I looked up and saw an aged and somehow unhappy person sitting there… I couldn't bring it up with him then."

Even when Boris found himself in a position of power, he didn't see himself as such. He was, they said, a good manager, and he did everything he could to make the region one of the most thriving in the country. He was interested in the construction sites, the manufacturing, the agriculture and, of course, people's lives – it was very important to him that their lives would be made easier. No matter what grand projects he had to undertake as First Secretary, he never forgot their impact on people – the logistics involved in getting stock to the shops, and the need for public transport and clinics.

The construction sites in Sverdlovsk at that time were famous throughout the country – the Nizhny Tagil Rolling Mill, for example, was the largest factory of its kind in Europe, and it used completely new technology.

At that time, there was a need for a new motorway to link Serov in the north to the rest of the region – in winter, the people living there were completely cut off. Under Boris's management, the motorway was built, despite the fact that the Soviet government refused to finance the project – Boris convinced some local firms to fund its construction from their own budgets. It was a very long stretch of motorway, and each firm sponsored a section of the road. Boris personally supervised the construction. He often visited the various sites, and in the end the scheme paid off and turned out brilliantly – and it is still in use today.

Since our region is an industrial one, food has to be imported. The steady supply of food to the city of Sverdlovsk was one of the First Secretary's chief concerns. In those days, produce came from all over the country, including faraway cities such as Stavropol. It was then that Boris became acquainted with Mikhail Gorbachev, who headed the Stavropol Party Committee.

Not all produce suppliers were noted for their helpfulness. Due to the time difference, late-night conversations on the phone were sometimes necessary – which is how I would learn that butter, sugar or meat was running low in the region, or that there was only three days' supply of bread left. I was always frightened to hear about these shortages – what if deliveries were disrupted? This was one of the main responsibilities of the First Secretary. Like me, Boris wasn't worried that it would be unpleasant for us, but rather that others would find themselves in a difficult situation – he did everything in his power to stop that from happening, but having to rely on other regions for food always bothered him.

Once, I found him reading a textbook about raising cattle. "Why are you reading that?" I asked, surprised. "I'm trying to understand how to increase milk production under the conditions we have in the Urals," he replied. Boris wanted the region to be able to sustain itself – at least in part. He took the initiative to build chicken factories, and before long we had local chicken and eggs in the shops. Reservoirs were put to use as fisheries – including those of the Beloyarskaya Nuclear Power Station and the Reftinskaya Thermal Power Plant. "No, not Beloyarskaya!" I said, frightened, when he told me. "Relax – there are clean parts there," he said. Fresh fish appeared in the stores – carp and pike, I think. Hothouses were also erected on an industrial scale. In the Urals, tomatoes, cucumbers and even watermelons can be grown. Even by the early 1980s, people came to us from other cities – Chelyabinsk, Perm and Tyumen – for produce.

Boris kept tabs on how things were in the shops – not from office memos, but from me, since I went shopping for food after work: we didn't have household help. We always preferred simple food: we didn't splurge on delicacies – we never felt the need to do so. In my youth I had eaten enough caviar to last me a lifetime – Papa had brought buckets of it from Guryev, which had saved us when we had nothing to eat at the dormitory. Sometimes I managed to bring something tasty home from my business trips to Moscow: I always went into the Yeliseyevsky shop and bought smoked sausages and frankfurters. I also bought caramels and toffees from the shop on the ground floor of the Hotel Moskva – you couldn't get them in Sverdlovsk, and the children really liked them – as well as Edam wrapped in foil: although you can find it everywhere now, back then it was hard to come by.

When I went shopping in Sverdlovsk, I tried to remember where everything was, what was missing and what people were queuing for, and I would feed the information back to Boris. He would usually reply, "I know" – and he really did. He would go into the supermarkets regularly so he could see with his own eyes what was on the shelves. He talked to people. The First Secretary didn't have bodyguards – he only had a driver.

*Questions on the Margins*

"Did you often discuss the region's problems at home?"

"Practically never. As I said, we didn't usually talk about work."

"That's hard to believe – you come home from work, you each have news from the day, but you don't mention it to each other?"

"People who get home from work at six o'clock probably have time to relax and talk about their day, but Boris would come home closer to midnight, and he'd be tired – exhausted, even. He needed a brief respite, at least, from work problems. I always understood that."

"Did you wait up for him to get home, or did you go to bed?"

"What do you mean 'wait up'? I had so much work to do at home that I had to finish it when Boris was asleep."

Boris had a notebook that he kept on his bedside table. If an idea came to him during the night, he would turn on the lamp and jot it down. I was always amazed by this – "How can you sleep if you never switch off?" He would just wave me away. And no matter how rough he felt, he would always get up early and go to work.

He once came home from a business trip with a temperature of 38°C, which continued to rise. I called our neighbours over – a doctor, Tamara Pavlovna Kurushina, and Valentina Korlyakova, who was a nurse. "Get me back on my feet so I can go to work tomorrow," he told them. Tamara Pavlovna tried to talk him into staying home – but it was in vain. She gave him a shot and a tablet to lower his temperature. While we waited for the medicine to work, Tamara Pavlovna, Valentina and I went into the kitchen.

"I know I'm a doctor, but there's little I can do," said Tamara Pavlovna. "And I'm his wife, and I can't do anything," I rejoined. There were tears of frustration in our eyes. "Let's have some tea with cognac to relax us a little," I suggested. Tamara Pavlovna had a great sense of humour, and her answer was, "No – let's have the cognac without the tea." So I poured the cognac – which we did drink with tea, after all. The next morning, Boris didn't even check his temperature before he went to work. There were times when things were even worse.

Once, he got an ear infection. He went to the surgery, hoping they would give him some painkillers so he could go on a business trip, but the doctor, Zoya Sergeyevna, firmly said: "You can't go." She must have realized that Boris had not taken her very seriously, because she came to our house that night and talked him out of going. "If the infection spreads to the inner ear, we'll have to operate," she said. "I can't not go – they're expecting me!" replied Boris.

In the morning, off he went. When he returned, he would usually call me from the car, as he had a radio telephone: "I'm nearly there." Sometimes his aide would call me from the reception at the Party Committee, saying, "He'll be there in fifteen minutes." And that's what happened this time.

Slamming the door to the foyer, I went out to greet him in the stairwell. I could see Boris there, climbing heavily up the stairs, one hand leaning on the wall and the other holding the handrail. Behind him was his driver, trying to hold him up. "Borya, what's wrong with you?" I shouted down the stairwell. He just shook his head. I ran downstairs, and could see that he was losing his balance.

He was tormented by pain all night, and in the morning he went to see the doctor, who referred him straight to hospital. For three days, the specialists debated whether they should operate or not – the infection had spread, and could no longer be treated with antibiotics. They did end up operating, but it wasn't very successful: Boris's hearing not only worsened, but he was left with damage in the vestibular apparatus of his inner ear. As a result, he even walked with difficulty. He was forced to go to the Central Clinical Hospital in Moscow, where he stayed for about two months. They could not restore his hearing completely – he remained partially deaf in one ear – but were able to repair his vestibular apparatus. It wasn't until he became President and some German doctors performed another operation that his hearing began to improve again. But he never learnt from this episode – he had no intention of changing his lifestyle.

One winter's day we were out walking around the dacha estate in our felt boots; the paths were icy, and Boris slipped and fell on his shoulder. It was broken. He was supposed to be going to Moscow – trying to talk him out of it was useless, of course. A plaster cast was put on, and off he went. I tried to make my own business trips coincide with his trips, so I went with him.

In the morning, he took off the cast and went to a youth forum he had been invited to speak at. In his opinion, the First Secretary of the Regional Party Committee shouldn't appear in front of the Komsomols with his arm in a sling. When he got back, I put the cast back on for the night. The forum was divided into two sessions – the first one in Moscow, and the second one in Ulyanovsk. Boris went ahead to the second session without me, and I returned to Sverdlovsk with his cast in my suitcase.

When Boris became Secretary of the Regional Party Committee, we moved to 8-Mart Street, where Boris had his own office. With his new job came another dacha – this time on Lake Baltym. It was very different there from the Istok dachas. Ryabov, the First Secretary, kept a certain distance from the others, but we always had very warm relations with his wife, Natalya Ivanovna.

I didn't like the tradition of all the men getting together from time to time at the First Secretary's house in the evenings. Ryabov would invite his colleagues to play billiards, and it was customary to celebrate a win with cognac. I didn't like it when the men drank – because of Borya's heart condition, I've always been against alcohol. Various doctors over the years told me that the strep-throat heart complication had left its mark – and his first heart attack happened before he was even forty. Sometimes, when the men were sitting up late at Ryabov's house, I couldn't stop myself calling my husband home. He reacted calmly – he would usually say, "Come and sit with us." Natalya Ivanovna understood my concern, and offered the guests tea – thus letting them know it was time to go home.

The Party Committee always welcomed the arrival of high-ranking guests with receptions. This tradition pre-dated Boris, and wasn't limited to Sverdlovsk. I didn't like this, either, but there was nothing I could do about it – having a banquet to mark the arrival of important guests was an important ritual at that time.

Even so, Boris always held up well – not just at work, but also when our friends would gather around a table on festive occasions. We had a coffee table with a bar, usually stocked with Georgian wines and cognac, which he loved to serve to friends.

Later, when we moved to Moscow, Boris was put under so much additional stress that alcohol helped him to relax. After the Party leadership conflict in 1987, he began to suffer from headaches and insomnia. We invited doctors in for consultations – one of them advised Boris to alleviate tension with cognac. A hundred to a hundred and fifty millilitres (a half-glass) before sleep, they said, was better than poisoning himself with chemicals. Of course, I was wary of such advice, but Boris would sometimes follow it. It really eased away the tension, and Boris would fall asleep. I don't know if this was the right thing to do. Perhaps it was – he had such burdens to carry – perhaps not: given his heart condition, alcohol – even in small doses – could have been dangerous.

I would not have written about this if it were not for the endless reports saying that Boris abused alcohol his whole life. Since I'm addressing this issue, I will try to do so fully.

The rumours that Boris was practically an alcoholic are nonsense. Of course, like most of the men in our country, he drank alcohol – when he got together with his friends on a festive occasion, with colleagues after work or at the dacha, at official receptions – but he never lost his self-control. If urgent papers were brought to the table, he would get up and read them carefully, and make annotations – even correct grammatical mistakes, sometimes.

Of course, alcohol could loosen him up a bit. I won't hide the fact that I got upset about it – I was worried about his health, and I didn't like it when people saw him excessively agitated and emotional. Such episodes were isolated, but the press would not forgive him these slips – and I suffered, knowing that the accusations were unfair.

\* \* \*

In those days, Party workers had special privileges, not so much in Sverdlovsk as in Moscow. There was the government dacha, the special clinic and the package holidays to health spas – these we could take advantage of. We usually took our holidays in Sochi or our beloved Kislovodsk. Sometimes we went to Pitsunda, too – our first trip gave us cause to laugh for a long time afterwards. At the time, however, I didn't find it very funny.

Boris called me at work, saying: "In three hours we're going on holiday to Pitsunda." What holiday? What's all this about Pitsunda? Boris always planned our trips well in advance, and I wasn't used to such improvisation. We had already thought about taking a holiday, but it hadn't fitted in with Boris's work, so we had forgotten about it. But now, it seemed, something had been cancelled in his diary. I had work too, however, and a meeting of the technical council that day. I couldn't see a way of dropping everything and flying off on holiday – I got upset, and tears sprang to my eyes. I tried to object, but Boris wouldn't listen. "I'm sending a car for you now. Make your arrangements quickly." He had never sent a car for me before.

I went to the Chief Engineer of the Institute, and of course the meeting of the technical council was postponed, and I was given leave. When I left the Institute, the car was already there waiting for me. I got home to find Boris packing up. When we were to travel, I would usually pack his things – even for his business trips. He looked rather flustered as he wrestled with shirts and socks – it was really rather funny. I burst out laughing, and so did he. I took over and threw some things into the suitcase myself. When I opened it in Pitsunda, I discovered that we had packed two black shoes for Boris – both for the same foot.

Our former classmates were still our closest friends: we continued to meet regularly, and we phoned each other very often, so we all knew each other's news. We continued to go on holiday together every five years, as we had planned all that time ago. Once, Boris, as First Secretary of the Regional Party Committee, used his position to organize a trip to Bulgaria – at that time, going on holiday abroad was not easy, especially in a large group. But Boris spoke to someone about it, and they managed to book all our friends into one tourist group.

We worked out a route – Sofia to Plovdiv, Stara Zagora, Kazanluk, Shipka, Nessebar, and finally on to Burgas. Boris and I couldn't go – the Olympic Games were on in Moscow, and Boris was a member of the Olympic Committee. Still, in the end we were able to get away. During the trip, the wife of Borya Kiselyov – one of our classmates, who later tragically died in the Hotel Rossiya fire in Moscow – turned fifty, so we tried to get there in time for the celebration. We couldn't be accommodated with our friends, however, but had to stay separately in the hotel of the Bulgarian Communist Party Central Committee, as Boris needed access to a government line. I remember the look of surprise on our friends' faces when they saw us – we hadn't warned them we were coming:

it was a surprise, Boris-style. We spent several days together, only returning to our hotel in the evening.

Boris and I were lucky, in that we shared all our friends. I can count on my fingers the very few times when I went somewhere alone.

One year, on the eve of 8th March, I was late going home, as we were celebrating International Women's Day at work. Evening came, and my colleagues and I left. It was already dark, and as I approached our building I could see Boris and my daughters in an illuminated window, looking out for me. As I entered the apartment I was met with: "We were making you dinner here, while you were there, chatting away with the men…" "It was Pronin, our director," I said, by way of justification, but I could see that Boris was annoyed – they had been cooking for me, after all, and waiting to celebrate. But, luckily, it didn't descend into an argument.

I always hurried back home from work, trying not to be late – there was more than enough to be getting on with. My colleagues would sometimes drink tea and chat in each other's houses after work, but for me that was out of the question. I once went to my colleague Ela's house – she lived across the road from us. On our way home from work, she invited me in to see some photographs – she had just got back from holiday. We sat there for an hour and a half – there was no reason to hurry, since I knew that Boris wasn't home, and the girls were in the country with their grandmother.

When I came home, the phone was ringing – Boris had been looking for me for some time, as he urgently needed some document from home. He had called my work, and was told that I had already left. He called home, and found that I hadn't returned yet. An hour – an hour and a half had gone… he began to worry. That evening, when he came home from work and I explained to him where I had been, he asked, puzzled, "But why did you have to go there at all?" I began to justify myself, and he said, "But I never go anywhere without you…" That was true.

Boris really loved his home. He was always pleased when we waited for him to get back from work. I would give him a kiss, and the girls would throw their arms around his neck – that's how it always was. When they grew up, Lena and Tanya would always wait up for him, no matter how late he was: they wouldn't go to bed until he got back.

We had a routine: I always knew where he was and he always knew where I was, and he would warn me if he was running late. If he was busy, his aide would call me. If he had guests with him, he would say: "Plan number one" – and I understood I was on dinner duty.

As the wife of the First Secretary, I had to take part in official functions. I was glad that these were rarely shown on television, so people didn't recognize me in town or stop me in the street. I can only remember being recognized once: I was on a trolleybus, and a huge crowd of people rushed on at a stop – there was such a crush that I could hardly breathe. Suddenly, I heard someone cry out: "Don't crush the First Secretary's wife!" – apparently I had been spotted. I got off at the next stop and walked the rest of the way – I was late for work, of course.

Once, the chairman of the Verkhnaya Salda Executive Committee visited me at the Institute. We were in the middle of a discussion about some issues with a project when he suddenly asked me, "Naina Iosifovna, are you related to the Secretary of our Regional Party Committee?" "We have the same surname," I replied. A year later we met up again, and he greeted me by saying, "I saw you in the theatre with Boris Nikolayevich – you were sitting next to him and chatting away. You said you weren't related!" "Yes, I am related to him," I said, and quickly changed the subject.

*Questions on the Margins*

"Were you happy about your husband's successes in his career?"

"I had mixed feelings. On the one hand, I was pleased to see him being appreciated – on the other, I knew this meant he would have less time for his family. But I realized it could be no other way – I saw it had to be like that. It was pointless trying to change anything."

"Were you always resigned to it, or did you come to accept it with time?"

"Oh, I always accepted it. As early as the Institute days I knew, after all, that he would totally dedicate himself to whatever he was doing – whether it was sports, studying or reading books. He always had the same kind of passion for his work."

I continued working at the Hydro Canal Design Institute. I remained Chief Project Engineer until we moved to Moscow. Around the time Boris became First Secretary, I think I subconsciously began to be more self-conscious – before that, for example, I would often go to the director of the Institute to discuss various issues, not just those concerning my projects. We had a good rapport, having studied at UPI together, and we used the familiar form of "you" – but now I worried that I might be misunderstood, and I began to go to see the management much less. This was a noticeable change – and once, when we left work together, the director asked, "Is there something wrong? You don't come to see me any more…" I laughed it off.

Soon after Boris's appointment, I noticed that my colleagues spoke to me more often about city problems during the "airings" (in line with sanitation regulations, we had to open the windows twice a day, and during this time everyone had to go out into the hallway). Perhaps it was just that I started to pay more attention to this. Either way, I would have to listen to tales about margarine or soap disappearing from the shops, about the issues with the housing management team… At first I pretended not to be too bothered, and, when pressed, I would say, "Well, I'm in the same position as you – I can't solve these problems, and Boris already knows about them."

In 1972, I had to join the Party. This had been proposed before, but I had made excuses, saying I wasn't worthy – but now it was too awkward to refuse. After a while, I was made the Party representative at the Institute. Nobody at the Institute was keen on having a Party position, so the role normally changed hands every year – with a few rare exceptions. At any rate, I only lasted a year – I wasn't very comfortable in the position, and it made me feel that way all the time.

In the autumn, all the local firms would go out to the kolkhozes and help bring in the harvest. Our Institute was responsible for a field in the Beloyarsky district.

I don't remember which year it was, but one autumn, when the harvest was particularly challenging due to the weather, Boris appeared on television to appeal to city dwellers for help. Everyone from our Institute set off – we were waiting for the commuter train on the station platform, when suddenly there was a heavy snowfall. As the Party representative, I said to my colleagues, "Let's call it off." But they replied in chorus: "But Boris Nikolayevich appealed to us – he asked us for help… we must go!"

That evening, I told Boris about it, and he laughed: "And you thought you could overrule the authority of the First Secretary of the Regional Party Committee?"

I conscientiously went to the Party's district committee meetings, wrote reports and followed the "socialist duties". I did all this patiently, like any other civic burden, but I soon came to feel rebellious.

A directive came from Moscow to our Institute about "economizing on metal", signed by Yegor Ligachev. "Who is Ligachev," I asked Boris, "and what's his job? How can you economize on metal if our pipes lie on rocky soil? And the climate is continental – there are frosts below forty degrees…" And that wasn't the only directive of that kind. So we cheated. In the design proposals we indicated that we would lay cast-iron pipes rather than steel. Then, after we had handed in our reports – supposedly after assessing the geological conditions – we would ask for permission to use steel pipes. I think the whole country worked that way – on paper it was one thing, and in reality, another.

Later came the so-called "personal programmes": "I pledge by 7th November to raise the productivity of my work." I couldn't understand why we had to do this – if you work with total dedication, how can you "raise the productivity of your work"?

How did everyone regard the political-information sessions that all workers had to sit through? They sat and pretended to listen – the women knitted, the men read books.

While I was on the District Party Committee, I was required to ensure these political-information sessions in every department.

I remember one evening, as I came out of the district Party building – I had just been to a meeting – looking up at the enormous whitish-grey edifice, which covered several floors, with dozens of lit windows, and thinking: so many people around the country – in district, city, regional committees – producing nothing else than papers no one needs. When I got home I said to Boris: "I don't understand why Party workers are paid a salary." He answered me very calmly: "Well, you see how I work, after all – what I do…" Yes, I saw how Boris worked, and I realized that, even in the Party Committee, he wasn't just shuffling papers but doing real business. I have to say, Boris's colleagues made a good impression on me, too.

Many of them, like Boris, came to the Party Committee with a great deal of experience in practical work. At that time, they began to invite people from industry – directors of factories, trusts and institutes – to work in Party bodies more frequently.

*Questions on the Margins*

"Did Boris Nikolayevich have enemies when he was First Secretary?"

"I don't know… I don't think so. At any rate, I never heard anyone say a bad word about him – only good things. I sometimes even felt a little uncomfortable. If they were being false, I didn't realize it."

"How did you feel when your husband did something at work that you didn't agree with?"

"I always tried to understand – I was never in doubt that he did everything in his power to make people's lives better."

My Party duties weighed heavily on me – I didn't have much spare time as it was. Like any woman, when I came home from the Institute, the second shift began – work at home.

I didn't use Boris's car. I walked to work or rode several stops on public transport. The only exception was our trips to the dacha – we usually went with Boris, but if he was away, the girls and I were driven in his car.

I didn't have any help with the housework. Our neighbour, the doctor Tamara Pavlovna, came to walk the dog in the evening, and she often asked me when I found the time to sleep. "Your light is on at two o'clock in the morning!" she said. In the evenings, I usually cooked the next day's food for my daughters. After that I would be up late sprucing up Boris's suits – I've always believed that the director's suit should look perfect. Sometimes Boris couldn't stand it, and he would come into the kitchen and unplug the iron from the socket. "That's enough – go to bed!"

I never sent out the laundry: I didn't like the fact that everything was washed together there – at least, that's how they did it in those days. It didn't bother me having to do housework until late at night – Mama had done so when I was young. Of course, my daughters helped me around the house – mainly with cleaning.

I got so used to going to bed late that I still can't shake the habit – I promise myself I'll be in bed by eleven o'clock, but every day I find something to do – I read books, leaf through newspapers and magazines, get lost in paperwork – and it's already past midnight. I know it's not good for me, but I've never been able to do anything about it.

No one at home ever knew if I was in pain or unwell – I was always thought to be the healthiest person. Perhaps I was just lucky, and God never sent me pain I couldn't endure.

## Questions on the Margins

"When you were busy with housework, did you ever seek your husband's sympathy?"

"It was enough for me that he understood that housework is work too."

"Was he ever unhappy if you didn't get something done around the house?"

"Not once."

"Did Boris Nikolayevich ever suggest that you quit work and spend more time with your family?"

"We didn't even have a conversation on this subject – it's how we were raised. We put heart and soul into work, and were very conscientious. We even tried not to take days off sick – we went to work with temperatures. Our whole generation was like that. All of my classmates worked after the Institute – we didn't sit home alone until we were retired. I don't think there was anyone who didn't work among the wives of Party workers in Sverdlovsk. It was hard to live on one salary."

I have always loved cooking – and I know how to cook. As soon as I was married, I bought *Tasty and Healthy Food*, which was the first Soviet cookbook – I still have it. We exchanged recipes at work, too – we wrote them down in special notebooks that we kept for years. We all tried to create something tasty from the few things available in Soviet shops – and we managed.

Nowadays, although it's no longer a problem finding the ingredients, I still use many of the same recipes. At the Yeltsin Center, the desserts are made according to my recipes – cottage-cheese biscuits, cherry pie and éclairs – and I'm told they're in demand. I'm pleased – although every time I go to the Center I look at the price tags. I'm opposed to my desserts being expensive. They normally listen to me, too!

Boris was very unfussy about food. I never heard him say, "I won't eat that." He ate everything – no matter what I cooked.

But he was especially fond of *pelmeni* and fried potatoes. He didn't eat sweets at all.

There was no delicatessen in Sverdlovsk. Some products could be bought in our dacha cafeteria – meat, for example, or the Sverdlovsk sweets which everyone loved, Meteorit. Even so, I tried to buy the meat for making *pelmeni* at the market – meat was very scarce in the shops. In Moscow, it was sometimes possible to buy cuts of meat in the shops, but in Sverdlovsk there were only convenience foods – mince or patties. Of course, chickens also began to be available in shops, thanks to Boris. The market was the only place where there was no problem buying meat – it was expensive, but it was always fresh, which was exactly what was needed for making the *pelmeni* or patties our family loved.

It never occurred to me to use Boris's position to buy things. There was a shop in Sverdlovsk which sold goods that were in short supply – but access was only by invitation from the ZAGS. At a friend's birthday party, we got talking about that shop to a former classmate, who said, "I have a relative who works there. They say that all the Party Committee wives go in, except for Yeltsina." "Why would I?" I said in surprise. "The only time I've been there is when we tried to buy shoes for Lena when she got married – but they didn't have the right size, so we bought two pillows instead." I didn't even know that the wives of other Party workers used the shop to buy hard-to-find items without having a ZAGS invitation.

At that time, using connections to buy clothes was the easiest way to do it. I once became acquainted with a nice woman who was deputy director of the Sverdlovsk Central Department Store (TsUM) when I had to buy Boris a suit urgently. We were introduced by the head of the Trade Department of the Regional Party Committee. A little later, I bought a coat for myself at the TsUM. I was never able to wear it in Sverdlovsk – many trade workers had the same one. If a batch was delivered to the city, it would immediately be distributed among insiders. In general, however, I didn't like manufactured clothes – there was always something wrong with them: either they were too big or the sleeves were too long… I usually had my clothes made at an atelier. Sometimes I would buy things in shops in the cities I travelled to on business, places where travel was restricted for security reasons – in Glazov and other places like that. The selection in these shops was better – but I soon realized that these weren't for me, either.

I once brought home a brown Crimplene trouser suit and a black dress with a rosette during a business trip to Glazov. I was so happy with them – Boris and I were planning a holiday to the Rossiya health spa in Sochi. On the first day, I went to a dance wearing my new trouser suit. As soon as we went in, I saw a woman wearing the same thing – horrors! I hurried off to change immediately. Several days later we ran into a woman who was wearing the same dress as me. This time, however, we laughed and made her acquaintance. It turned out she was the wife of a major Party boss from Kyrgyzstan and had bought these items in a special sort of shop which they had in Soviet republic capitals. Apparently, these shops had the same supplier as those in the cities with restricted access.

In short, after that trip I didn't risk it again. Of manufactured clothes, I only wore what my sister bought in Germany. She brought two or three suits from there, which were enough for several years.

Boris also brought me things home from his trips. Amazingly, he always guessed the size correctly. He'd say, "I asked a sales clerk with the same figure as you to try it on." It wasn't just my dress size, but even my shoe size that he guessed!

* * *

Lena announced that she wanted to apply to the Leningrad Ship-Building Institute. I tried to talk her out of it – Boris didn't want to interfere. "Let her go where she wants!" he said. In the end, she saw the wisdom in my reasoning and went to our Institute, enrolling in the Faculty of Construction, and on the same course as Boris – Industrial and Civil Construction. When she was in the first year, I bumped into an old classmate of ours. "It turns out my

Olga is in the same group as your Lena," she told me. "And how is she doing?" I asked. "At first the girls thought she had got in using her connection as the daughter of the Secretary of the Regional Party Committee," she said. "But it turns out that Lena is better than all the others in descriptive geometry – she helps everyone."

At dinner, I recounted this conversation. Tanya reacted sharply: "Now I definitely don't want to go to school here. They'll always say that I only got in thanks to our connections."

I was very upset by this, because I didn't want Tanya to go away to some other college. Boris reassured me, saying, "She'll forget about this a hundred times before she gets there!" But she didn't forget, and in 1977, when she graduated from school, she went off to the Faculty of Computer Mathematics and Cybernetics at Moscow State University (MGU).

I enquired among our Moscow friends, and found out that the son of one of them studied there. I tried to talk Tanya out of it with my new-found information: "For each place there are eight applicants, and they give priority to Muscovites because they won't need a dormitory. Stay here!" But she was having none of it.

My colleagues laughed at me when, on the first day of Tanya's exam, I said: "Lord, please give her a two!" They gave Tanya a three – I was delighted. "There we go – come home," I said. But Tanya explained that a three was good – that half the applicants got a two. The next exam was the maths oral. She told me that they questioned her for a very long time, and in the end gave her a five. She got two points above a pass, so she got into MGU.

Boris and my former classmate Tamara Sisina, who lived in Moscow, watched over Tanya at first, at my request. "She's such a little fish in a big pond!" Tamara told me on the phone. "Such a homebody," she said.

I was upset, but Boris was firm: "She is independent – she will get along without us," he said, and kept repeating: "Do you want them to live their own lives, or are you going to live it for them?" Of course I wanted them to live their own lives, I said, but I still worried.

To my surprise, Tanya really did turn out to be a homebody – she was homesick for Sverdlovsk, especially in the first year. As soon as she received her stipend, she spent it on a ticket home, every time, and she usually stayed for the weekend. Sometimes she would stay a few more days, which worried me – it wasn't good to miss classes. In those instances I had to buy her return ticket and give her money to take with her. I tried to persuade her to move back to Sverdlovsk. "I'm only saying it for your sake," I told her. She did go to several lectures at the local university, but when she returned she said, "The authors of the textbooks they study from in Sverdlovsk are our lecturers in Moscow." She didn't move back – she gradually got used to Moscow, and soon she only came home during the holidays.

No one at Tanya's university knew that her father was the First Secretary of the Regional Party Committee. Whenever anyone asked her about her father, she would say, "He is a construction engineer by trade." Whenever Boris or I went to Moscow on a business trip, Tanya would come to the hotel, and we sometimes went to the theatre together – but during all her years of study, I never once went to her dormitory. Boris, however, did go once, to bring her a present – a set of pots and pans which one of the defence factories had produced for the consumer-goods shop (at that time military factories had started to manufacture consumer goods in order to overcome the shortfall in production). At the dormitory entrance, Boris was asked for his ID, and he showed his work ID to the lad on duty at the desk – who just so happened to be from Tanya's friendship group. Soon it became known that Tanya was the daughter of the First Secretary of the Regional Party Committee.

In the third year, Tanya married her classmate, and in 1981, little Borya was born. Her first marriage didn't last long, and they divorced before their graduation. She finished her studies with a baby in her arms, which was not easy at all.

Lena's first marriage was also unsuccessful, but in 1979 she gave us our first granddaughter, Katya. Her second marriage was a happy one, and she has spent the rest of her life with Valera Okulov. After Katya, they had two more children: Masha and Vanya.

My daughters have suffered many trials – the whole family has. But everything has turned out well.

# By an Oppositionist's Side

Boris did not try to move to the capital, despite the fact that he worked as First Secretary for nearly ten years. He was offered a transfer to Moscow a number of times, but he never took it up. In 1985, however, he was no longer able to say no. Viktor Ivanovich Dolgikh, Secretary of the Central Committee of the Communist Party of the Soviet Union, called him and offered him a position as head of the Department of Construction at the Central Committee. As always, Boris tried to decline, but then Yegor Kuzmich Ligachev, another secretary of the Central Committee, called him and reminded him of Party discipline. There was no way out of it – he had to agree, although first secretaries of the major regional Party committees were usually transferred to higher posts in Moscow.

Boris brought business in Sverdlovsk to a close a few days later, and we flew together to Moscow. We travelled light, and took with us only the necessities – we didn't have time for packing anything else. Before too long, I wanted to go home to get a few things, but Boris said: "They can do it without you. You are not leaving me, are you?" That was enough for me – I knew he couldn't live alone – so I asked my sister to pack up our old home, and some other relatives helped her.

I thought I would find work in Moscow in my field – our head office was there, and I had often visited on business. But then I realized I couldn't – the sort of atmosphere we had at our Institute was not easy to find elsewhere, and at the age of fifty-three it would be hard to adapt to a different one – especially because it would only be for two more years, since I had always said I would retire at fifty-five. I dreamt of finally having time to myself, so that I could read what I had never had time to read, I could go to museums, to concerts, to the theatre. I decided to take early retirement.

I didn't like Moscow – I had realized this when I visited in the past, and knew I didn't want to live here. Once I dreamt that we were moving there, and I broke down in tears in my dream. Boris had woken me up, asking, "Why are you sobbing?" For me, the move was a real tragedy.

## Questions on the Margins

"You always speak of Sverdlovsk as a place where everything in your life was perfect – the people, your job, your relationships. But you describe Moscow as the absolute opposite. I wonder if your memory is deceiving you…"

"I don't think so. For the first fifty-three years of my life, there were no squabbles, there was no gossip, and we were always treated with respect. My student years were perhaps the happiest, although my work at the Institute was a pleasure, too – and during all those years I was surrounded by wonderful people. In Moscow, it was completely different. But we stuck it out, all the same. And how much filth was thrown our way in Moscow… I don't even want to remember."

"Were you hurt by the press?"

"I was, yes. Sometimes I said to Boris, 'That's a lie – you should sue them!' He never agreed – he used to say: 'It'll blow over.'"

"What if it wasn't a journalist lying, but Boris's political opponents?"

"Even then he would wave it away, and would say, 'Don't stoop to their level.'"

For the first few weeks, we lived in a new hotel – the Oktyabr on Dimitrova Street (now called the "President Hotel" – the street has been renamed "Bolshaya Yakimanka"). Boris went to work in the morning, and I remained alone. I had no idea where to go – or what to do either. We ate in a restaurant, and I didn't have any housework to do. Tanya bought me an electric hob after a few days so I could cook something.

Sometimes Tanya would stay with us overnight – little Borya was in day care at the dacha in Kratova. After breakfast, she and Boris would leave, each for their jobs, and I would go out into the street, feeling terribly alone. I yearned for Sverdlovsk, for my Institute and my colleagues, and I would burst into tears. After crying a little and talking to my family, things would feel a bit better. I told myself I should calm down and try to settle in. It wasn't easy, but I persevered.

In late May, we were sent to view two apartments. When we got to the first address, a building for high-ranking officials near the Belorussky station, we found that the apartment was convenient – it had four nicely laid-out rooms – and we liked it straight away. We didn't even go to see the second apartment – which is a shame, as it turned out to be unpleasant living next to a railway station. There was always a thick layer of soot on the windows, and the trams woke us up in the morning as they passed under our bedroom windows.

However, we were glad to have our whole family back together again. Some time before, Lena's husband, Valera, had applied for a transfer to International Flights in Moscow. Management agreed to the transfer, but Aeroflot couldn't find him an apartment – so when Boris was transferred to Moscow, an opportunity opened up for Valera to finally make the transfer too. So we all moved to the capital at the same time. Since Lena lived with us in Sverdlovsk, we were given not just one, but two apartments in Moscow – we took one, and Lena, Valera and their children settled in in the other apartment, which was nearby on Dostoyevsky Street. Tanya returned her room in the communal apartment to the authorities (that was the procedure then), and moved in with us, along with little Borya.

The only new furniture we needed was kitchen furniture – the rest we brought with us from Sverdlovsk. All our furniture was bought from a Dnepropetrovsk factory Boris had visited on one of his business trips – he had liked the factory's products, so we decided to order our furniture there. We didn't regret it, either – it served us several years in Sverdlovsk, then in Moscow, and after that it went to Lena's dacha, except for the dresser and coffee table, which are now museum exhibits.

We quickly settled into the Moscow apartment. We arranged the bookshelves, unpacked the crockery and hung the curtains – and once again we had our home. I felt better. As well as little Borya, my granddaughters Katya and Masha were put in nursery in nearby Snegiri, where they went five days a week. They liked it there. This gave me time to walk around Moscow, and I explored the city centre – from Belorussky Station to Red Square – on foot. Sometimes I walked for hours – I didn't feel so alone, and I took great pleasure from doing so.

As was required of a pensioner, I registered with the Party's housing office, and I went to their meetings, where elderly people sat and discussed in all seriousness why residents made a habit of throwing rubbish from their windows on the heads of passers-by – a strange topic for a Party meeting, in my view. But what can you do? I went – I listened.

I gradually grew accustomed to Moscow life. I was pleased to learn that our neighbours from Sverdlovsk – the Petrovs and the Zhitenevs – had been transferred to Moscow a little earlier, and they lived in the same building. We socialized, going over to each other's houses, and soon Moscow didn't seem such a foreign city any more.

At first it felt as though I was finding a new routine, but I slowly came to realize that work had meant more to me than I thought – without it, there was a void that was hard to fill.

Boris did not spend long as head of the Department of Construction, and he was quickly made Secretary of the Central Committee of the Party – and, in late 1985, he was made First Secretary of the Moscow City Party Committee and a candidate member of the Politburo. This was a very high position, and an enormous responsibility: the capital was huge, teeming with millions of people, and it had a complex economy. But Boris, with all his experience in Sverdlovsk, was not frightened by the scale of his role – he liked it. He loved being involved in important business.

Along with the Politburo role, Boris was offered a dacha, which was called "5 Moscow River". Up until now we couldn't have imagined such comfort – luxury, even. The Party Committee dachas in Sverdlovsk were ordinary little wooden cottages with simple furniture – but here, you could get lost. There were many rooms, and large grounds with a greenhouse and a fruit garden. A full staff came with the estate, too, and security was always nearby. We weren't accustomed to this, and it was rather unpleasant – when I tried to cook something using ingredients bought in a shop, the cook gently but firmly stopped me. "God forbid that you are poisoned – we would all be fired!" she said. It wasn't just me – our whole family had great difficulty getting used to this new way of life.

In the summer, Lena and her family went to Valera's parents' house in Kirov. They had an allotment beside their little house in the suburbs – a plot of about four hundred square metres. Mikhail Vasilyevich, Valera's father, kept several beehives. We went, once, and saw the beehives and the garden, and we showed the children where the bees lived. Then we went to have lunch in the house, where we had trouble fitting around the table. Masha, who was four years old, looked all around and said to her grandparents: "They told me you have bees living here – but where do you live?" – apparently comparing the size of the government dacha with this house. We laughed for a long time – we still tell this story today.

We usually spent the week in Moscow – Boris and my daughters worked, and I kept the apartment tidy – and we normally spent the weekends together outside the city.

There were some funny moments in our new life in Moscow, and I often found myself in situations that would never happen in Sverdlovsk. Once, for instance, I went into a shop near our building, where there was a long queue to buy chicken. In the middle of the queue was a neighbour I recognized, and he gestured to me to stand in front of him. I did as he suggested, and when my turn came, I politely pointed at the chicken I wanted, which didn't have as much of a bluish tinge as the others. The woman behind the counter rudely grabbed a different one and threw it onto the scales. I began to object, and my neighbour said, just loud enough for others to hear, "If she only knew that she was being rude to the wife of the First Secretary of the City Party Committee!"

It was even funnier another time, when friends came from Bulgaria to visit Tanya and I discovered that we didn't have any sour cream at home. I ran to the shop, and decided to buy butter and sausages as well – which at that time were rationed. The queue wasn't long – about ten people – and I waited in line. When it was my turn, the woman serving said "Wait a minute, please" and hurried off, returning several minutes later with a big package, which she handed to me, naming a price. I realized that the package was too big and the price was higher than I had expected, but in confusion I just said "Thank you" and took the package and paid her. When I got home, I discovered that I had come away with quite a bit more sausage, butter and cheese than was allowed by the ration cards. Tanya and the kids laughed, and said, "They recognized you!" I didn't agree, and thought the woman who served me must have made a mistake – I went back two days later at the same time, hoping to catch her. When I found her, I asked her what had happened. "You're the wife of the First Secretary of the City Party Committee!" she said. What could I do? I simply asked her never to do that again – but even so, I always avoided that shop afterwards.

There were more queues in Moscow than in Sverdlovsk, but I still went to the normal shops anyway. I didn't like the delicatessens, which did exist in Moscow, unlike in Sverdlovsk. I did go several times, but found that everything was divided into "us" and "them". One time, for instance, I wanted to buy Malyutka sausages, which were a delicacy in the Soviet years. In front of me, the wife of some big executive bought them – but when my turn came and I asked for these sausages, the woman behind the counter said they didn't have any – even though she had just weighed them out before my eyes. It was terribly unpleasant.

During the first year of our Moscow life, I couldn't rid myself of the feeling that it would all soon end, and that we'd find ourselves back in Sverdlovsk. Of course, I didn't talk about this with anyone – but I really hoped it would happen.

Meanwhile, I acquired a new social calendar, since the wife of the General Secretary, Raisa Maksimovna Gorbacheva, regularly invited the wives of the members and candidate members of the Politburo to tea parties, usually at the House of Receptions on Lenin Hills (now Sparrow Hills), or even at the Kremlin. She was forever planning trips to museums and theatres, and once even a trip to Star City – but for some reason, that never went ahead.

Raisa Maksimovna always stood out among the wives – and not just because of her elegant dresses: it seemed to me that she wanted to make the relationships between the wives of the Party leaders more informal – she tried to maintain a relaxed tone in conversation. Once she came up to me and said, "Naina Iosifovna, you look well – that's a very elegant suit you're wearing." At these meetings, everything seemed normal – but even so, it was very tense. I think it was perhaps because the wives tried to conduct themselves in a way they thought fitting with the ranks of their husbands – this was manifested in everything: how they sat, how they talked to each other, how they spoke with the wife of the General Secretary. This was all unfamiliar to me, and I felt out of my element. At these meetings, I tried to sit close to those I felt comfortable with – Ludmila Fyodorovna Talyzina, Tama Veniaminovna Kapitonova, Valentina Avraamovna Zimyanina and Mariya Nikolayevna Demicheva – and we would usually take the seats at the end of the table. The wives of Eduard Shevardnadze and Yegor Ligachev would always sit next to Raisa Maksimovna.

When Boris became President, I recalled this tradition, and invited the wives of the vice premiers and ministers to the Kremlin several times. We went to the theatre together, and even went to Gzhel, a small pottery town not far from Moscow, once. It seemed to me that our meetings were less formal than in the past – I hope that was the case. I formed lasting relationships with many of the wives at these tea parties.

When Raisa Maksimovna died, I felt I had to bid her farewell, despite the difficult relationship I had with her husband. I believe that Raisa Maksimovna deserves respect for the huge efforts she made not only for her family, but also for her country. I was sincerely sorry that she departed this life so early.

Boris was enthusiastic about his new job – he was full of energy and plans, and he liked to socialize with his colleagues. We visited the Kapitonovs, the Dolgys and the Lukyanovs. Under Gorbachev, informal socializing with Politburo members became customary – before, under Brezhnev, we were told this was not encouraged. At first Boris had quite a normal relationship with Gorbachev, Shevardnadze and the other Politburo members. His friendship with Alexander Nikolayevich Yakovlev only blossomed much later, I believe – at that time, they were not close. Very soon relations with Ligachev grew tense.

I noticed that something was bothering Boris – he had started to sit for hours at a time deep in thought. Once, returning late from a meeting of the Politburo, he said, "You know, in our Regional Party Committee meetings, the atmosphere was always business-like. We would discuss a problem, set out deadlines for solving it and appoint people to be responsible for solving it. Everything was concrete, focused. Here people can talk for hours about who knows what, drinking tea with pastries."

The Politburo meetings were held on Thursdays, and Boris would often come home depressed. I remember he couldn't fall asleep – he would sigh, toss and turn. Something was clearly worrying him. "What happened?" I asked once. He replied: "I can't go on like this. I don't want to ruin the country with this gang." These words made me remember my dream of leaving Moscow – it seemed like it might happen at any moment. As I've already said, Boris just didn't discuss work at home – that night-time conversation was the first exception. He didn't mention it again, and I stopped worrying. However, in September 1987, he wrote a letter to Gorbachev in which he asked to be relieved of his duties as a candidate member of the Politburo and First Secretary of the Moscow City Party Committee.

He didn't show the letter to my daughters or me – but before sending it, he mentioned it first to me, then later to Lena and Tanya. He spoke with each of us separately. I remember my conversation with him very well.

It was in the evening, and we were getting ready for bed when he said, "There may be some serious changes in our life. I want to leave the Politburo." "But where will you work?" I asked. "They will always take me on as the head of a trust," he replied. I doubted that: they wouldn't hire someone who was out of favour in Moscow, and they wouldn't let him return to Sverdlovsk. "Then we'll go North," said Boris. This was a fairly calm conversation, but I saw that his mood was black.

"What's the problem, really?" I said. "Our children are grown – they'll feed us. If the worst comes to the worst, I'll go and mop floors – we won't be destitute." I tried to dispel the tension with a joke, as Boris usually did.

That evening, I had the impression that he was hoping to stay on the City Party Committee – he liked the work there, the relationships in the group were good. I had heard his colleagues speak warmly of him – and they seemed sincere. It's possible that Boris was counting on the Committee not accepting his resignation – or perhaps that's just how it seemed to me.

Boris asked Gorbachev again and again for a meeting, both before writing his letter and afterwards – but the meeting kept being postponed.

None of us knew what the letter said exactly, until Boris quoted it in full in his book *Against the Grain*. I tried to find a draft of the letter for the museum, but it looked as if it either was lost or never existed. The archivists, however, insisted that he must have kept a draft, since Boris had quoted it in the book. We went through all the boxes of documents, and in one of them we found not just a draft, but a Xerox – it turned out that Boris had made a copy before sending the letter to Gorbachev.

*Questions on the Margins*

"You didn't try to talk him out of sending the letter?"

"It didn't even occur to me to do so – if he had decided he needed to do so, then that's how it had to be."

"You weren't afraid for him?"

"No, I didn't have any fears – and, well, if he left his post, to be honest, it would only have made me happy. He would no longer be so overloaded with work. I wasn't afraid of any possible terrifying consequences – it wasn't the Stalin era, after all."

Without waiting to meet with Gorbachev, Boris decided to speak at the October Plenary of the Central Committee of the Communist Party of the Soviet Union (CPSU). He didn't share this plan with me, and I only read his speech a year and a half later, when the transcription of the Plenary was finally published. The essence of the speech, in short, was that Perestroika was progressing too slowly and had no concrete results – that there was still a lot of formalism, that the General Secretary was glorified and there was little constructive criticism. After his speech, a break was announced.

I have no doubt that during the break the Central Committee members were told to condemn Yeltsin's speech – not to discuss it, but to condemn it. More than twenty people spoke, and their speeches all seemed to be carbon copies. Boris was accused of betraying the interests of the Party, of apostasy, of aiding and abetting the West. I was amazed to hear someone say: "Yeltsin's speech is a knife in the back of Perestroika." Let us suppose that they sincerely believed that his speech was wrong – if that person had already resigned from the job, wouldn't it be easier to accept it and move on? But a real show trial had been prepared for Boris, and there were several hundred people from all over the country in the hall – many of them knew Boris well from work, but not a single person supported him.

Boris later told me that people with whom he had worked side by side for many years avoided him during the break and after the meeting. His speech was declared "politically wrong", and the Moscow City Party Committee was recommended to find a new First Secretary.

On 7th November, Boris went to Lenin's Mausoleum to take his place on the tribune as head of the Moscow Party organization, along with members of the Politburo, Central Committee secretaries and leaders of communist parties in the socialist countries. No one spoke to Boris. It was only the Cuban and Polish leaders, Fidel Castro and Wojciech Jaruzelski, who decided, unexpectedly, to support him – they both went up to him and gave him a hug. Fidel said something in Spanish, and Jaruzelski said in Russian, "Boris Nikolayevich, hang in there!"

Boris hardly slept those days – his nerves were on edge. On 9th November, he suffered a heart attack in his office. When the doctors came, they discovered a cut on his chest. We were told this was a wound made by a pair of scissors. An ambulance took him from the City Party Committee to the Central Committee hospital on Michurinsky Avenue – that's when the story that he had tried to commit suicide cropped up. I never believed it – it wasn't in his nature; he wouldn't even think of it – and if he did, he would not try to end his life in such an awkward way: he had a pistol in his safe.

He was given huge doses of strong sedatives in order to ease off the stress. As a result, he had difficulty talking and almost didn't get out of bed.

Gorbachev called Boris at the hospital – at that very moment a consultation was underway under the direction of Yevgeny Chazov, who at that time was head of the Fourth Main Medical Directorate. Gorbachev told Boris that he must be present at the Plenary of the Moscow City Party Committee. I was there while they had that conversation – I had hardly left the hospital ward since his admission.

"The farthest I can go is the toilet, with difficulty," Boris said, barely managing to get out the words. "Don't worry – the doctors will help you," Gorbachev said.

"I have to go," Boris told me.

I nearly shouted. "You won't make it… Over my dead body – you're not going anywhere!"

He tried to explain why he thought he had to go. "I'm worried that this will turn into a 'Leningrad Affair'." He repeated that several times.

To be honest, I had no idea what the "Leningrad Affair" was – I knew that, under Stalin, a large number of innocent people were persecuted in the Leningrad branch of the Party – and I understood that Boris was afraid that his colleagues at the City Party Committee would also be under attack because of him. I couldn't stop him going – but I did make an attempt, and spoke to his personal physician. "We'll inject him with enough medication to keep him up and about for an hour," he said. It became clear that he had to go.

The Plenary lasted several hours. I sat in the hospital all that time, drinking valerian and waiting for Boris to return. He later told me that the speech at the Plenary required enormous efforts on his part. He was only just able to speak, and the effects of the medications wore off after an hour, as the doctor had said.

Not a single person spoke in his defence. It was a betrayal. Those he wanted to protect from the Politburo gave incriminating speeches and criticized him on points which they had previously supported him on.

He was brought back to the hospital ward on a stretcher, and he was very pale. When I saw the condition he was in upon his return, I was in despair. One of the heads of the KGB's Ninth Directorate, which was responsible for guarding top officials, accompanied him. I didn't hold back, and gave him a piece of my mind – I couldn't restrain myself any more. I remember I was almost shouting: "Tell Gorbachev that even the Fascists during the war didn't treat prisoners of war in this way!" Really – it was pure sadism to drag a person out of an intensive-care ward to the podium of a plenary. I also remember saying to the doctor angrily, "What about your Hippocratic oath?" "I have my own Hippocrates," he replied, not looking me in the eye.

Several days passed. Then there was another call from Gorbachev. Once again, it came during a consultation led by Chazov – it was hardly an accident. The conversation took place in my presence. Boris held the receiver, but far enough from his ear that I could hear everything.

"I propose you go into retirement," said Gorbachev.

"I don't intend to do that," Boris replied.

I grew worried, but pulled myself together and went and faced the consultation panel.

I tried to speak calmly. "Mikhail Sergeyevich is proposing that Boris Nikolayevich go into retirement. You know well what condition he is in – he can't make decisions at the moment. Let him recover before forcing him to have this sort of conversation – especially as he is not of a pensionable age yet."

The consultation panel have to be given their due – they assured me that the question of Boris going into retirement would not be decided for the time being, and they kept their word.

After a while, Gorbachev called a third time. This time he said he was transferring Boris to another job, at Gosstroi – the State Committee for Construction – and he added, "I won't let you back into politics!" He didn't ask for Boris's consent, and didn't offer him any other options.

Many years later, I watched a talk between Gorbachev and the journalist and presenter Vladimir Pozner, where Gorbachev said he believed that one of his biggest mistakes was that he had not banished Yeltsin for ever to some far-off country to "harvest bananas". I was shocked. How can you talk like that – even if you still haven't let go of your resentment? Had understanding really not come with the years? It was so clear that back in October 1987 the Politburo, headed by the General Secretary, ruthlessly and in the tradition of Stalin, destroyed a man who, more than most others in the Soviet leadership, supported reforms. And wasn't there a shred of regret? I can't understand that.

The girls and I sat at the hospital from dawn until dusk – it was only when Boris fell asleep that we would leave him alone. He got better, but there wasn't a massive improvement. As before, they injected him with medication to help relax him. One day a doctor – the same one who had brought Boris to the hospital from the Plenary – pulled me to one side to have a chat outside the room. "If you want him to get out of here on his own two feet, it's better that you take him now," he said.

I was frightened. I had an urgent discussion with Lena and Tanya about what we should do. We decided that we would take him home immediately. I told the doctors at the next consultation that we were discharging him – they agreed surprisingly easily, although they thought it was still too early for him to go home, and they suggested he finish his treatment in a health spa in Barvikha, outside Moscow. I agreed to this on the grounds that there were fewer medications, doctors and consultations at the spa. But on the other hand, there was more fresh air and freedom. After a while, Boris felt more lively. It was then that I decided to keep far away from hospitals.

A week or two passed, and we brought him skis, and gradually he was able to get into cross-country skiing, which reassured me. I brought food from home every day – bouillon, meat patties and *pelmeni*. When he first fell ill, he ate next to nothing, but his appetite slowly began to return with his health.

During this difficult time, Lena and Valera moved to an apartment closer to ours – now they lived just a block from our house on Alexander Nevsky Street, so we didn't even have to go on the tram – we could get together at any time of the day or night with our daughters, and with their husbands (by that time, Tanya had married Lyosha Dyachenko). Lyosha and Valera were always nearby, and they supported us as much as they could – even though being a member of the Yeltsin family was not very comfortable and not without danger in those days.

Boris began to receive letters from various cities around the country after the Moscow City Party Committee Plenary when he was still in the health spa. A lot of letters came. We couldn't have imagined such a thing happening. They didn't fit in the post-office box, so the postman brought them to the door. We put them in piles and sorted them into cardboard boxes. First Tanya and I would read them, then we would read them aloud to Boris. It was as if a dam had burst – there were so many kind words and so much sympathy in those letters. Here are some of them:

> We don't agree with the accusations that have been made against you. We're puzzled by the position taken by those at the Moscow City Plenary, who were unhappy with your policy… Muscovites have grown too soft in their posts and don't understand work around the Urals. We would like to see and read your report, so that we can make our own conclusions – rather than accepting the conclusions of Muscovites, members of the Moscow City Party Committee and the Politburo… We support Yeltsin's policy fully, and think that he is right.
>
> TENTH-GRADE STUDENTS
> School No. 10, Nizhny Tagil

> My son studies in Moscow, and he and some fellow students were present at your meeting. They are in a state of utter amazement, and are touched by your directness, honesty, openness and acute mind. It's only pathetic dullards and fanatics who can't see the greatness of your speeches or recognize your fight for the truth. You're the only bold and honest one among the whole lot of them. You sincerely believed in Glasnost ("transparency") and the other nonsense which they fool people with, and you paid for it. I and millions of other Soviet citizens bend our knees before you. Courage to you! Strength! Honesty!

The scientists working in Moscow have reacted extremely negatively to the recent changes that have taken place, and even more negatively to the new terminology that has been coined... Only a few weeks after you arrived in Moscow, lively conversation about your work sprung up. There hadn't been such things before. My wife sighed every time, bitterly, and said: "The man will burn out, or they will put him in his grave." The things that were threatened by your speeches – patrimony, the clans, the mafia – believed you had come to take away the privileges they believe to be God-given... Transcripts of your speeches are going around Moscow – I read them. If they are full and accurate, then our worst fears are confirmed: a new unit of Glasnost really has been introduced, equal to one Yeltsin. It is hard to believe that you're so politically immature that you didn't realize the consequences of speaking out. Indeed, everything said there hit the target. But you hadn't expected to be accused of putting a knife in the back of Perestroika by delivering a speech at a closed meeting. We hadn't expected that, either. It is most likely a push-back against the undesirable, a nod to those who don't want to see anything and hang on only thanks to their clan.

Those were the kind of letters that we received. We have kept them all.

When we went to Kislovodsk that summer, for the first time we met hundreds of people who were prepared to support Boris. We would go out for a walk, and it would end up turning into an impromptu rally. And it was like that every day. It was very unexpected for us – and also very pleasant – to see that people trusted Boris and supported him.

\* \* \*

When Boris started working at Gosstroi, I think it helped him recover from the stress, to some extent, and he gradually found a new routine. The construction topics under discussion were as interesting to him as before, and he felt as though he had found a good place to be. I didn't think he intended to get back into politics – but I was mistaken.

In the summer of 1988, the 19th Party Conference was to take place, and, for the first time in a decade, the delegate nomination at a Party event of this level was not a formality – many Party branch committees wanted Boris to be their delegate. I was proud to see him secure the nomination of almost all the major industrial plants of the Sverdlovsk region – but, each time, high-ranking Party officials interfered, and refused to confirm his candidacy. Even so, bowing to the pressure of Uralmash (Urals Heavy Machinery), Uralkhimmash (Urals Chemical Machine-Building), Verkh-Isetsky Electrical Mechanics Plant and other firms, eventually even the Sverdlovsk City Party Committee came out in support of Boris. The Regional Party Committee had the last word, and it delayed its decision – but then workers threatened a strike, and the Central Committee was forced to reconcile itself to the fact that Boris would be a delegate. However, instead of allowing him to stand for his native Sverdlovsk, he was to represent Karelia. Karelia's plenaries – where the composition of the delegation was decided – were among the last to be held, long after the other districts and regions. As a result, Boris didn't end up in the front rows at the Kremlin, among the Sverdlovsk delegation, but on the balcony, in the Karelia delegation.

Boris prepared long and hard for his speech at the conference. After his Gosstroi appointment, we moved to Uspenskoye, where we had a little wooden cottage. At the weekend, as we had done before the move, we got together with our daughters' families. During one of these weekend gatherings, Boris read us the speech he had prepared for the Party conference. We were worried that someone might eavesdrop, so we shut ourselves into a tiny room which had a bed and table crammed into it.

Boris said that the speech he was reading to us was a rough draft, and he still had work to do on it. In his speech, he intended to mention his "Party rehabilitation". This came as a surprise to us – the word "rehabilitation" was associated with victims of the Stalin repressions – but Boris thought it the right phrase to use. He continued to work on the speech, and when it was given a second reading, we took even greater security measures – we went outside late at night, taking an electrical extension cable with us, which we used to power a light that we hung from a tree.

Boris chopped and changed the text every day. The final version had to be typed, but he could not entrust an outsider with this task – he was maintaining the strictest secrecy around the speech, as he believed that, if his plans were discovered, he would not be given the floor – so Tanya brought an old typewriter along, an old present from some of her friends, and Lena typed it up.

As I accompanied Boris to the party conference, I tried to prepare him for the worst: "They probably won't let you onto the podium," I said. But I was mistaken – he forced his way to the podium and gave his speech. It was quite the event. After the Party conference, there was really a sense that Boris's supporters were increasing in number by the day. Even among the delegates a supporter – Vladimir Volkov from Sverdlovsk – came forward to back Boris publicly.

Muscovites began to invite Boris to their meetings. His speeches grew sharper and sharper. I was worried – but there was no stopping him. In the autumn of 1988, he met with the students of the Higher Komsomol School. The speech he gave, for those days, was very bold: he spoke about the benefits of a multi-party system, about the need to reject the monopoly of the Communist Party of the Soviet Union and to hold presidential elections with more than one candidate. He had never said anything like this before – and I was afraid that, after that speech, he wouldn't be coming home afterwards. When he returned, the first thing I said was, "I thought you would be arrested!"

At about that time, a documentary was made about Boris by the journalist Valentin (Valya) Yumashev, who worked for one of the most popular magazines in the country, *Ogonyok*. The filming took place at our house, at Gosstroi, in Boris's government car and on the tennis court. It was the first documentary about Boris. Later, when he became President, others appeared. I particularly like two films by Alexander Sokurov, *Soviet Elegy* and *An Example of Intonation*, as well as the television interview by Eldar Ryazanov: *A Day in the Life of the President*. Of course, these directors are very different, and their work cannot be compared, but Sokurov's films and Ryazanov's interview were both made honestly, with a desire to understand Boris's character and appreciate the depth of his personality. It's interesting that in these films Boris speaks a lot about himself – in general, that was not typical of him. The directors must have been able to find the right tone to talk with him. Alexander Sokurov also managed to capture Boris's pauses – that was really amazing: only those close to him know that his silence can say a lot.

While he was filming with Boris, Valentin tried to persuade him to write a book – and he eventually succeeded. They began work together on a manuscript, which eventually became *Against the Grain*. Valentin helped Boris a lot with the writing, and he became a frequent guest in our home. We became friends – at first I was wary of him, but he turned out to be a lovely person.

Boris didn't want people to know about the manuscript – he was worried that he'd be banned from publishing it – so we tried not to talk about the book, even on the phone. His concerns weren't unfounded – I was convinced we were being followed everywhere we went, and once, when she came home from school, our granddaughter Katya called me in fright: "Someone has been in our house! They were looking for something…" I tried to calm her as best I could, and I asked her not to touch anything while I ran over to her house. Lena's apartment was always in perfect order – everything in its place – but now all their stuff was scattered across the floor. We called the police, and they came to the apartment. It didn't look like a robbery – only a few random things were taken. We were sure they were looking for Boris's manuscript, having learnt that he kept it at his daughter's house – but they got the wrong daughter: it wasn't at Lena's, but at Tanya's. Even I didn't know that.

Boris's book of memoirs – or rather "confessions", according to the Russian title – was intended as an answer to all the lies that had been written about him in the Soviet newspapers. Valya introduced Boris to the British literary agent Andrew Nurnberg, who was surprised to learn that an oppositionist was side by side with the Party leaders of the USSR. He came to visit Boris at the Gosstroi, and told him that the whole world was waiting for such a book. From then on we were convinced that it would be impossible for Boris to publish his book in the Soviet Union.

Boris dictated the text of the manuscript into a tape recorder in snatches, taking himself off to a place where he thought no one would be able to listen in. Sometimes he went to the dacha of Nina Alexandrovna – Lyosha Dyachenko's mother – which had an attic: I was amazed how he could squeeze up there on the narrow staircase. Sometimes he went to Kirov to Valera's parents' house, and took the tape recorder to the hayloft.

Boris took his duties as First Deputy Chairman of the Gosstroi very seriously, like everything he did, but it required finding the time to meet with people in an era when his public appearances became more and more frequent. The burdens on him grew, and he knew he had to keep himself in shape – which is when he started playing tennis.

He hadn't played tennis before. In 1988, when we were on holiday in Jūrmala, we became acquainted with the tennis legend Shamil Tarpishchev – he had come up to Boris and introduced himself, and had invited him to the Davis Cup, which was being held that year in Jūrmala. We took him up on the offer, and watched a match with great pleasure. It was at Shamil's suggestion that Boris gave tennis a go, and he picked it up quickly. I also tried to play, but I wasn't a natural, and I dropped it quite quickly, but Boris began to play regularly.

Boris got little Borya into playing tennis, too, and Tanya along with him. Even when he played against his grandson, he played for real, with passion. Borya also tried to play as best he could – neither of them liked to lose. At the weekend, the entire family went out to the courts – Boris senior played Boris junior, and everyone cheered for them, while I rode a bike along the paths.

We had always dreamt of building our own home, but never had the time or opportunity. But in 1989 we bought a wreck – you couldn't call it anything else – in a village not far from Zelenograd, on a little patch where there had once been a nursery, then some sort of workshop: eventually, only a ruin remained. First, we took apart what was left of the building, planning to make a garage out of the broken bricks, or perhaps a little driveway. Work began on the house: we hired a team of carpenters, and we bought new bricks – more than were needed for the house. But there was no one to oversee the construction – Boris had begun his election campaign, and the First Congress of People's Deputies was approaching. Tanya and Lena and their husbands were busy with their jobs.

We discovered that the builders had built the external walls using the new bricks, while all the partition walls had been made from the broken bricks. They had sold off the rest of the new bricks. So we hired another team – but, as before, there was no one to oversee the construction. The house was broken into, and a boiler, two doors and some windows were stolen. The project was put on hold – we had run out of money.

Despite everything, Tanya and Lyosha finished building the house and planted fruit plants on the grounds – raspberries, currants and gooseberries. All that was left to do was the interior. We could have picnics there, and could come and breathe a bit of fresh air – but we couldn't yet live there.

* * *

The political landscape was in a state of turmoil. Gorbachev understood that change was about to shake up our political life, whether he wanted it or not, and there was a general feeling that the country was on the verge of something big. The First Congress of People's Deputies was announced, and preparations began. For the first time, elections were promised where a choice was offered – never before in the USSR had there been more than one name on the ballot paper. It must be difficult for those who didn't live through the Soviet era to imagine such a thing.

Boris decided to run for the election. By that time, he had a group of assistants: Vladimir Mikhaylov, Valentin Latsev, Lev Sukhanov, Viktor Yaroshenko and many others worked for him on a voluntary basis, and they often met up at our house. This was essentially his campaign staff – just a handful of people who stood in opposition to the Party machine. They found it impossible to plan anything ahead of time – organizational issues continually arose, which were hard to resolve without the government's support. Sometimes there were so many of these problems that they had to work around the clock. I didn't take part in this, but was witness to all of it: there was no other "Yeltsin HQ" besides our apartment.

When in 1994 we moved from 2nd Tverskaya-Yamskaya Street to Osennyaya Street, I found several packets of dried-out Korovka sweets on the shelves – an unexpected reminder of the days when the campaign was underway! We bought those sweets in 1989 with our ration cards, instead of sugar, and we fed the whole campaign staff with them if there was nothing to serve with tea. While I emptied and packed up the cupboards, I found other relics of those years of rations. There were packets and packets of coffee, for instance, which Tanya, being a coffee connoisseur, had brought home from her business trips.

We had to have more and more ration cards, and there was less and less food on the shelves in the shops: there were ration cards for sugar, grain and vodka. In Moscow, groceries were sold only to those with special "Muscovite cards". I kept all of our cards and gave them many years later to the museum. Mine were more worn than Boris's, of course, and my grandson Borya was included on them. These "Muscovite cards" were introduced to prevent residents of other cities buying food in the capital: rationing had been reintroduced in the country.

But everything was different for Party leaders – the special distribution system for the elite operated just as before, along with special clinics and boutiques. Through this system, you could buy not only food, but also clothes, shoes, furniture, household appliances – even books and theatre tickets – and the medical care was incomparable with that offered in ordinary surgeries. The battle against Party privileges was one of the main points in Boris's manifesto. He refused to register at a special clinic, which he could have joined as First Deputy Minister and Member of the Central Committee, and instead signed up at the district clinic near our house.

Boris's election campaign was tense, and there were a lot of problems. The first among them was: where would Boris run? Districts all over the country wanted to nominate him – he had to choose.

Boris's Berezniki support group was headed by our former classmate Sasha Yuzefovich. Boris flew out for a meeting there. He was to be nominated as a candidate in the deputies' election. He didn't fly from Moscow, but from Leningrad, on board a military plane carrying some sort of missile, and he took a roundabout route – he had heard that there were forces trying to prevent his nomination taking place by any means necessary. He arrived safely, and the meeting passed uneventfully.

Usually, however, in the districts in which he was nominated, it was a very different situation – sometimes the meeting was moved to another building just an hour before it was due to start, sometimes people blacklisted by the Party would be denied entrance, and provocateurs were brought in to try to compromise Boris. These meetings went on for six, eight – sometimes even ten hours.

*Questions on the Margins*

"You didn't take part in your husband's election campaign. Why?"

"To be honest, back then, it didn't even occur to me."

"But you went to the candidacy meetings, at least, to cheer him on?"

"Not once – I cheered him on from home."

I once asked Alexander Mikhailov (the head of Boris's election campaign in the Ramenki district in Moscow): "Will Gorbachev really let Boris get to Congress?" He laughed: "Gorbachev has no chance of stopping him!" Boris and his aides were confident of victory. The tense atmosphere, however, led to Boris being tormented by insomnia once again – but he endured it: he didn't have time to visit doctors. Each step towards Congress took a great effort.

After a campaign meeting at the Likhachov Plant (ZiL), Boris came home absolutely exhausted – his suit was drenched, as if he had been caught in a downpour: there had been so many people packed into the room that the heat was terrible, and the meeting went on for several hours.

Everything was decided at a meeting at the Hall of Columns in the House of Unions – the names which would end up on the ballot paper in Moscow were chosen. Dozens of candidates were discussed, but only two had the support of the government: Yevgeny Brakov, Director General of ZiL, and the pilot and cosmonaut Georgy Mikhaylovich Grechko. According to the rules at the time, these two were offered the choice whether to include all the other candidates on the ballot as well, or just to run against each other. Boris knew that the Party apparatchiks would do everything in their power to limit the choice to Brakov and Grechko, but they hadn't counted on Georgy Mikhaylovich disrupting the course of events. Just before the final vote, he withdrew his candidacy, which meant that Yeltsin and Brakov ended up on the ballot paper. Boris's victory in the Moscow election was amazing: about ninety per cent voted in favour of him – more than five million Muscovites.

The meeting of the First Congress of People's Deputies was shown live on television from morning until night. There had never been anything like that before: it was impossible to tear yourself away. Everyone suddenly became obsessed with politics. We had a TV set in front of the dinner table, and during those days it was almost never turned off. In order not to miss the broadcast of Congress, I adapted my cooking and did all the preparation at the dinner table, and only ran into the kitchen to tend to the stove.

We were very worried about Boris and his supporters – we were outraged when they weren't allowed to speak, or when they were rudely pushed away. I remember a powerful feeling coming over me when I watched Gorbachev driving Andrei Dmitrievich Sakharov from the podium. I couldn't understand – Gorbachev had released Sakharov from exile, and now he was subjecting him to public humiliation…

Meetings of the Inter-Regional Deputies Group (MDG) – which became the first legal Soviet opposition – began, and those in favour of reform joined up. The meetings took place in the House of Cinema, and the entrance was free. So many people were packed into the hall that they had to sit on the steps. I went to the meetings, listened to the speeches, and worried – it was all so unusual and interesting. Boris, along with Sakharov, Gavriil Kharitonovich Popov, Yury Nikolayevich Afanasyev and the Estonian deputy Viktor Palm, became co-chairmen of the Inter-Regional Deputies Group.

1989 was probably the best year in Boris's political career. Even with all the hardships, the feeling that everything was changing for the better never left us. Quite often, Boris's colleagues came over to our house after the meetings – the future mayor of Moscow, Gavriil Popov, the future mayor of St Petersburg, Anatoly Sobchak, the future State Secretary of Russia, Gennady Burbulis, as well as the future deputy mayor of Moscow, Sergei Stankevich, and Arkady Murashev, a Parliamentarian, who were both quite young then. Andrei Dmitrievich Sakharov even called Boris at night sometimes, if there was an urgent matter. Once I had thought that our life in

Moscow would require us to socialize with the top Party bosses – but it turned out that our circle was the opposition politicians, whose names no one had heard until recently. They were people of varied ages and life experiences, but they were all educated and thoughtful, and had an unusual way of thinking. Sometimes they were very naive – they believed that our country had to be reformed and that it could be done very quickly.

After Andrei Dmitrievich Sakharov died at the end of 1989, Boris and I met with his widow, Yelena Georgievna Bonner – and later, when Boris didn't have the time, I visited her on my own. We talked a lot about the future of our country. At some point, at an event – I think it was the launch of Boris's book – Bonner approached Boris and asked him to read a letter. He took the envelope and hid it in the pocket of his jacket. "Be sure to read it, Boris Nikolayevich," she persisted. "I always read your letters," he replied – and that was true. He was always very attentive to her requests. The letter, I later learnt, related to the Memorial Society – Boris was on its supervisory council, and was convinced that all the victims of Stalinism had to be immortalized in some sort of memorial. He did everything he could to make this happen.

In the autumn of 1989, Boris accepted an invitation to go to the USA to give a series of lectures in American universities. On the eve of his return, an article about his trip, full of fabrications, appeared in *Pravda*, which claimed that Boris had bought a box of shirts and several video recorders, and that he had drunk whiskey by the crate… In short, a lot of nonsense. The article, it noted, was reprinted from the Italian newspaper *La Repubblica*. In later years, I found out from journalist friends that the KGB often used the foreign press in this way during the Soviet era.

When Boris got home, I asked him jokingly, "But where are your boxes of shirts? And the video recorders?" Of course, he had brought gifts – ordinary souvenirs for us and the grand-children and he had bought himself a cowboy hat. He had a lot of stories – the trip had made a very strong impression on him. He told me how amazed he was by the supermarkets, where the shelves groaned under the weight of goods. He said he felt an enormous sense of hurt on behalf of our people – didn't they deserve a better life? He managed to include impressions from this trip in his book, which came out later that year.

Despite my fears, the book wasn't banned by the censor – and it generated enormous interest. At first it came out with the publisher Ogonyok in paperback, printed virtually on newsprint – but the first print run sold out instantly. After a short while, the book was published abroad – in England, Spain and other countries – and Boris was invited to speak at various events.

Boris flew to London in late April 1990, and from there he went to Barcelona. He flew on a small private aeroplane with his aide Lev Sukhanov and Viktor Yaroshenko, a people's deputy. Upon landing, the plane was unable to lower its landing gear, and it hit the ground heavily. Fortunately, everyone survived, but Boris felt a sharp pain in his back. He tried to endure it, but it was impossible, and a few hours later an ambulance took him to a hospital. One of his vertebrae was dislocated, and this injury was on top of an old volleyball lesion he had suffered in his youth. The Spanish doctors made the decision to operate – they couldn't delay, or he could lose the use of his legs at any moment. He was very lucky – one of the best surgeons in Spain was on duty that day.

I learnt about the accident and the impending surgery from Lev Sukhanov, who called me from Barcelona. Needless to say, I was on tenterhooks waiting to hear how the operation went. I was fully aware of the danger of the situation in which Boris had landed. Not long before I had heard about someone who, after a similar injury, had wound up stuck in a wheelchair. But Boris was on his feet already by the second day, and he called me himself. By the fifth day, which came around surprisingly fast, the doctors let him return to Moscow, and sent him away with a whole set of binding materials – we didn't have such things in our country. When he got home, we covered him with plaster, as directed. We were eternally grateful to those Spanish doctors. After a while, when they finally took up Boris's invitation to come to Russia – by which time he was Chairman of the Supreme Soviet of the RSFSR (Russian Soviet Federative Socialist Republic) – we received them at home with great joy.

Unfortunately, Boris's back pain remained for the rest of his life, although it was only particularly acute for a few years after the accident. I don't know how he coped with it. I remember well the First Congress of People's Deputies of Russia meeting a month after the accident: the night before, his back had begun hurting badly again, but – of course – he went to the meeting anyway. He was barely alive when he came home that evening – his forehead was beaded with sweat. It was the first time I had seen him in such a state. I remember thinking how many times my daughters and I, trying to support him, had said to him: "People are counting on you… you must – you really must look after yourself…" And I said to him then: "You don't owe anyone anything – you are already doing more than you can! Don't go in to Congress any more. Do I have to ask you on my knees?" And I did just that. Tanya was just coming home from work, and arrived in the middle of this scene. She asked us in fright: "What's wrong with you?" I explained, and then, together, we tried to talk Boris into staying home. But he went to Congress the next day anyway. We were lucky that a young doctor, Andrei, lived in our building, and our families were friends. When Boris needed relief from the severe pain in his back, Andrei could give him an injection – this was usually late at night. In the morning, Boris would get up feeling energetic, but by the end of the day the pain would catch up with him again.

After the accident, healers and psychics got in touch and offered their services, but Boris didn't believe in them, and never took them up on their offer to help. I mention this because there have been many claims that he was treated by healers – even Djuna (Eugenia Davitashvili, a Russian faith healer of Assyrian descent) told such a story, although Boris met her only once, when he presented her with an award at some ceremony or other. Djuna went so far as to claim that she had not only healed Boris, but also provided counsel to him about Chechnya, for which he gave her a nickname – "Total Delirium". The healers were really very persistent. I remember one of them, Ludmila Kim, tried to persuade me to exert my influence on Boris. She even tried to demonstrate her abilities to me, standing behind my back and moving her hands around, saying "Do you feel the warmth?" I didn't feel anything – and told her so.

Ludmila then decided to visit Baba Vanga (Vangeliya Pandeva Gushterova, the blind Bulgarian mystic). Before the trip, she asked me if she could put a sugar lump under Boris's pillow – this way, she claimed, Vanga would be able to predict whether Boris would be elected President or not. Knowing how my husband would react, I didn't even mention this to him – but in order to avoid any more discussions with her, the next day I gave her a lump of sugar – I have that on my conscience. Ludmila returned and said: "Vanga said Boris Nikolayevich will be elected President." When I told Boris about this later, he laughed.

* * *

On 29th May 1990, the First Congress of People's Deputies of the RSFSR elected Boris Chairman of the Supreme Soviet. This was a very important event for him, and for our whole family. When he decided to run for this post, he understood that there would be much resistance from the Soviet government. In itself, the position wasn't very significant. Now it's fashionable to write about Boris striving for power at any price – but whatever people say, that wasn't in his nature. Power for him, both in Sverdlovsk and Moscow, served only as a tool – he needed it to complete the tasks that he set himself.

Once, before his election as Chairman of the Supreme Soviet, Boris came home late, very tired. He had supper, and we talked about domestic affairs – the usual evening conversation. Suddenly he said, "Russia must be saved." This caught me off-guard: no one ever talked about "Russia" – usually it was "the Soviet Union" – but I soon realized that that was exactly what he meant to say. There were conflicts brewing between the various republics and the main body of the USSR. It had become clear that a compromise had to be reached, or the country would be dragged into civil war – and this prospect seemed more and more real every day.

After the People's Deputies of the USSR and RSFSR elections, Boris's popularity grew by the day. This frightened the Party leadership, of course, and it turned out to be quite difficult for him to win the post of Chairman of the Supreme Soviet. Voting in the election was done at the Congress of People's Deputies of Russia, and in order to win, you had to get 531 votes – one more than half of the total number of deputies. The first vote took place on 25th May. Boris's main opponent was Ivan Polozkov, leader of the Russian Communists – a very conservative man who was not very exciting, but had the backing of the Soviet government. As had become the custom, we watched the whole thing on TV. It almost felt as if we were participating.

We were terribly worried about Boris. He spoke animatedly and convincingly before the deputies, touching on some of the country's most troubling issues, and proposing about twenty laws which needed to be passed in the interests of Russia. Polozkov, of course, in contrast with Boris, looked dull, and was clearly losing: his speech was inexpressive and formal. We thought, however, that the leadership would be exerting pressure on the Communist deputies behind the scenes – and that turned out to be the case, although we found out about this only later. Before the vote, the Communist deputies were summoned to the Kremlin, and it was strongly suggested that they support Polozkov. Nevertheless, the result of the first vote was in favour of Boris, with 497 votes for him and 473 for Polozkov.

The second round of voting took place on 26th May – once again, Boris was ahead, and once again, neither had a majority: Yeltsin had 503 and Polozkov had 458. The result surprised me – I knew, of course, that the Soviet leadership would do everything in its power to prevent Boris from becoming Chairman of the Supreme Soviet of the RSFSR. These results, however, suggested that Congress was starting to come out from under the Kremlin's control, and that the deputies were voting with their consciences, rather than following the orders of the General Secretary of the CPSU Central Committee. It no longer mattered now whether they had Party cards in their pockets or not – and, of course, this confused the Party leadership.

On 28th May, another round of candidate nominations was held, and the 29th brought with it a new round of voting. The situation had now changed: Polozkov withdrew his candidacy at the last moment, lending his support to another protégé of the CPSU Central Committee, Alexander Vlasov, Chairman of the Council of Ministers of the RSFSR. Vlasov wasn't as odious a figure as Polozkov – he was simply a high-ranking bureaucrat who said the right words… but with no follow-up. To be honest, I was confident of Boris's victory – and I wasn't mistaken: with the third vote, Boris secured 535 votes – a healthy majority. It was clear that a strong and popular leader had emerged – one that could promote Russia's interests in the dispute with the Soviet Union's leadership. Our family was, of course, delighted for Boris – but I immediately began to think about the increase in his workload, about the additional effort the new position would require, and what toll that would take on all of us.

Just over a month later, in July 1990, Boris left the Party. He announced this during the 28th Congress of the CPSU. In his speech, he said he could not defend the interests of the RSFSR while remaining a member of the CPSU and obeying its Charter. Boris didn't tell the family that he planned to do this: we found out from his speech on television along with everyone else. My first thought was that it must have been a difficult decision for him to make – he had been a member of the CPSU for so many years, and had given so much to the Party… I wasn't mistaken: when he came home, he seemed deeply distressed by what had just happened. This was quite clear to me, and to both of our daughters, but, as always, we supported his decision. Not long ago I learnt that the first person in our family – before Boris – to leave the Party was Lena's husband, Valera Okulov. Lena didn't tell me about it at the time, presumably in an attempt to stop me worrying unnecessarily. Like Tanya, Lena was not a Party member.

During Congress and immediately after it, thousands of Party members followed Boris's example, including me – although I didn't write a statement or give a speech: that was when I stopped going to Party meetings and paying my dues. I kept my Party card, however, and still have it today.

1990 saw much opposition from the republics – even so, Boris's position remained unchanged, and, as before, he advocated preserving the Soviet Union, whilst remaining convinced of the need to reform it. The Union could only work if the republics – despite having to relinquish many of their powers to the central government – were considered equal to Russia. That year, the preparation of a new Union Treaty came under threat.

In early 1991, the Soviet leadership sent troops into Vilnius. This wasn't the first conflict – before that there were tragic events in Kazakhstan, Azerbaijan and Georgia. Shooting broke out at the Vilnius Television Centre, and people were killed. The situation grew worse in the other Baltic republics. There were demonstrations in Moscow in support of Lithuania, Latvia and Estonia, and Boris went to Tallinn to express his solidarity with the cities of these republics – that was a brave act.

The leaders of Latvia, Lithuania, Russia and Estonia put out a joint statement, officially recognizing each other's sovereignty, and asserting their readiness to help one another fight off anyone who would challenge their independence. That day, Boris appealed to Russian soldiers in the Baltics, asking them to refrain from following orders and using force against the civilian population. The Presidium of the Supreme Soviet of Russia joined Boris in calling on the Soviet Union's leadership to forbid the use of force, and to begin talks with the lawful representatives of the republics in order to find a way out of the crisis.

After his resignation in 2006, Boris received the highest state award of Latvia – the Latvian Order of Three Stars of the

First Rank – and in 2011 he was posthumously given the Lithuanian Order of the Grand Cross of Vytis. A commemorative bas-relief in his honour was unveiled in Tallinn's city centre. Thus the Baltic governments recognized the contribution of the First President of Russia in helping them achieve their independence.

The early months of 1991 were very tense. Living standards deteriorated – the once-unified economy fell apart before our eyes: the shelves were empty; people had to queue for everything.

Once, in the 1990s, I went on a business trip to the Netherlands with Galina Starovoitova, a people's deputy, and Irina Shushkevich, wife of the Chairman of the Supreme Soviet of Belarus. Every day, as spending money, we were each given the equivalent of $100 in guilders. When I went into a supermarket I was dazzled – none of us had such bulging shelves in our countries. I asked those accompanying us to help me buy something tasty for my grandchildren. They filled a huge bag – on top of which, I remember, were bright-yellow bananas. I returned home, and with a sweeping gesture poured the bag's contents onto the worktop. Fruit, chocolates, cookies and chewing gum spilt out… My grandchildren had never seen such abundance, and they jumped for joy.

\* \* \*

In February 1991, Boris turned sixty. We celebrated his birthday at the holiday home of the Supreme Soviet of Russia, and gathered a fair number of guests. Our former classmates came, and, of course, people from his new Moscow team. It was a sunny day, but absolutely freezing. Boris was in fine spirits – joking and raising toasts. We talked a lot about the future that day. I don't remember the details, but I remember the general mood: hopeful.

Just a couple of months later, on 12th June 1991, Boris won the presidential election.

*Questions on the Margins*

"Did Boris Nikolayevich consult with you before deciding to run for President of Russia?"

"No – he presented me with a fait accompli."

"How did you take it?"

"I told him the election to the USSR People's Deputies had been enough for me, and that I wouldn't survive the presidential election."

"What did he say?"

"He said: 'When did you become such a wimp?' I tried to say, more gently: 'I don't think I can go through all that again.' He immediately grabbed on to that 'think' and broke into a smile. 'I *think* you can.' As it turned out, he was right – as always."

Nowadays they say that Boris sailed through the first presidential election. Of course, that's not how it really was. First, there was a battle to introduce the election itself – there had never been a leadership election in any of the USSR republics by direct, universal vote. Gorbachev became President of the USSR by election at Congress – he had not risked a universal election. But Boris did that – he believed that if the President of Russia was elected democratically, it would make him strong and capable of defending Russia's interests, and he was prepared to start a national discussion on the institution of the presidency. On 17th March 1991, seventy-one per cent of voters in a referendum supported the idea of direct elections for President. Boris was thrilled – although he realized that the election itself would not be easy.

The election campaign was extremely intense. There were demonstrations in support of Boris across the whole country, and about a million people gathered in the squares of Moscow, chanting "People's Deputy to People's President!"

Boris was opposed by Nikolai Ryzhkov, Vadim Baktin, Aman Tuleyev, Albert Makashov and Vladimir Zhirinovsky. Ryzhkov was supported by Gorbachev, and was probably the most serious threat to Boris – the Party machine, as before, was busy against him. This didn't frighten him: he plunged into the campaign with enthusiasm, and felt uplifted by the support of people across the country. He didn't take part in televised debates, considering it more important to spend time talking to people. One trip around the country was followed by another – now no one could stop him from meeting with voters, talking to them and answering their questions. People could speak to him about their problems; they wrote letters to him with words of support; there were even touching signs of affection – an elderly couple once brought a jar of jam and some cucumbers for Boris to the security guards at the Supreme Soviet.

The election campaign was short but intense. Unlike during the second presidential election, I kept a low profile. The victory was impressive – more than 57 per cent of the vote. Of course, we nervously awaited the final result. When it was finally announced, we didn't even have the strength to sit down at the table and celebrate properly – we just managed a glass of champagne.

The inauguration took place in the Kremlin. Patriarch Alexy II took part – as did other religious representatives – and the clergy sat in the first row. Of course, everyone who had worked in Boris's team was present too – including Gennady Burbulis, Sergei Shakhrai, Ruslan Khasbulatov, Alexander Rutskoi and Ivan Silayev. Even Gorbachev said a few words.

No one quite knew what form the inauguration should take – everything was being done for the first time. In the end it was based on the protocol service, but with input from the President Elect. The ceremony itself was short, but solemn – Boris swore an oath to the Constitution of the RSFSR, and everyone stood in front of an enormous Russian flag (the Soviet flag, not the tricolour). Boris wore a dark-red tie and his best suit. We didn't have one specially made – there wasn't time for that – and he wore the suit for many years afterwards; it is now in the museum. I wore something from the best side of my wardrobe, too – but I no longer remember what.

# By the President's Side

Boris had a lot more work to do now. A desk was moved into our bedroom – he would often wake up at about four o'clock in the morning and get up to work. The focus of Boris's attention during the first stage of his presidency was preparing the new Union Treaty. These days it is fashionable to say that Yeltsin and Gorbachev "destroyed the Union", and in writings about that era it is often claimed that the sour relationship between the President of the USSR and the President of Russia prevented them from agreeing on Union reform. That's nonsense. Boris was able to forget about personal problems when dealing with government issues, and he was not vengeful at all – in Boris's opinion, Gorbachev put the brakes on the negotiations and tried with all his might to hold on to the former powers of the Union government. The republics didn't agree to this – they wanted more independence. Boris said a number of times: "Gorbachev is waiting for the republics to run off."

In his battle with Gorbachev, Boris defended the right of Russia to be an independent sovereign republic, an equal among equals, and to enter into a new union on those conditions. Few today recall that, before 1990, Russia did not have its own leading Party bodies in the USSR – the RSFSR did not have a republican Communist Party, its own central committee or First Secretary. The President of Russia was supposed to defend his voters' interests, just as other Union republics' leaders did – and that is exactly what Boris did, although his role in the negotiations, of course, was different from those of the republics' leaders. He took upon himself the coordination of the republics with the central government of the Union, and to that end was in constant contact with the republics' leaders as well as Gorbachev, doing everything in his power to avoid the negotiations coming to a dead end. Despite the difficult relationship he had with Gorbachev, he managed to smooth conflicts between the various sides and coordinate their efforts.

But negotiating the new treaty was, of course, very difficult. We didn't know the details – many of the discussions with the republic leaders took place face to face. Of course, some details leaked to the press and became common knowledge – we all lived for political news then: we read the papers, and never missed the news programmes. I could only judge the difficulty of the negotiations from Boris's condition – even compared to his previous periods of stress, this era seemed particularly tense. But in the end the work yielded results, and a draft of the new Union Treaty was prepared, with its signing scheduled for 20th August. Boris was confident that no one would interfere with it. I was too, for that matter.

We spent the summer of 1991 in the Council of Ministers' dacha in Arkhangelskoye. Of all the government dachas we lived in, I liked Arkhangelskoye the best. There was a particularly peaceful atmosphere there, and there was a large apple orchard and a creek, and fragrances which, I am sure, have never seen their equal anywhere else. The neighbours – Sergei Shakhrai, Gennady Burbulis, Viktor Yaroshenko, Nikolai Fyodorov and Alexander Shokhin – were wonderful… It was very modest: nothing luxurious in the two-storey brick home we shared with another family – no fence, not much security. You felt absolutely free. I even started a garden here – in August, large yellow and red tomatoes grew ripe in our home-made greenhouse. My sister had sent me the seedlings from Sverdlovsk.

Sunday 18th August came: Boris was on a trip to Almaty, and the rest of the family – except for Valera, who was away at the time – was waiting for him in Arkhangelskoye. We were told that Boris's flight was delayed, and that he would fly into the military airport instead, for some reason. There were no bad premonitions, and we weren't particularly surprised – any number of things could be responsible for this. I later learnt that Nazarbayev had caused the delay.

Boris arrived at Arkhangelskoye late, and went straight to bed. On Monday 19th August, at 6 a.m., the phone rang. Our bedroom was on the first floor, the phone was on the ground floor, where Tanya was sleeping, so it was she who picked up the receiver. It was Boris's office calling, and they just said four words to her: "Turn on the television."

I always left the bedroom door open, just in case my grand-children needed us. Suddenly, I heard someone's step on the stairs. Tanya came in and turned on the television. "What are you doing? Papa is sleeping!" I said, surprised.

"Mama, something's happened," Tanya replied, and woke Boris.

I looked at the screen: *Swan Lake* was on. At six in the morning. We knew that this was the signal of some emergency. Then the anchor appeared, and announced that Gorbachev was ill and a state of emergency had been declared. "It's a coup," said Boris.

Boris's security guards said that Arkhangelskoye was surrounded by machine-gunners. Boris's security team at that time was small, but they were dotted around the house. We quickly learnt where the assault team was located – and that the muzzles of their guns were trained on the windows. And, I thought, there were children in the house. I felt awful.

Boris asked me to call his colleagues who were staying nearby while he shaved. I couldn't get Ruslan Khasbulatov on the phone, so I ran over – their dacha was just across from ours. Quite quickly, Burbulis, Shakhrai, Shokhin, Poltoranin, Yaroshenko, Silayev and Khasbulatov gathered at our house.

Together they wrote an appeal to the people of Russia – each added a phrase, and they edited it together. We didn't have a typewriter, so Khasbulatov wrote down the text – he jotted down notes, but didn't write it in full, he now claims – and, when it was ready, Lena took Mikhail Poltoranin – the Minister of Press and Mass Media – to the service part of the house and started typing it. Poltoranin dictated it, and Lena typed several copies. They called acquaintances and read the appeal over the phone, asking them to disseminate it. The first person they spoke to was a relative of Valera's who worked in a ministry, where there was a fax machine. Tanya also sent the message to acquaintances who had a network through which they could distribute it.

Anatoly Sobchak dropped by on his way to the airport – he was supposed to be flying to Leningrad – and he and Boris had a brief conversation. I remember he said, "There are convoys of tanks everywhere." I went to see him off – it wasn't clear if he would be able to get home. On the porch he said to me, "God save us, Naina Iosifovna." It gave me the shivers.

The grounds of the Arkhangelskoye dachas were open, and the assault team didn't want to risk an open battle with the security of the President of Russia. It turned out that the Spetsnaz never received the go-ahead from KGB Chairman Kryuchkov to storm Arkhangelskoye.

Boris decided to go to his office in Moscow, the White House. The car was driven up to the porch, and the guards suggested he put on a bulletproof vest – it was too small, and it made his jacket bunch up.

"Well, it's good that you have a bulletproof vest, but your head is unprotected!" I told him. He tried to reassure me in a few words – there wasn't time for long conversations.

Boris went off, taking several copies of the appeal with him, and we remained at the dacha. We were terribly worried – would they let him reach the White House? Horrible thoughts filled my head as we counted down the minutes. I sighed with relief when they called to tell us they had got there.

We decided to go to Moscow too – we had to pack quickly, and I suddenly realized that, instead of packing clothes, I was tearing tomatoes from their stalks and throwing them into a basket. "Mama, have you gone mad?" my daughters shouted. It's true, I wasn't thinking clearly – although later they happily ate the tomatoes I picked. The ones we didn't manage to pick were sold: when we returned to Arkhangelskoye, the greenhouse was empty.

We were soon faced with a big question: where should we go? The security team told me to take our grandchildren to the apartment of Boris's bodyguard, Viktor Kuznetsov, in Kuntsevo, rather than go home. It was brave of him to offer us a refuge, under those circumstances. Lena, Tanya and her husband Lyosha decided to go to our Moscow apartment.

We grabbed what we needed and put the children in a van. One of the guards said, "If they shoot, lie down on the floor, face down." Borya, who was still quite small, heard this, and asked loudly, "Mama, will they shoot us in the head straight away?" Lena and Tanya, who were getting ready to leave in Lyosha's car, turned pale. At the dacha's security checkpoint, the officers looked into the van, saw the children and me in the back, and let us through without a word.

That first night, I didn't sleep at all. I sat in the armchair in front of the television. It was quiet in that unfamiliar apartment, and there was nothing to keep myself occupied with. The children slept in their clothes wherever they could – in an armchair or on the sofa.

That evening, I went outside to make a call from a phone booth – I had been told not to use the home phone – and, as I reached the middle of the street, I suddenly realized that I didn't have two copecks to pay for the call. I asked a passer-by, who gave me enough to call the office. Someone answered and told me that everything was fine, but they couldn't put me through to Boris. In the morning, I decided: "That's it! I can't stay here any more – I'm going home." I called Lena and Tanya; the security team didn't object.

We spent the second night in our own apartment, along with the armed guards. We had heard that thousands of people had turned out to defend the White House – this filled us with hope, but also with alarm. We were terrified – a tragedy could occur at any moment.

The security team asked us not to go near the windows. "Why?" I asked. "There's a bread truck in the courtyard – we think it might be full of machine-gunners," they said.

That night was even more terrifying than the first – a rumour was going around that the White House would be stormed. Masha, our youngest grandchild, kept asking what would happen to us.

I eventually managed to put the grandchildren to bed – but that night we were woken and told we had to leave the apartment.

We waited. There was some kind of hold-up. The situation was nerve-wracking. I remember saying to the security team: "If they shoot at us, don't shoot back. You have families. You won't be able to hold your own if there are machine-gunners out there." But they said, "This is our job." Nobody panicked – we kept calm and waited in silence.

The security team was waiting for a signal. Then a telephone rang – the White House wasn't going to be stormed. Everyone sighed with relief – that meant we were in the clear, too.

Early in the morning of 21st August, Boris called to wish Lena a happy birthday. "I'm sorry I couldn't get you a present," he said. Lena replied: "You've given me the most important present of all: freedom." That phrase sounds a bit melodramatic now, but it was absolutely sincere, and it was how we all felt at the time.

Now, recalling those days and that night, I shudder to think how close we were to the edge.

\* \* \*

The coup pushed the republics into leaving the USSR, and the signing of the Union Treaty was abandoned. What Boris feared had come to pass: the country fell apart before our eyes, and it was no longer possible to preserve the USSR – one after another, the republics passed declarations of independence. I am amazed that people can believe the myth that the leaders of Russia, Belarus and Ukraine gathered in Belovezhskaya Pushcha and "broke up the USSR" with the Belovezha Accords. What sort of great country can be "dismantled" with one document? In actual fact, at the end of 1991, the country was slowly imploding by itself. Everything was falling apart – and this was a nuclear power! If the leaders of the republics had not interfered, the consequences could have been terrible – for the whole world. Of course, it would have been better if the USSR had been gradually reformed, if the new Union

Treaty had been signed, if the rights of the republics had been extended, if coordinated economic reform had been initiated. But after the coup, it was only possible to watch while the country rolled towards the abyss – or try, by any means necessary, to slow its descent. Boris, along with the leaders of Ukraine and Belarus – and, later, the other republics – took the responsibility upon themselves. I know how hard it must have been for Boris to make the decisions that were made in Belovezhskaya Pushcha – but he couldn't do anything else. He had to do everything he could to stop the country disintegrating.

Boris tried to organize a transfer of power from the President of the USSR to the President of Russia, whilst still showing consideration for Gorbachev. At the end of December, he held talks with Alexander Nikolayevich Yakovlev, a close colleague of Gorbachev, and many issues were settled – concerning, above all, the government, of course. But some decisions concerning Gorbachev personally were also made: he was provided security, a presidential pension, a dacha and a building to house the Gorbachev Foundation. It was important to Boris that the head of the USSR leave his post with dignity. This was not staged for the public – Boris believed it was a humane thing to do, as well as being right from a government point of view.

On 25th December, the President of the USSR addressed the citizens of his country and announced his resignation. Later that day the Russian flag was raised over the Kremlin.

It was a very difficult time: Russia did not have its own government institutions, and it was in a parlous economic situation – the Soviet economy was built in such a way that all of the republics were interlinked economically, like different departments in a big factory: the raw materials were in one republic; the factories to process them were in another. Suddenly, all these links began to break. A ration-card system had been in place for several years already, but by the autumn of 1991 the situation was catastrophic. The shops were empty – the only help was from humanitarian aid, and that was limited. I remember well having conversations about whether humanitarian aid would be enough. Boris travelled the country a lot, and saw the horror first-hand. A famine wasn't far off – action had to be taken, and quickly.

At around that time, Boris became acquainted with the economist Yegor Timurovich Gaidar – Gennady Burbulis, a friend of Boris's, introduced them. Later, he held the post of State Secretary. I remember the first time Boris met with Gaidar at our residence. They spoke for a long time – several hours. When he left, Boris said: "There is a blockage in the economy. We'll break through it." They had evidently discussed a plan of action, and Gaidar had convinced Boris that his programme could save the country – Boris believed in Gaidar, and didn't doubt his choice.

## Questions on the Margins

"You weren't surprised that Boris Nikolayevich trusted the economy to a person with no management expertise?"

"No – Boris became a manager very early, and he always trusted young people. That's how it was in construction, and at the Regional Party Committee. That was his principle."

"But here it was surely different – was he aware of the risk?"

"I can't say. All I know for sure is that Boris was rarely mistaken in his choice of people – he always had a good gut feeling."

"He accepted the fact that Gaidar knew better than he did when it came to the economy – in the sense that he was more educated?"

"Boris always said that he wanted smart people around him. It was better if they were smarter than he was."

Boris grew calmer after Gaidar's appointment – he evidently felt supported by him. He wasn't the only one, either – it seems to me that the appearance of Gaidar and his team in the government to some extent reassured everyone with any common sense. It was clear that the professionals had taken charge of economic reform – and prospects began to look brighter.

Of course, when they started talking about free markets, everyone had doubts. Like many others, I couldn't see the situation changing overnight: one day there were empty shelves – the next, if pricing regulations were removed, would they fill up? With what? Where would the food and goods come from?

But after the new free-market regulations were announced, the shelves really did fill up rapidly – although they were still painful times: food and goods may have appeared, but there was no money to buy it with. Boris worried a lot: he realized how hard it was for people – what difficulties were weighing on their shoulders. But he also understood that, without resolving the problems which had accumulated for years, it would be impossible to make their lives easier. If the leaders of the country were indecisive, it would be even worse for ordinary people.

The year 1992 was a turning point for the economy. Boris did everything he could to implement the reforms Gaidar's team had conceived. It was not easy – the situation was so dire that it was impossible to plan ahead: first one region, then another, was on the edge of famine; factories came to a halt; oil was only $10 or $15 a barrel; power and heat outages were reported... At the same time as making these reforms, the country had to be saved from economic collapse.

Gaidar's team coped admirably with the difficult task, despite the fact that there was huge resistance to reforms. Instead of uniting people at such a challenging time for the country, the Communists aggravated the situation: Congress, which was under their control, rejected the laws that were necessary for the reforms, and Party functionaries put people on the street calling for the resignation of the government. Boris realized that he was the only person who could defend Gaidar's team – and he did so as best he could.

Ruslan Khasbulatov, Chairman of the Supreme Soviet, and Alexander Rutskoi, Vice President, who had only recently supported the President, betrayed him at the very first hurdle, and stood in opposition to the course Gaidar was taking. This aggravated things no end.

For me, as for everyone else, the 1990s were very difficult. I saw how hard it was for everyone we knew – our former classmates in Sverdlovsk, my sister, my brothers and their families, Boris's relatives and all our friends and acquaintances suffered a lot during the 1990s. It wasn't just from newspapers that I knew what people were going through. But we very much hoped that our sacrifices would not be in vain. Hope – that's perhaps the most important word in understanding the 1990s, those years which now people have begun to call "wild". Of course, there were disappointments, there were mistakes: we wanted to press ahead quickly and without damage. But that only happens in fairy tales – in real life everything is more complicated. But the fact that people no longer have to bustle in humiliating queues is a result of the reforms that were rolled out in the early 1990s; the fact that people can own apartments and plots of land, that someone can open their own business – it's all down to the reforms. On the whole, the fact that we now live in a modern, civilized country is also to the credit of the 1990s – if we hadn't had the "wild" 1990s, there wouldn't have been the prosperous 2000s. Yes, it was hard for everyone, but Boris, Yegor Timurovich and other members of the team did everything in their power not only to bring the country out of the crisis, but also to lay a solid foundation for the future. And they managed to do this.

*Questions on the Margins*

"Did Boris Nikolayevich come to regret that he chose the path of shock therapy?"

"Why would he regret it? There was no way out. He couldn't say: 'Be patient for a year or two while we gradually reform the economy.' People had to be fed that day – not in a year's time."

"Did he understand that no one would thank him or Gaidar?"

"He knew what he was getting himself into – he even said to Yegor Timurovich: 'Everyone is going to attack you.'"

"Gaidar wasn't afraid of this?"

"He believed they had to get the job done. And, in my view, he wasn't afraid at all."

It upsets me to hear people speak scornfully of the 1990s or curse those who took upon themselves to drive reform. They somehow forget who drove the country to the point where it was put on ration cards in peacetime, where the gold reserves were exhausted – that didn't happen under Yeltsin and Gaidar, but under the Communists.

Boris very much wanted Gaidar to become the Chairman of the government – and I continue to think that if Yegor Timurovich had remained at the head of the Cabinet of Ministers for another two or three years, the economic reforms would have been less painful. But it didn't work out.

I remember well that December day, in 1992, when a vote was held in Congress to choose a candidate for the Chairman of government. The deputies had been elected back in 1990, and among them there were still many Party functionaries of various levels – there were many Communists in the First Congress of People's Deputies, and it was clear that Congress would put up a fight against the President and his team. When Boris left home, Tanya and I said, almost in chorus: "You have to defend Gaidar!" Boris was silent, and we didn't expect an answer – we understood that he would do everything in his power. He went to Congress that day very troubled. We all sat at home in front of the television, worrying – so when he returned, we already knew that he hadn't managed to get Gaidar elected as Prime Minister. Boris came in the door and immediately said, "I did everything I could, but it wasn't enough." That was the end of the conversation – so saying, he went into his office; he was clearly very disappointed.

Although Gaidar continued to work in the government, Boris was troubled that he wasn't able to complete what he had begun – work he considered necessary. But I think the country was very lucky that Gaidar stood beside Boris – history will be the judge, and I am certain that Gaidar will have monuments erected in his honour as a great Russian reformer.

Boris always kept up with Yegor Timurovich, both before and after his departure from the government – and Gaidar came to our home both before and after his resignation. He amazed me with his calm smile, which he always had, no matter how difficult the situation he found himself in. He had very warm eyes – his gaze would melt whomever he was speaking to. How unjust it is that he died so young, at just fifty-three years old!

Although Boris was now President, Lena and Tanya continued in their jobs – Lena was still at the construction exhibition at the VDNKh, and Tanya worked at the Salyut Space Design Bureau, where she calculated satellite trajectories. She often went on business trips to the spaceship-tracking station at Yevpatoriya. Her husband, Lyosha, also worked at the design bureau. Lena's husband, Valera, worked in the Central Administration of International Air Services, before he was made the lead navigator trainer at the Aeroflot training centre. Several years later, in 1996, Yevgeny Ivanovich Shaposhnikov – Aviation Marshal and the head of Aeroflot – called Boris to ask if he would be opposed to the appointment of Valera as Deputy Director. "That's up to you," replied Boris.

My daughters did their own shopping and used public transport – in those days they had no security team. No one recognized them in the street. Our grandchildren – Katya, Masha and Borya – went to special schools in Moscow with advanced-language study, but no special arrangements were made for them either.

Sometimes we'd laugh at some of the things that happened to us. Valera once bought a sheepskin coat for Lena from Bulgaria, but he guessed the size wrong: it was too big. Lena decided to sell it, so she went to a second-hand shop; on her way to the shop, a woman stopped her and asked to see the coat. Suddenly, a policeman appeared. Lena was horrified – now they would find out that she was the President's daughter! She grabbed the coat and ran into the shop. The woman went after her, shouting – apparently she liked the coat – and trying to stop her. Lena came home exhausted – but when she told us what had happened, we all had a good laugh.

\* \* \*

Towards the end of December 1991, we moved to the former residence of the USSR President in Barvikha: special-communication equipment was already installed there, and security was provided – everything that was necessary for an official residence. There was no question of building a new residence – there was neither the time nor the money for that. Only a small cosmetic renovation was done in Barvikha.

After Gorbachev's resignation, we discovered that there was a special apartment for the President – the so-called "living quarters" – at the Kremlin. Boris and I visited, but we never spent the night there – I very much regret that now: it would have been interesting to walk around the Kremlin at night.

I didn't want to move to the residence in Barvikha, knowing that Gorbachev had lived there before his resignation. We had in the past been offered an apartment in the building where he lived. I was categorically opposed to the move, not wanting to live next door to him, so we had turned down the apartment at that time – only to find ourselves moving into his old residence.

The house seemed gloomy to me – the windows didn't let in much light. The house had not prepared for our arrival – except for furniture, there was practically nothing. There wasn't even any crockery – Boris went to the kitchen to get some water, but there wasn't even a glass. We had never experienced this at any other government dacha: there were usually dishes in the kitchen, tablecloths on the tables and curtains at the windows. Here there was none of that – and there were even loose wires where lamps should have been, and holes in the walls from nails.

On the first night, I couldn't force myself to get into bed, and I dozed in the armchair until the morning. Soon after that, they brought our furniture from the previous apartment – but even after that, I spent as much time as I could at the Moscow apartment. When Boris went to work, I quickly got ready and headed to Moscow to visit my daughters and grandchildren, and I only came home just in time for his arrival.

We saw in the New Year in Moscow, but we all gathered at Barvikha for Christmas. Despite the fact that the new residence didn't feel lived in, it was cheerful when the whole family got together. The Christmas dinner menu was simple, just as it had been in Sverdlovsk: Olivier salad, "tenderness" salad – made from eggs, onion, apples and grated cheese – and *pelmeni*. We didn't have a cook then, as the service personnel didn't come straight away, but I didn't consider this a problem.

When Boris was First Secretary of the Moscow City Party Committee, we had helpers, and cooks who worked on shifts, but for several years after that I did it all myself. Now we had to become accustomed again to have someone working in our home – and we all had to obey strict rules relating to the security of the President. Gradually the staff at Barvikha increased, taking in additional officers of the Federal Protection Service (FSO) – waiters, security, drivers and adjutants. We were lucky that they were all very nice people – and we treated them warmly and with respect, which I think was mutual – but I never did get used to the constant presence of security.

Lena and Tanya and their families moved in with us at Barvikha about a year and a half later, and our three families started to live together, which was easier for everyone. When Boris came home exhausted, the children's presence was better for him than any medicine. It was easier for me to help the girls with the grandchildren as well – my workload had increased, and getting to them in Moscow had become more and more difficult. The grandchildren were a source of joy for all of us – they wouldn't ever let us become despondent.

Once, as I rode up to the house, I saw someone hanging by a rope – he was wearing my grandson Borya's scarf, hat and tracksuit.

I was horrified. Another person was falling off the roof, all bloody. I looked around wildly and saw Masha and Borya off to the side, laughing. I turned my head to the other side, and saw Katya peeking out from behind the bushes with a video camera which they had been given recently. They had dressed a scarecrow in their clothes, and the blood turned out to be ketchup. I needed a little time to calm down before I could laugh about the whole thing – imagine thinking this up! They didn't part from the camera for quite some time. They filmed each other, interviewed us and recorded shows they put on – it really is a pity that the tapes were lost somewhere.

*Questions on the Margins*

"You weren't afraid that your grandchildren would feel a sense of entitlement, growing up in the presidential residence?"

"No. Lena and Tanya never developed such a thing – they never behaved like the daughters of Party bosses – and I was certain my grandchildren would be the same."

"Was any special effort made to ensure this wouldn't happen?"

"No. My daughters simply knew that their papa's job placed certain restrictions on their lives – that's how it was."

"And with the grandchildren, too?"

"Of course. Katya, my eldest grandchild, for example, was categorically opposed to being accompanied by security. I think that's probably why she got married so early – to get rid of the security team! In 1999, we were travelling with Masha in the car when she suddenly asked: 'Grandma, how long will Grandpa be President?' I replied: 'A little longer… be patient – it's only until June 2000.' Masha replied: 'Oh, good! Then we will only have rights and no duties?'"

"Did you explain to your daughters and grandchildren that Boris Nikolayevich's position would mean restrictions for them? What did you tell them?"

"Not really – we just lived with a sense of heightened responsibility. It was clear to everyone that the family of the President is always under public scrutiny. No one needed to be told, everyone understood. The grandchildren, too – although they would have heard the words 'not allowed' very occasionally. They didn't need lecturing, though – sometimes it even seemed to me that we were too strict. We never took our children or grandchildren with us on trips abroad – they never flew in the presidential plane. But Bill Clinton came to Moscow with his daughter, Chelsea – that made me think, and I asked Boris: 'Why can't we take our grandchildren with us on trips?' 'When they grow up,' he said, 'they can go where they want.'"

Boris strongly believed that the President's family shouldn't be isolated from the problems that other people faced. He never informed us of any decisions ahead of time – in that sense, the painful steps the government was forced to take were as unexpected for us as they were for everyone else.

For example, in July 1993, Boris and I were having lunch at the residence in Valdai. We wouldn't usually be disturbed during meals, but this time I was called to the phone, where an anxious Lena said: "Mama, did you know that the money was being exchanged today?" "What do you mean, 'exchanged'?" I said, not understanding. Soviet roubles were being exchanged for Russian roubles, she explained, but the amount each person could exchange was restricted. They were just going on a camping trip to Karelia with their Sverdlovsk friends – who had already set off. Valera had been granted leave the day before – he was well remunerated as a navigator, and he had promised to loan some money to some of the friends they were going with. What could they do? They couldn't exchange enough roubles – the exchange itself was a problem, too: the queues were so long, they wouldn't be able to do it before they had to leave. Lena was nearly in tears.

I went back to the lunch table and asked Boris, "Did you know that the money was being exchanged today?" He answered quietly: "Yes." "Why didn't you tell us?" I asked. "No one was supposed to know," he said. "Including you."

I told him what Lena had said, but he told me firmly that the President's family shouldn't receive special treatment. We began to think aloud together. It must have inconvenienced many – there must be lots of people in situations like Lena's. Someone was going on holiday, someone else was ill, someone wasn't physically able to wait in a long line… What were people supposed to do?

The government prepared an amendment to the presidential decree, softening the regulations for exchange and extending the deadline.

There were other cases when important decisions for the country came as a complete surprise to us – but everyone in the family understood Boris's position and accepted that it couldn't be otherwise.

\* \* \*

Despite the difficult situation in our country, Boris, as President of Russia, had to go on official visits to meet with the heads of foreign states. This was not just a formality – the welfare of our country depended on the relations between the new Russia and the rest of the world. We needed help – the country was on the verge of famine – but it upsets me to read pieces claiming that the President of Russia went around the world in the 1990s with his hand out. That's not true. Boris did everything he could to portray Russia as an equal to those he visited – and he succeeded in this. Wherever we went, we were met with a great deal of respect.

The European and US leaders understood what a difficult situation our country was in, and tried to help. Helmut Kohl told me years later that Germany had sent us humanitarian aid, including entire truckloads of women's underwear, during the years of Perestroika. I told him that we appreciated the gesture – but we didn't feel an improvement in our lives at the time. "I understand," said Kohl. "We – West Germany – put so much funding into East Germany, and still couldn't solve all the problems." "What can we do, Mr Kohl?" I asked. "We have no West Russia – we only have one Russia." "I agree – it's much harder for you," the Chancellor replied.

I always felt that all the leaders we met in the 1990s were united by more than formal obligations – there was a lot of trust and respect, and a genuine desire to warm the relations between their country and Russia. Without this, there couldn't have been the "informal meetings" which became a tradition.

## Questions on the Margins

"From the outside it seemed as though the first Russian President easily formed friendships with world leaders – or was that just appearance, a show for the public?"

"No, it wasn't a show. In those years, the world leaders were all very strong and responsible people who understood what was happening in Russia. There were such strong personalities among them, too – Bill Clinton, Jacques Chirac, Helmut Kohl…"

"There was a sense that, besides official relations, there was mutual respect between the Russian President and many world leaders."

"Yes, there was. I remember that Klavdiya Vasilyevna began to have serious problems with her heart in the early 1990s. Boris mentioned this in conversation with the US President, George Bush, as the Russian doctors were not sure of the diagnosis. Bush offered to send a medical plane with special equipment – Boris thanked him, but didn't take it seriously. He returned to Moscow, and soon received a call: an American plane was flying to Sverdlovsk. The doctors on board conducted tests and reassessed her treatment. They said they were amazed by the Russian doctors – they were doing everything correctly, despite the fact that they lacked modern equipment."

Boris prepared carefully for his trips abroad. It wasn't easy for him, as the only experience he had of international relations was through the Central Committee. His trip to America while serving as Chairman of the Supreme Soviet of Russia had been unofficial.

1. Naina Yeltsina, 1990s

2. (above) In a cowboy-town museum. Kansas, USA, 1992;
3. (below) Boris ad Naina take Queen Elizabeth II of Great Britain
on a tour of the Grand Kremlin Palace, 1994.

4. (above) With Hillary Clinton at the children's hospital of the I.M. Sechenov
Moscow Medical Academy, Moscow, 1995; 5. (below) Before the
military parade in honour of the 50th anniversary of the victory
in the Great Patriotic War, Moscow, 9th May 1995.

6. (above left) With Pope John Paul II, Vatican, 1998;
7. (above right) With Patriarch Alexei II, Moscow, 1999;
8. (below) With South African President Nelson Mandela
at the Kremlin, Moscow, 1999.

9. (above) At the reception for famous actresses (see pp. 200–1), Kremlin, 1994;
10. (below) Family portrait on New Year's Eve 2003.

11. (above) With Boris at the Barvikha residence, 2005;
12. (below) With grandchildren Masha Yumasheva and Vanya Okulov, Barvikha residence, 2012.

13. (above) With Russian President Vladimir Putin, Prime Minister Dmitry
Medvedev, head of protocol Vladimir Shevchenko and daughter Tatyana
at the opening of the B.N. Yeltsin Museum, Yekaterinburg, 25th November 2015;
14. (below) Vladimir Putin hands Naina Yeltsina the Order of
St Catherine the Great Martyr. Moscow, Kremlin, 14th March 2017.

15. Fifty years together. Barvikha residence, 2006

He learnt the finer points of protocol on the fly. Luckily, from 1992, Boris had the help of Vladimir Nikolayevich Shevchenko – an experienced, brilliant diplomat who had previously served as the chief of Gorbachev's protocol service. Boris regarded Shevchenko with deep respect – he knew how to appreciate professionals.

On presidential trips the schedule was unforgiving, with many official meetings and negotiations, and much document-signing. For some reason, people often think that leaders only sign documents, and that these are prepared by diplomats and aides – that is not the case. Aides reported to the President on the situation of ministries and agencies, provided him with memos and coordinated the drafting of documents. But the most important part came later, behind closed doors, when the aides and journalists left. Whether or not an agreement was reached was often not clear until the last minute.

Between 1991 and 1993, we visited Italy, Germany, the USA, Great Britain, France, Belgium, Poland, the Czech Republic and the republics of the Commonwealth of Independent States.

During those years, Russia began to take part in summits – at first by invitation, as a guest at the informal club of great powers, the G7, and later as a member, when the G7 became the G8.

Protocol dictated that I had to accompany my husband on all his official trips. Being the First Lady was work, of course – and it wasn't just formal duties. I knew I was also representing the country – a vast, complex country with a mass of problems, but which I loved very much. Like Boris, I wanted Russia to be treated with respect, its citizens considered with warmth and sympathy for the problems that had befallen them. I didn't find it hard to be sincere in my role – I think this is probably because I don't put on airs. I believe a person should always be what they are.

I always prepared for the trips, and read the material that was prepared for me by the protocol service – I couldn't go to a country without knowing anything about its political system, customs or culture. I wanted to socialize with the leaders of the country and their wives, as well as with ordinary people.

Of course, back then, in the 1990s, none of us knew how the First Lady's work should be organized – we worked it out as we went along. I didn't have a press secretary or assistants – Vladimir Nikolayevich Shevchenko filled those roles. I am so grateful to him – he helps me even now. Of course, I was assigned security by the FSO as well, but that was all there was to the First Lady's team.

With Vladimir Nikolayevich's help, and thanks to his conscientious approach to his work, I coped with my new responsibilities – although in other countries I saw that the presidents' wives had a whole staff of specialists working with them. Some had a bigger staff, some smaller, but each had their own team. Hillary Clinton's aides worked with particular care, it seemed to me. Maybe she's not the most typical example – she had her own political ambitions, which was evident even then. Later, when she ran for President twice, I wholeheartedly wished her success.

During the G7 summits, the first ladies had their own programme, and we formed warm, informal relations. I became friends and stayed in touch with many of the first ladies for many years – with Madame Chirac, for example. I visited her and Jacques at the Élysée Palace with Boris, even after his resignation, and she once gave me some rose cuttings from a wonderful bush which grew in their garden. Unfortunately, they didn't survive in our climate.

The First Lady's official programme was quite different from the President's: there were fewer official functions, but more meetings.

As a result, I was in a better position to get a feel for people's lives. For me, this was very important. I visited hospitals, schools and care homes. I didn't shy away from asking questions – I wanted details, I wanted to delve into things. Of course, it's impossible to know everything, and pointless to pretend that you aren't surprised by some things – I always thought it best not to fake it. The main thing is always to be yourself.

I discovered much on our trips around the world. In the USA, I was shown a rehabilitation centre for children with cerebral palsy. Expecting to find the visit very difficult, I steeled myself for what was to come. But the children were all in wheelchairs, and were lively, mobile and cheerful. There were ramps everywhere, they all had computers and everyone was alert. I was glad for them – but I worried, and thought to myself, "How much there is to be done so that we can have this in our country!"

This clinic made a big impression on me. I have seen hospitals in Sverdlovsk and Moscow, many of them in very poor condition, with dated equipment, rooms holding four to six people and repairs going unmade for years – that was how it was in the old days. Boris had to drag clinics out from the basements in Sverdlovsk. Of course, there were better medical facilities for officials – but even those didn't compare with what I saw in the West, both in terms of equipment and the attention paid to the patients. Computers were still a rarity in our country, but in the West they were in the most ordinary of hospitals.

The most noticeable difference was how people were treated: in those hospitals, people didn't feel torn away from their ordinary lives – they felt comfortable. I remember going to a maternity ward in Norway – I didn't have to wear a gown when we went into the room where new parents were sitting with their babies. I went up to one family; the father told me that he had been present for the birth, and that he was now helping his wife. A baby of about three or four days lay on his chest in a romper – there was no swaddling; we didn't have rompers for newborns in those days – they were swaddled, and as tightly as possible. The homely environment of the maternity ward amazed me.

In Marseilles, we were taken to a private clinic which also housed a restaurant, hotel and post office. If people came to visit someone at the clinic, they could stay in the hotel; patients could join relatives and friends in the restaurant.

Of course, our country now has much of what we saw in other countries in those days but sadly the medical equipment and the rehabilitation centres for those with limited abilities still aren't accessible to everyone.

All those we visited noted Boris's punctuality – and of course, I always tried not to let him down, but life is life, and sometimes unexpected things happen.

Usually I helped Boris get ready – I chose his suit and tie, and sometimes even combed his hair – and only then would I get ready myself. Once, before we left, I decided to wash my hands, but I got the taps confused – and the shower above my head came on. I had to fix my hair again before I could leave, which took time. Boris couldn't wait for me, and went out to meet the public; Vladimir Nikolayevich had to explain to journalists why I was late – and he didn't opt for a cover story. When I got home, my former class-mates called me to tease me: "Naya, how could you mix up the taps? Your career was in 'water supply and sanitation', after all!"

It took some adjusting to the rhythm of presidential life. Sometimes I had to do my manicure myself on the plane – Boris would grumble: "You're going to cut all your fingers!" – and once I even had my hair styled in the car: Irina Baranova, my hairdresser, worked away in the back seat.

Our first trips abroad made a very strong impression on me, and highlighted the vast difference between everyday life in our country, which was in a very difficult economic situation, and life in prosperous Western countries. After the fall of the USSR, there was nearly a famine, and there was terrible inflation, so no one had enough money for anything. In the West, they had an enormous selection of food, beautiful clothing and clean streets. It was pain-ful to notice the contrast. Our people, of course, deserved better.

In the autumn of 1991, we went on our first official visit to Germany. The wife of the Lord Mayor of Cologne suggested we go for a walk around the market – I had never seen anything like it in my life. There was a huge pavilion, where everything was astonishingly clean, and appetizing aromas filled the air. On some shelves there were meat and poultry; on others there was fish; others were brim-ming with berries and fruits. Just the day before I was in Moscow, where food was only available with ration cards. The only fruit available was apples, and that was only because it was autumn and they had just been picked. Not long before our visit, I had watched a television programme in which a well-known paediatrician said that the reason our children were often ill was because they didn't get the vitamins they needed in winter. Standing in the middle of such abundance in that Cologne market, I nearly cried.

In the evening, Boris and I went out for a walk. We went past one glittering shop window after another – it was like we were on a film set. Next to a pair of shoes there was a handbag in the same colour – I had never seen such things. Of course, we could do without these things – unlike vitamins – especially since we had been raised to be indifferent towards them. Boris and I were like-minded in that sense – clothes didn't mean anything to either of us. But there and then, we so wanted all that for our people. "So much for cursed capitalism!" I remember joking – but I didn't feel like laughing at all.

When I returned to Moscow, I went into a shoe shop. They had felt ankle boots made by a cooperative – and that's it. I stopped by the linen shop near Tishinsky Market – they had two or three nylon fabrics in a toxic colour, and that was the extent of the selection. No other fabrics, sheets or pillowcases. All of this is not essential in the grand scheme of things, but it helps to paint a picture of the state of the country the new government inherited – and the plight of its citizens. This was the everyday life of the people, and Boris thought about it constantly – no matter what some have written in recent times.

I didn't go shopping during our visits – I had neither the time nor the inclination, and I found it hard to imagine making purchases in front of journalists and the curious public. Of course, I always wanted to take something home for my grandchildren. Sometimes I asked people in my security team to buy some chewing gum for them, or perhaps a toy car – the grandchildren were always very happy to receive such presents.

I can only recall once or twice buying something for myself. One of those times was in Paris. Madame Chirac suggested we visit a department store. We went up to the first floor and found ourselves in the homeware department. It was just at that time that we had a Russian stove installed at the dacha, and it needed cast-iron pots. I wanted the sort we had in Titovka – other pots often have enamel inside, which cracks in the oven. We didn't have this kind in our shops. But there I saw a large cast-iron pot – the kind we call a "duck roaster" – with no enamel. It was just what I needed. Of course, I was too shy to buy it in front of Madame Chirac, but I remembered the name of the shop and its location, and the next day I asked someone to drive there and buy it.

Another time, during a visit to the USA, I was looking out for a particular Estée Lauder perfume I remembered from the 1970s in Sverdlovsk. I remembered the little bottle, tied with silk threads, and the little brush it came with. I didn't end up going into a perfume shop, however – although I did meet Mrs Lauder, and asked her whether that particular perfume was still made: it turned out that it wasn't.

I looked after Boris's wardrobe, as well as my own, by myself. When we moved from Sverdlovsk to Moscow, my husband had about five suits, some of which he had worn for years. He was of average build and had a good posture, and he was six foot two. We could usually buy his suits off the rack.

In Moscow, however, we started to have his suits tailored by a dressmaker in the presidential-office building. Gerasim Alexeyevich Gradov, a wonderful tailor, had a very good sense of his figure, and had a talent for taking into account all of a person's features – even his gait and manner of holding himself. We used him a lot for Boris's suits. The fabrics were good, but the accessories were of average quality. We had no yardstick to compare against.

After Boris was gone, I sometimes opened the wardrobe and looked at these suits – some of them had little notes pinned to them: "FIRST INAUGURATION", "SECOND INAUGURATION". I would never have thought that one day I'd give them to a museum – but that's where they are now. I imagine I could recognize these suits by touch – especially the ones from the Sverdlovsk period – because I ironed them every evening.

Although he was indifferent towards clothes, Boris loved ties, and had lots of them – but only a dozen or so favourites. This was the only detail of his outfit to which he paid any attention. But even with his love of ties, he easily parted with them. He had a habit of exchanging ties during a meal with friends. I did his tie for him – not on him, but in my hands: he never learnt to do his tie up. I once looked at the drawings of tie knots in a magazine, chose an ordinary knot and learnt to tie it perfectly. Now even my grandchildren sometimes ask me to do their ties.

Boris usually wore what Lena, Tanya and I advised him to wear – but he always had a neatness about him: during his student years, he ironed his trousers every evening – he simply couldn't bear to go out in wrinkled ones.

I had my clothes made by the same dressmaker who tailored Boris's suits. I never wore fashionable designer outfits – either from Russia or abroad: it's something that never occurred to me to do. I am very grateful to the dressmaker's manager, Galina Ivanovna Titkova, and the fashion designer Larisa Sergeyevna Khinyavina. Their seamstresses were highly professional, too. We discussed styles and fabrics and many of the details together. I preferred suits in the Chanel style. Nowadays, top government officials and their wives use this dressmaker – I think it very unfair that clothes designers do not receive state prizes.

It wasn't possible to buy expensive branded clothing at that time, and I didn't have suits and dresses made very often. Sometimes, even on official trips, I wore the same suit twice. This didn't bother me too much – I didn't worry about my appearance or my clothes. At that time, it was sometimes even difficult to find stockings. I remember once, during a visit, just before I was due to leave our hotel room, I discovered a ladder in my stockings. I fixed them using an old Soviet method: I painted the ladder over with nail polish. It was a good job that my skirt covered up that spot!

I've never felt the need to put on airs. One time when we visited the USA, for example, I brought a silk suit with me which Lena had bought in Greece for the equivalent of about $30. I still have it in my wardrobe. I have always relied on my own taste – and, of course, consulted Vladimir Nikolayevich Shevchenko. If the official programme indicated "ordinary-length dress" or "evening dress", I understood what it meant – but beyond that, what exactly should be selected? The colour, for example – what colour should the dress be? And did all this change when meeting royalty? I couldn't have coped on my own.

December 1991 marked the first time a Russian leader had visited the Vatican. I wore a cream-coloured suit to meet Pope John Paul II. When I got there, I discovered, to my horror, the Pope was also wearing white. Had I made a mistake? But I tormented myself for no reason – upon enquiry, I later found out that protocol does not prohibit women wearing white in this situation.

I always took an iron with me on our trips abroad: during the first presidential term, we didn't have assistants to iron clothes for us. In the early 1990s, we often stayed in embassies, which was cheaper than renting a hotel. The rest of the members of the delegation also stayed in embassy rooms or apartments – it was comfortable enough. There you could usually get an ironing board to iron what you needed to.

When we stayed in hotels, I sometimes sent shirts or suits to be pressed – but even so, sometimes I had to iron them myself. Only in Japan did shirts come back in perfect condition. I have never seen such quality of work in any other country.

\* \* \*

I must also mention our dealings with monarchies. To someone who had grown up in the USSR, royals seemed like fictional characters. Boris had no experience on this front, either.

One of our first royal meetings was in Belgium, where Boris was due to speak to delegations of the European Union. A royal luncheon was part of the programme. I was nervous – but Queen Paola turned out to be a gentle and friendly woman, and everything was almost homely.

In June 1993, during the G7 summit in Tokyo, we became acquainted with the Japanese Imperial family. I didn't notice any stiffness in the emperor – although, without question, the respect felt for him and his family by those around him was palpable.

In 1994, Queen Elizabeth II came to Russia on a state visit. According to protocol, the monarchs of Great Britain can only make a state visit to a country once during their reign – and the Queen had never visited the Soviet Union. Another protocol stated that, if a country has an outlet to the sea, the monarch must arrive and depart on the royal yacht. This protocol was relaxed a little, however, and Queen Elizabeth and the Duke of Edinburgh flew to Moscow on a plane, although they went back on the royal yacht *Britannia* from St Petersburg. Boris and I met the Queen and Prince Philip at the airport: Boris travelled in one car with the Queen, and I rode in the other car with her husband.

Before then, the new Russian government had not received royal visitors. Queen Elizabeth and her retinue stayed in Kremlin suites; the rest of the delegation stayed at the embassy and in hotels. British cooks prepared the Queen's favourite dishes, with the help of their Russian colleagues, in the Kremlin kitchen. The British "reconnaissance" delegation responsible for the state visit came to Moscow six or seven times beforehand, and they coordinated every detail. The Russian men, for example, were surprised to learn that, for the Kremlin reception, they were supposed to don tuxedos – so thirty-five tuxedos had to be ordered from abroad. This was the first time Boris put on a tuxedo. The British also coordinated not only the colour of my dress, but also the size of the bouquets. This came at a time when we had to economize on everything. I had a long evening gown which I had worn on a trip to the USA, so I wore that for the reception – and, ever since, I have called that dress "the one I wore to meet the Queen".

Before sailing from St Petersburg, the Queen gave a farewell reception on her yacht. In addition to politicians, she invited many cultural figures, such as Maya Plisetskaya, Rodion Shchedrin,

Hermitage director Mikhail Piotrovsky and academic Dmitry Sergeyevich Likhachov.

I saw Dmitry Sergeyevich sitting alone, away from the din, and fell into conversation with him – I will always remember that conversation, despite the fact that we met by accident. He stunned me with the depth of his thinking and, at the same time, his simplicity and sincerity. Boris and I met up with him again a number of times in Moscow.

That same year, we travelled to Spain to meet King Juan Carlos and Queen Sofía. We were flown by helicopter from Madrid to the Zarzuela Palace, where we had been invited for breakfast by the King and Queen. For the first time in my life, I began the day with *jamón ibérico*. An enormous platter of finely cut slices was brought out, and we sat at a coffee table and chatted. There was no silverware on the table – what should we do? I watched the King take a slice of meat with his hand and eat one, two, three pieces with great appetite, without ceremony. We didn't fall behind. The *jamón* turned out to be truly amazing; we were brought a second platter. Before our flight back to Moscow, two whole legs of *jamón* were brought out from the King's reserves, and he gave them to us as a present. When we got home and unwrapped them, we discovered to our horror that they were covered with mould. We didn't realize that they were supposed to be like that – but we decided to take a risk, and we tried it. The whole family liked it. Now, whenever my daughters go to Spain, they always bring back *jamón*. But I must say, I never had any as tasty as the King's.

This was our first experience with food that was unfamiliar to us. On our first visit to Japan, we were given a selection of sushi and sashimi in very beautiful black lacquered boxes. When we returned to Moscow we decided to try it… we couldn't get on with it, though – everything smelt like raw fish. We threw it away – we didn't realize that sushi and sashimi had to be eaten with wasabi and soy sauce.

*Questions on the Margins*

"Did that heightened sense of responsibility you talked about ever get in the way?"

"I can't shake it off. I give an interview, and then I torment myself for two or three days analysing it. I said this wrong, that wasn't right... Constant self-consciousness is a terrible thing. Maybe others don't have it – good for them – but I can't switch it off."

"Do you keep everything inside, or are you able to share with those close to you?"

"I keep it inside – I never discuss personal things with anyone."

"Do you make an effort? Or is it just your character?"

"It's just my character – I've always been like that."

During the first years of Boris's presidency, I became good friends with some famous Soviet actresses who had fallen on hard times, and I tried to help them.

In the daily *Moskovsky Komsomolets* I had read an unpleasant, even insulting, article on the relations between the wonderful actresses Marina Ladynina and Lidiya Smirnova – they had fallen out with each other when they were working at the National Film Actors' Theatre – and, realizing that they were in difficulties, I decided to go and see them.

Someone found Ladynina's phone number for me, and I called her, asking permission to visit. She lived in a little two-room apartment, and she was alone and ill... It was so strange to see her in those conditions, given that she had been the darling of millions of fans. The second time I went to see Marina Alexeyevna, we talked about the poet Sergei Yesenin. "Would you like to hear 'Hooligan' now?" she said, and recited the whole poem from memory. What an inspiration! After all, she was over eighty years old. During our later meetings, she recited poetry for me a number of times – more poems by Yesenin, as well as by Alexander Blok. And she always did it so wonderfully – I loved listening to her.

I admired her independence. Ladynina was the wife of the famous Soviet director Ivan Pyryev. She was in many of his films, including comedies and melodramas of the Stalin era – *They Met in Moscow*, *The Country Bride*, *Cossacks of the Kuban* and others – but it transpired that she didn't share her husband's views at all. They had disagreements, especially about Stalin. In the harshest years of his dictatorship, she supported political prisoners, and sent them packages and gave them money. She hid this from Pyryev. Despite their divorce, despite the fact that he ruined her later career, she always spoke of him with respect, and her memoirs were honest. She described how, on the day of Pyryev's death, he appeared to her in a dream and bade her farewell.

While I was with Ladynina, I discovered that these wonderful actresses never met up, even though they lived in the same building – the skyscraper on Kotelnicheskaya Embankment. I had also made the acquaintance of Lidiya Smirnova after seeing the article in *Moskovsky Komsomolets*, and began to visit her, too. Of course, I never went empty-handed – I always brought something tasty with me. When I couldn't go myself, Tanya would visit her.

Visiting them and other actresses of their generation, I realized that – even taking into consideration all their rivalries, which are not rare in their world – they didn't socialize much at all with each other. I had an idea: I should organize a reception for them at the Kremlin. I called an actress from the Moscow Art Theatre, Sofya Stanislavovna Pilyavskaya, another of those I visited at the time, and consulted with her.

The Kremlin has a winter garden, and that's where we had our reception. Mariya Mironova, Galina Volchek, Liya Akhedzhakova, Vera Vasilyeva, Irina Miroshnichenko, Elina Bystritskaya, Marina Ladynina and Lidiya Smirnova... there were twenty-three actresses in all. It was a miracle to get them all there. That was the first time since the filming of *The Ballad of Siberia* that Marina Ladynina and Vera Vasilyeva had seen each other – and that film had been made nearly fifty years before. We had lunch, looked around the Kremlin and drank tea. We went to the Tsar's chambers – "his half" – where the Tsar used to receive his closest guests. We weren't allowed to touch the furniture there, but Mariya Vladimirovna Mironova wanted to be photographed on the Tsar's throne. I asked our guide, and he looked the other way while she sat on the throne and cried theatrically, "I am the Tsarina!"

I wanted a group photograph as a souvenir, so we posed together up the stairs, and I gave each actress a rose to hold. When the photograph had been taken, we came down the stairs again; Sofya Stanislavovna Pilyavskaya was just ahead of me. Suddenly, someone touched my arm and nodded in her direction. In front of me stood Sofya Stanislavovna, wearing just her lace slip – her skirt was on the floor. Apparently, the hook holding it together had slipped open. I reached out and touched her shoulder, and said softly, "Sofya Stanislavovna – your skirt!" She remained absolutely calm, and artistically raised her hands and said, "Oh, I haven't lost my skirt in the Kremlin before!" There was such laughter...

Dmitry Donskoy, Boris's personal photographer, had managed to immortalize the moment. When the photographs were developed and I was about to send copies to all those who had been there, I saw this one, and asked Sofya Stanislavovna, "What do you think – should I send this one out, too?" She replied, "Naina Iosifovna, they may forget everything else, but this they will remember for ever. Of course you must send it."

A few years later I tried to set up another meeting with the same people – I began to phone around, but found that one was ill, another was on tour, another one on holiday – it just didn't work out. And now half of them are no longer with us.

But I did manage to continue meeting up with many of them, and I tried to help them as much as I could – I got them into hospitals and health spas, if they needed it. Boris was able to pass a law which entitled the People's Artists of the USSR to a supplement to their pension.

I remained on very friendly terms with Galina Volchek, the artistic director of the Sovremennik Theatre. We switched to the familiar form of "you", and if I forgot and used the formal "you", she would laugh: "There you go again!" She was very busy at the theatre, so we didn't meet very often, but we spoke on the phone regularly and at length. We sometimes started talking at eleven o'clock at night and finished at two in the morning. I often invited her over to my house, and if she had the time, she would come.

\* \* \*

In the autumn of 1992, we persuaded Boris's mother to come and live with us. She usually came to stay with us for a few months during the winter, when there was no work in the garden to do, but her health had grown worse, and housework was becoming too much of a strain for her. We were all very glad she came – things were calmer when she was around. Klavdiya Vasilyeva suffered terribly seeing what happened to Boris after 1987 and during the tempestuous 1990s.

## Questions on the Margins

"Did Klavdiya Vasilyevna follow politics?"

"Of course – we all did. She watched television and read the newspapers. She got very agitated whenever she saw something bad about Boris. We sometimes had to ask Boris's brother, Misha, when Klavdiya Vasilyevna went to live with him, to hide the newspapers. I often said to her, 'Don't read the newspapers – you'll get upset.' But she did read them and got upset. I did, too."

"How did she see his presidency?"

"She was proud – but also very worried for Borya. When she lived at our house, she often stayed up and waited until he got home – it was important for her to see him. They had a very warm relationship. I remember once, when he came home exhausted from Congress, Mama went up to him, kissed him and said, 'Hang in there. God sent you these trials.' This wasn't for show – she meant it."

"How did your mother react to Boris Nikolayevich's election as President?"

"She said, 'What a yoke you have put on yourself!'"

Klavdiya Vasilyevna had her own room at the residence, on the ground floor, near the quarters of the on-duty doctor and nurse – they were obliged to be near the President round the clock.

March 1993 was a very difficult month: the President's relations with the Communist Congress became more and more tense.

One morning, I looked in early on Mama, and she was still sleeping. The rest of the family was sitting in front of the television, following the news. Boris was still at home. Suddenly, the door burst open, and a nurse beckoned me out of the room. She was holding a glass of medicine. "Drink this," she said. It was valerian.

I understood then that something had happened. "Klavdiya Vasilyevna isn't feeling well," the nurse said quietly. They didn't tell me the truth straight away, but I guessed that it was the worst.

I had to decide whether or not to tell Boris immediately – he was about to leave for an Extraordinary Meeting of the Supreme Soviet, so the day ahead would be a difficult one. I was afraid that his heart wouldn't be able to take it – he was already under terrible stress – so I thought it was better to talk to him in the evening, and perhaps to try to prepare him. I was tormented – I had no idea how to tell him about his mother's death. It was an immense grief for both of us, of course, but I knew that it would be a dreadful shock for him.

During the day, I cautiously told him that Klavdiya Vasilyevna wasn't feeling well. He called back a while later, and I told him that an ambulance had taken her to the hospital. By evening, we had informed Boris's assistants and Viktor Stepanovich Chernomyrdin – I asked Viktor to accompany Boris that evening to help comfort him.

Despite our efforts, this came as a terrible blow for Boris. He couldn't talk to anyone, and he retreated into himself and went to bed. I worried that before long he would need a doctor himself.

I think the crisis of 1993 ruined his health even further – although he held up, as always, and I never saw him depressed or gloomy, and he never broke down. As a rule, he didn't speak about what was really worrying, bothering and tormenting him.

I was amazed by his reaction to the slanderous insults hurled at him by the media: he never showed any sign that he was hurt by them. He calmed me, saying, "Forget it." He gave a characteristic wave of his hand – that's it, the conversation's over.

It seemed to me that he made all his decisions with absolute calm, and in the face of difficult situations he was composed – he didn't succumb to fear or pain. I never sensed even a smidgen of perplexity. The events of 1993 were no exception.

I took these events very hard, and probably not as stoically as Boris – and not just the most difficult days of the crisis in October, but also all the preceding months. Boris received widespread support in the referendum, but even so, he didn't want to resolve the conflict between Congress and the Supreme Soviet by force – for which many reproached him at that time. It seemed to me, however, that he couldn't do anything else: he must try to avoid military action if possible – and at times it seemed that a compromise was indeed possible.

I was strongly in favour of the drafting of a new Constitution that had been announced. It had long been clear, even to me, that the current Soviet Constitution was a constant source of conflict in the government, and a brake on progress. Unfortunately, work on the new Constitution stalled – the various political forces couldn't agree among themselves. Boris was continually, tortuously looking for a way out of the increasingly difficult situation – he was looking for it, but could not find it. This was very painful for him – by nature he was a person of action.

During the summer months, the crisis grew. The deputies' aggressive position prevented the establishment of a dialogue. On all sides, people spoke of the necessity of extreme measures. I was very worried, of course – Boris was under constant stress, and consultations with members of the government and advisors were unrelenting.

By 20th September, the conflict between the President and Congress reached its climax, and on the 21st Boris signed Decree 1400 and appealed to the Russian people on television. I didn't know this was going to happen – but I can't say it came as a complete surprise. It was clear that an impasse had been reached and decisive action on the part of the President was necessary.

In his address, Boris announced the suspension of Congress and the Supreme Soviet's activity, and stressed the need for a new constitution, which would entail a new Parliament and a snap presidential election.

The deputies, of course, didn't accept the plan, and they refused to leave the White House, into which they had come, armed, to declare Vice President Alexander Rutskoi "Acting President". The situation was on the verge of descending into violence – and horrible thoughts filled my mind.

Boris didn't want to introduce extraordinary measures – he didn't want to involve the army or impose a curfew. There were protests in various parts of Moscow: these were allowed to go ahead. Boris felt it was important to show people that it was business as usual. He ordered the police not to use firearms – they could carry only rubber batons on duty – to avoid any tragic accidents. But the crowd Rutskoi and Khasbulatov gathered grew more and more aggressive by the day: stones were thrown at policemen, who could only shield themselves with their hands.

The cellist Slava Rostropovich and the singer Galina Vishnevskaya, who had already showed their support for Boris back in 1991, flew to Moscow on that day. I was so worried at this time that a tragic turn of events was just around the corner – the atmosphere was uneasy in Moscow. Slava had come to arrange a public concert in support of Boris on 26th September. There was much debate around whether it was safe to have such a crowd of people in Red Square – but Boris insisted that it must go ahead.

Tchaikovsky's music was wonderful, and Slava was amazing – but even so, it was difficult to enjoy the concert given the general feeling of unease. Afterwards, we had hoped to invite Slava for tea, but he had disappeared. Half an hour had gone and there was still no sign of him. An hour passed... an hour and a half... We began to worry. But in the end it turned out that he got so cold he had to run back to the Hotel Rossiya to warm up. That evening, he and Galya were our guests. We sat up until one in the morning, and talked about everything, including the state of affairs in Moscow. I remember Slava saying, "Remember, Borya, they will go to any lengths."

Rostropovich and Vishnevskaya spoke in no uncertain terms: they said that this was the Communists and the KGB wanting to return to power – that it would be impossible to avoid clashes, and that Boris must display resolve. Their support was very important to him.

Many members of the intelligentsia shared Galya and Slava's point of view – forty-two people signed a letter in defence of democracy. Among them were the academic Dmitry Likhachov, the writers Ales Adamovich, Boris Vasilyev, Vasil Bykaŭ, Alexander Gelman, Daniil Granin, Yury Davydov, Viktor Astafyev, Yury Nagibin, the poets Bella Akhmadulina, Bulat Okudzhava, Alexander Kushner, Grigory Pozhenyan, Yury Levitansky, as well as many others.

On 29th September, there was a glimmer of hope that a peaceful outcome to the crisis could be found – Patriarch Alexy II offered to serve as an intermediary in consultations between the President and representatives of the Supreme Soviet, and these meetings began at the Danilov Monastery. I always had enormous respect for Alexy II – he was an extremely virtuous person, and was well disposed towards people. Despite his high ecclesiastical rank, I never had any difficulty talking to him. I spoke to him about many different things, and was always met with understanding and support. I know he enjoyed enormous respect from Boris as well.

When I heard that the Patriarch had taken upon himself the difficult role of an intermediary, I felt somehow calmer. The talks at the Danilov Monastery seemed to signal a compromise. However, Khasbulatov and Rutskoi walked out of the meetings. The feeling of impending disaster returned, and haunted me day and night.

The leaders of the countries of the Commonwealth of Independent States came to Moscow as well, and there was an important meeting at our residence in Barvikha on 3rd October. As soon as it ended, Boris got a call from the Kremlin. "I'm on my way," he said. A little while later I heard an unusual noise – a helicopter had landed on the square near our house. "In a helicopter?" I was barely able to ask. "You can't get through Moscow in a car at the moment," he replied as he left. That's good, I thought – it's less dangerous in a helicopter. Luckily, it was only later that I found out how much more vulnerable a helicopter is than a car. That was the only time in his entire presidency that he went to the Kremlin in a helicopter.

I was worried, and I waited anxiously for news. Finally, there was a call from the office: everything was fine – Boris had got there safely. I called the Kremlin throughout the evening and night, trying to find out what was going on – but I couldn't get through. Finally someone answered. "Just tell me – is Boris Nikolayevich all right?" A cheerful voice answered: "Yes, Naina Iosifovna, of course." Still, I demanded the phone number of the doctor on duty at the Kremlin and called him too. He also reassured me. I called all night, but I didn't manage to speak to Boris.

I had seen on the news that thousands of people were lighting campfires on Tverskoy Boulevard and in the Alexander Garden, as well as many other districts of Moscow. Just as they had done in August 1991, the people were crowding the streets again. Yegor Gaidar, Liya Akhedzhakova, Nikolai Svanidze and many other members of the intelligentsia went on air calling people to the Moscow City Council to defend the President and democracy, and to stop the Communists from returning to power. And people responded – this was very important.

During the evening and the night of 3rd October, and into the morning of 4th October, just like the rest of the country, I was glued to the television. When the tanks fired the first volley at the White House, I was horrified. It turned out that the military had fired shots at windows on floors where there were no people, and not a single deputy was wounded. But during many of the violent events provoked by opponents of the presidency, to our enormous regret, people were killed – 158 in total, twenty-seven of whom were policemen.

We knew that Boris was doing everything he could to avoid casualties. Tanya and Lena, their husbands and I supported him unconditionally – we didn't for a second doubt that he was right, knowing what we did from our own experience rather than from the accounts of other people.

Boris said in a televised address: "There are no victors or vanquished here." Those were my feelings, too. He called on everyone to help stop such events ever being repeated.

In December 1993, a new constitution was passed in a referendum. Boris attributed great significance to this event – he believed that a document sanctioned in this way could unite people, and give them security as well as confidence in the future. For him, it was also very important that it would be impossible to use the new Constitution for political opportunism, and when he was pushed to make amendments to the Fundamental Law of the country, he refused to do so.

In December 1993, the first elections under the new Constitution took place – for the State Duma and the Federation Council, the lower and upper houses of Parliament. The results of the Duma election turned out not to be very good for the President. The Liberal Democratic Party of Russia (LDPR), headed by Vladimir Zhirinovsky, won huge support, and it was only thanks to the success of democratic candidates in single-mandate districts that the largest party in the Duma became Russia's Choice, headed by Yegor Gaidar. But the Communists, agrarians and the LDPR, who made a united front, outweighed the democrats.

Of course, we had all hoped for a more peaceful period after the upheavals of 1993 – but that didn't happen. I couldn't have imagined the first term of Boris's presidency being so stressful. Every day, new problems cropped up – there was never any peace.

Only later did I understand that it couldn't have been otherwise: he was leading a country that was entering a new chapter in its history in the most difficult economic circumstances. But the opposition from the Communists was so fierce and the difficulties were so many that at times it seemed to me it must be an impossible burden to bear.

Of course, our family was passionately involved with everything that was happening in the country, but we only discussed politics when Boris was out. We did, however, ask him questions – he would usually answer us with "Later" and make his characteristic hand gesture. We understood what it meant: the conversation was over – there wouldn't be a "later".

His schedule was intense. When we lived in Sverdlovsk, I thought it was impossible to work more than Boris did as First Secretary of the Regional Party Committee. I was wrong.

The President's day began at seven or eight in the morning, after he had got up at 6.30 a.m. or before. I saw him off to work all my life. Even when I worked, I made arrangements at the Institute so that I could be fifteen minutes late in the morning if I needed to be.

## Questions on the Margins

"What would you talk about at breakfast?"

"Nothing substantial – the usual things. I told him to take care of himself, not to work late."

"Was Boris Nikolayevich not very talkative in the mornings?"

"It was just that he was immersed in his work – I always understood that."

Boris's work day ended no earlier than 8 p.m. – sometimes much later. He could receive phone calls at any time of the day, and his urgent intervention was usually required. I'm not saying that his aides abused this – they only called in emergencies. It's just that there were a lot of emergencies.

\* \* \*

Boris tried to plan his foreign trips in such a way that he could visit several countries in one trip. This put quite a strain on his body. Sometimes he had to visit two countries in one day, which meant a change in time zones and sleep deprivation. As a result, he got severe headaches. Once, on the way home from the United States, a few hours before the stopover in Ireland, Boris fell ill. Doctors came to his assistance, but despite their solicitude, he was not in good enough shape to meet the Taoiseach. Boris didn't like to show any weakness, so he and his aides thought up a story about how he had overslept. It would probably have been better to tell the truth.

The reason Boris arranged his trips in this way is that he believed that he couldn't leave the country for long, in case his political opponents tried to exploit his absence – and they did. The conflict between the President and the legislative body of the government remained, especially in the Duma, where the Communists and agrarians had gained a considerable majority – and, as before, they prevented the President and his team from conducting reforms.

In October 1994, another financial crisis occurred – the so-called "Black Tuesday", when the exchange rate of the rouble collapsed.

In December, the war in Chechnya began. I don't know all the details leading to the decision to start a military operation there, but I know for a fact that Boris tried in every possible way to avoid a military response to the Chechen problem.

And it was, without a doubt, a problem. Suffice it to say that, by that time, tens of thousands of ethnic Russians had been forced to flee Chechnya. Violence had escalated in the republic – yet, even so, I saw how difficult it was for Boris to have to make the decision to start a military operation. I believe that when Boris said in his last speech to the citizens of Russia "I beg your forgiveness..." he was referring to the Chechen tragedy.

*Questions on the Margins*

"Did you often hear criticism of the President from people who had previously supported him?"

"No – in conversation with me, they tried not to mention such topics."

"Even Yelena Georgievna Bonner, who was an implacable opponent of the war in Chechnya?"

"Yes, even Yelena Georgievna. We still had conversations – although not so frequently as before – and she always showed her respect for Boris Nikolayevich."

"Did he sense that the attitude towards him changed due to the war in Chechnya? Did that affect him?"

"Of course. But that wasn't his principal concern – the main thing he worried about was people suffering during the war. That pain remained with him for the rest of his life."

1995 was very hard. There was Budyonnovsk hospital hostage crisis. Civilians were killed. The military action in Chechnya worsened the political situation. The reformers did badly again in the Duma election, which took place in December. The pro-President bloc Our Home Is Russia, led by Chernomyrdin, took half as many votes as the Communists. I began to worry about how the next Presidential election would go, although I was certain that Boris would not take part in it.

# By a Candidate's Side

So the second presidential election was approaching.

At first, Boris said that he wouldn't run for a second term – he thought he should yield power to the next generation. Our family was supportive of this – but the Communists' success in the early stages of the election alarmed us. It became clear that Gennady Zyuganov, the leader of the Communist Party of the Russian Federation, could become President. I was afraid that Boris might change his mind, given the circumstances – and that's what happened. Reports started to appear in the press: "YELTSIN SAYS NOMINATION FOR SECOND TERM STILL POSSIBLE".

I tried to talk him out of it, repeating again and again: "Think of your health." At a certain point he said quietly to me: "All right. Zyuganov will be President."

He cited opinion poll predictions: if Chernomyrdin, Gaidar or any other politician from Boris's team ran, Zyuganov would win.

We talked about the election at home. At first, Boris didn't intervene in our political conversations – he listened silently. I was anguished – I knew that there was no easy way out of the situation. On the one hand, I couldn't imagine him being able to make it through another election. On the other hand, I realized he didn't want to lose to the Communists – losing to Zyuganov would mean undoing everything he had done, and he couldn't stand the thought.

At that time, the approval ratings of the various candidates began to be published. Boris's ratings were the lowest of all – it was upsetting and unfair, but those numbers calmed me, to some extent. I hoped that pride would prevent his taking part in an election where the chance of success was pretty much zero. But he was built for victory – he couldn't be otherwise.

No one then – not I, Lena or Tanya – suspected the doctors feared for his health. But it was revealed much later that, in late 1995, Sergei Pavlovich Mironov, head of the Presidential Medical Centre, briefed Alexander Vasilyevich Korzhakov, head of the Russian Federation Presidential Security Service, on the results of an official medical consultation on the critical state of Boris's heart. Korzhakov didn't tell us anything – and, to be honest, I don't understand why the consultation's conclusions weren't shared with the family.

Boris read the letter himself, of course, but didn't take it seriously – he always believed that he had an iron constitution, and the doctors' prognoses didn't frighten him.

About a month and a half after the parliamentary election, Boris made the decision to run, and on 15th February he made an official announcement in Yekaterinburg.

A week later, on 23rd February – Red Army Day – at the Russian Army Theatre, there was a gala evening. I went alone, as Boris had to go to a reception at the Kremlin. One of the generals raised a toast during the buffet, calling out: "To our past, to the Soviet Union, when we lived well!"

I knew from my sister, however, whose husband was a military man, what the life of a Soviet officer was really like. In most cases, they were given rooms in dormitories or communal apartments; sometimes these weren't available, in which case they had to arrange their own private accommodation and pay for it themselves. I remember how happy Roza was when her husband was sent to serve in Germany.

I couldn't hold back, and said, "If life was so good in the USSR, why did you all try to serve abroad?" To be honest, I felt uncomfortable saying this to a general, but I just couldn't help it.

This episode made me realize how difficult the election campaign was going to be. In actual fact, it turned out to be even harder than I had imagined.

*Questions on the Margins*

"What was your reaction? Was it a disaster?"

"The disaster wasn't so much the decision to run, but the election campaign and, to be honest, the second term. But I had to accept it."

"Do you regret not talking him out of it?"

"It would have been impossible to do so – he couldn't hand the country back to the Communists. But I still think that if Boris hadn't run again he would have lived longer."

A campaign HQ was set up under the leadership of Oleg Soskovets. Korzhakov played a leading role there, too. The headquarters seemed to be functioning, but it turned out that work was done in an excessively formal way, which hampered progress.

Korzhakov had worked with Boris from the days when he was a candidate member at the Politburo. When Boris fell out of favour, Korzhakov came to him at Gosstroi and offered his help. Then, for many years, he was by his side – both in August 1991 and in October 1993. When Tanya had her second son, Gleb, in 1995, and we were very worried about his health, Korzhakov's wife, Irina, arranged a baptism with the priest in the church she worked in, and Alexander Vasilyevich became Gleb's godfather. Even so, I regarded him with caution – it's hard to say exactly why. My granddaughter, Katya, felt the same way, and didn't hide it. When I tried to convince her to be nicer to him, she replied, "Grandma, look in his eyes."

In the winter of 1996, Korzhakov came to our bedroom when Boris wasn't there, put an envelope on the bedside table and asked me to show it to my husband. It seemed strange to me – why put a letter on his bedside table? Why not give it to him at work or in the car? Even so, I pointed it out to Boris when he was getting ready for bed. He opened the envelope, read the letter quickly and then threw it on the floor by the door and said, "Let him have it back!"

"But who will give it to him?" I asked, trying to defuse the situation. "Not me… You took it – you return it to him," he replied abruptly. I picked up the envelope and went out of the room. It was unsealed, and for the first time in my life I read someone else's letter – I needed to understand why Boris was so upset.

In his letter, Korzhakov was stabbing Viktor Stepanovich Chernomyrdin in the back. I didn't believe a word – the decent and honest Viktor Stepanovich always had my full confidence.

Soon after this, Boris invited the Chernomyrdins to our residence in Zavidovo. That day, some documents had been delivered to Boris and he was in his office for a while. In the meantime, Viktor Stepanovich and I spoke about Korzhakov – Chernomyrdin said that both he and Boris's first assistant, Viktor Vasilyevich Ilyushin, were an obstacle for Korzhakov and Soskovets. I realized that Viktor Stepanovich knew about Korzhakov's letter, yet I didn't say anything to Boris about our conversation at the time.

At a certain point in the campaign, it became clear that communications at the campaign HQ had to be looked at again, and Valentin Yumashev suggested Tanya come on board – they needed someone who could talk straight to the President, without worrying about their position or the consequences for their career. I was against it – little Gleb was only six months old, and he had health problems. My grandson was born with Down's syndrome, and the doctors doubted that he would live long. They even spoke of giving up the child for adoption, but I couldn't think of such a thing. Nor could Tanya – she did everything she could for her son. Of course, when she was asked to work for Boris's campaign, it was a great dilemma for her. Eventually, we started looking for a nanny, and in the end Gleb's other grandmother, Nina Alexandrovna, helped out.

While Tanya was thinking about the offer, she made a trip to Paris to talk with Claude, the daughter of French President Jacques Chirac, who had been her father's personal advisor. Claude told her that at first it wasn't easy, but in the end everyone got used to the situation and she became a fully fledged member of the team and was much help to her father. The decision was made: Tanya began to work for Boris. She was horrified when she discovered how the headquarters operated – she later said it reminded her of Party meetings in the Soviet era: everything was done very formally – no ideas were discussed, and no one thought about strategy. But Tanya couldn't change the headquarters on her own.

After a while, Boris, too, was left without any doubts as to the headquarters' efficiency – so a restructure was called for. Viktor Ilyushin, the President's first assistant, headed up the restructured headquarters. A strategic group headed by Anatoly Chubais became the think tank at its heart. Now that Tanya had like-minded people working on the team, I gradually came to realize that I was wrong to resist her taking part in the campaign – she really helped Boris, and tackled things no one else could have.

*Questions on the Margins*

"So Tatyana could broach difficult subjects with Boris Nikolayevich?"

"Of course – that was very important. And Tanya had more opportunities to do so than others, and she could do it in a home setting."

"Did they have any conflicts during the campaign?"

"Not anything serious. Of course, they sometimes argued, but it was never about any fundamental issues."

"Did you ask Tanya to keep an eye on Boris Nikolayevich, to ensure he didn't overdo it?"

"I didn't need to ask her – it went without saying. Of course, it was reassuring for me to know a member of the family was with Boris."

In March 1996, the Communist-led Duma denounced the Belovezha Accords. This was a clear provocation. They didn't intend to restore the USSR: the deputies simply wanted a political crisis. Soskovets and Korzhakov's response plan was to dissolve the Duma and postpone the presidential election for two years. Chubais, Chernomyrdin, General Anatoly Kulikov (the Interior Minister) and the President's aides sharply opposed this. I didn't know the details, but I heard conversations about possible constitutional amendments. Boris didn't like these proposals. I remember him once abruptly breaking off a conversation on this subject during a family lunch. He got up from the table, saying: "I will not change the Constitution. No more discussion!" But as I understand it now, Soskovets and Korzhakov's supporters continued to lobby him to cancel the elections – and at that time Boris wholeheartedly trusted Korzhakov.

A decree dissolving the Duma, banning the Communist Party of the Russian Federation and postponing the election was practically ready – but Boris hesitated. His closest aides and the Interior Minister Anatoly Kulikov were categorically against this step – Tanya was too, and she persuaded Boris to meet with Chubais at that critical moment. Chubais's arguments were convincing: Soskovets and Korzhakov's plan was discarded, and the election went ahead.

An intense election campaign began. The campaign team decided I had to run my own campaign too. My schedule was fairly packed and emotionally difficult. I had visited orphanages in the past, but this time I had to see what I had not seen before. It was especially difficult at the homes for chronically or terminally ill children. In 1996, I visited two of these homes in the Sergiyev Posad district.

I went to a special boarding house where I met children with severe, incurable psycho-neurological diseases. They had been tied to their beds since birth. They were terribly thin – they couldn't even eat without assistance – they didn't talk and didn't seem to have any perception of the outside world. It was very painful to see them.

I went to another boarding house in Sergiyev Posad, where I met deaf children. They were amazingly courageous, despite their situation. The children were taught using special methods

– I must say, their teachers were remarkable. There was a concert for us – one young boy performed part of a Tchaikovsky concerto, which he had learnt through sound vibrations. It was impossible to watch him without tears welling up. Vera Kuzminichna Vasilyeva came with us on the trip, and she read poetry and sang – but that was a present for the caregivers, since the children couldn't hear her.

During a trip to Vorkuta, I went to an orphanage for healthy children – and what poverty they lived in! There was only one television in the whole home, which the children had to share, even though they were such different ages – and some wanted cartoons, some films, some football... When I got back to Moscow, I told Pavel Pavlovich Borodin, Manager of the President's administration, about the orphanage, and asked him to buy them several television sets. I found out later that nine sets had been sent to Vorkuta.

On each of these trips, I tried to help those I met – I helped with nappies, medication and medical equipment. In one children's home I saw that they were playing on a bare, cold floor. I agreed with Boris that one of the rugs from our residence would be sent there. I was anguished that I couldn't do more – I tried to involve businessmen, hoping that they would donate money, but it didn't work. Business in Russia was only just starting to develop, and entrepreneurs were not yet prepared to give money to charity. I didn't think I could insist, using my position, and I felt help should come from the government as a principle – otherwise, one orphanage would be lucky enough to have donors and would be fine, while others remained in poverty. That would not be fair.

During Boris's presidency, there were people like Galina Karelova and Ella Panfilova who worked on social issues, so I turned to them for help.

Once, I remember, Shamil Tarpishchev called me and said, "We can transfer about $100,000 from the National Sports Fund to charity – where would it be best to send it?" I put him in touch with a children's ophthalmological clinic, which was able to order some equipment for that amount, and the National Sports Fund paid for it. I asked Shamil to make sure he checked that the subsidy reached its intended recipient. He told me later that it had indeed been received by the clinic.

It didn't always go so smoothly, however. Once I went to a care home in Moscow. A businessman who had offered to help came with me. I was glad at the time, but he later asked for tax breaks. I had to tell him: "If you want to help, help. But no strings attached."

Once a well-known charitable foundation offered me a place on the board. I honestly admitted that I wouldn't be able to give much time to their foundation – especially since I was still working. The person I was talking to said, "What do you mean? You won't have to do anything – it's just, if I go to the bank and say you're on the board, they won't reject my loan application." That spelled the end of our conversation: "After what you've just said, there can be no question of my being on the board. I will help you where I can, but not as a member." With that, we parted. That was a useful experience for me: I never agreed to be an honorary member of any charitable foundation, although I received many offers. I didn't want anyone using my name in any way.

Wherever I travelled, I never met with either hate or aggression towards Boris, even though the previous years had been extremely difficult. There were many questions, of course, and dissatisfaction too – but that's normal, that's life. I tried to answer every question and explain my position. More often than not, they listened to me, and all went well.

In almost every city where there had been factories in the Soviet era things were very difficult. I was often asked the same question: "Under Stalin, they built DneproGES (the Dnieper Hydroelectric Station), Uralmash (Urals Heavy Machinery), the Chelyabinsk Tractor Factory – now they don't build anything any more. Why?" I had to remind them how those factories had been built – by a huge multitude of prisoners with wheelbarrows. If we used free labour with modern construction technology, we would build even better, bigger structures – but do we want that? It often turned out that people simply didn't know the country's history: they had studied Soviet textbooks, and therefore had no idea what price the country had paid for Stalin's industrialization.

I was often faced with resentment that change was coming too slowly. I understood how they felt. At one of the meetings I went to, military pensioners complained that their housing and medical-care problems were left unresolved. "We hoped that the new government would fix the situation quickly," they said. What could you say? We all thought that there would be a rapid change for the better. But it turned out that four years were not enough to fix what had been neglected over the previous decades. I said what I thought, which is probably why all my meetings were amicable.

The atmosphere in Boris's campaign remained tense, and there was a follow-up to Korzhakov's letter. The election campaign was already in full swing, and we had travelled extensively around the country. In Khabarovsk, after a hustings meeting, we got back late to the hotel, had dinner in its restaurant and decided to head off to sleep. I was about to go up to bed after Boris when Korzhakov came up to me and said, "We need to talk." I was frightened, and thought it might be about Boris's health, but instead he tried to convince me: Chernomyrdin had to be removed from his post immediately – he wasn't able to cope with his responsibilities. I objected. Knocking back a shot of liquor, he said: "You have to help me." I answered rather abruptly, "I don't have to do anything for you." Korzhakov wanted to replace Prime Minister Chernomyrdin with Soskovets. I didn't think Soskovets was suitable for the position. I told him, and in order to cut off our conversation, I left the restaurant. When I entered the room, Boris was already asleep. I couldn't settle down. I suddenly realized that Korzhakov might go to extraordinary lengths to put his plan into action – which meant there was a threat hanging over Boris. I went to look for Tanya. After dinner, she had gone down to the hotel's basement, where the campaign staff had been discussing the itinerary for the following day. I listened – but it was all quiet. I thought everyone must have gone to bed. I went back upstairs, but I couldn't fall asleep. At about five in the morning, I went downstairs again, wondering if Tanya and her colleagues had already begun work. Hearing voices, I knocked on the door. It turned out they had not gone to bed: when I had previously come downstairs, they were silently working on some documents. I called Tanya into the hallway and told her about my conversation with Korzhakov. "They want to oust Chernomyrdin and replace him with Soskovets – then it'll be only a question of time before something happens to Papa. Soskovets will end up as head of the country, and Korzhakov will be next to him…" I realized that Korzhakov could easily have exploited Boris's heart condition. Tennis, then the banya – and after the banya, alcohol. And that would be it… his heart wouldn't be able to take it.

Tanya listened to my apprehensions with a grave expression on her face. We decided not to say anything to Boris in the meantime, so as not to alarm him. He already knew what Korzhakov thought of Chernomyrdin anyway. Fortunately, everything worked out, and Korzhakov was never able to secure Chernomyrdin's resignation.

In May, Boris decided to visit Chechnya. This was very risky: the war was dragging on for a second year, and no one had managed to stop it, although Boris very much wanted to. Yet one day I heard in the morning: "I'm flying to Chechnya!"

Even Tanya, in her role at the campaign headquarters, didn't know anything about the plan – Boris had kept it secret. His closest aides and Boris Nemtsov flew with him. Nemtsov was Governor of the Nizhny Novgorod region at that time. He opposed the war and had gathered a million signatures to try to stop it.

I had no way of communicating with my husband. I watched the news on television all day – what else could I do? – but there was no report of the President's trip. Finally, on the evening news, they showed some clips from Chechnya. There was Boris, signing documents on a tank; there was his helicopter, rising into the air – and finally there was a call. Thank God – he was back! It was very important for Boris to stop the war. He was haunted by the fact that people were being killed, and that it was dragging on for so long. May 1996 was a significant step towards peace in Chechnya.

As the campaign drew to a close, the burdens grew, and I sometimes feared for Boris. In the breaks between meetings, his personal physician had to be called more and more frequently. Although I didn't know the alarming results of his tests, I felt that he was only just hanging on. I don't know how he endured it, but he did.

The first round took place on 16th June 1996. Boris beat Zyuganov, but only by a slim three-per-cent margin – so they both went to the second round. Boris greeted this news calmly – at least on the outside. The campaign staff expected an outburst of temper from him – after all, Boris had told people: "We'll win in the first round." But there never was an outburst – he simply said: "We'll keep working."

But three days later, on the orders of Korzhakov and Mikhail Barsukov, who was then the Director of the Federal Security Service (FSB), two members of Boris's campaign staff, Arkady Yevstafyev and Sergei Lisovsky, were detained while they were carrying a box of Xerox paper filled with campaign cash. This cash was from sponsors, and was intended for performers who took part in concerts. Korzhakov knew all this perfectly well.

Tanya phoned me late that evening, briefly explaining what was going on, and asked me to get hold of Korzhakov via the special-communication system – it would have been impossible to reach him in any other way. But Korzhakov didn't come to the phone, even though I kept calling. I knew that he and Barsukov were together, but each time I called, Barsukov took the receiver and said, "Korzhakov is busy." Finally, he rudely added, "Please don't interrupt his work." I was outraged – Mikhail Ivanovich had never behaved like this before.

Only then did I guess what was happening at the other end of the line. Apparently they had been drinking, celebrating their success, and Korzhakov didn't want to have to explain things to me.

They were buying time. I don't think Barsukov would have acted this way on his own initiative – Korzhakov forced him to do it.

It was already midnight when Tanya came to Barvikha. "Mama, I have to talk to Papa," she said. Boris had just gone to bed, and I really didn't feel like waking him, but what could I do? I woke him up, and Tanya said: "Papa, your campaign is on the verge of collapse." She described the situation in detail. Boris called Korzhakov straight away; Tanya and I left the room, so we didn't hear the conversation, which was very brief. I can only guess what Boris said. I know how hard it must have been for him to accept that he had been betrayed. The next morning, Boris summoned Korzhakov and Barsukov to his office. The decision was made: Korzhakov, Barsukov and Soskovets were fired.

After a while, I found out that Korzhakov, now off work, had been showing up at our gates in Barvikha. I don't remember exactly who told me about this – but I asked the security not to allow him in the residence grounds.

*Questions on the Margins*

"After he was dismissed, Korzhakov spoke out repeatedly against the President. Was Boris Nikolayevich upset by this?"

"Boris was not vindictive, but he could not forgive betrayal. He was lucky that there were very few situations like this in his life."

"For you, as I understand it, Korzhakov's actions were not unexpected?"

"Not completely, no – although I didn't think he would turn out to be such a dishonourable person, even pulling our grandchildren into it. He said in an interview that Tanya had given Gleb to an orphanage. How could he, as Gleb's godfather, lie so blatantly? I just couldn't understand. He said so many awful things about my family that I just don't want to think about it. I understand he wanted to have his revenge against Boris, but God punishes such things. I have no doubt."

Many years before, we had came home from Zavidovo by helicopter with Korzhakov and his wife Irina, and I invited them in for tea, along with Barsukov and Pavel Borodin. The conversation touched on Gorbachev, and Barsukov mentioned that the former head of presidential security, General Medvedev, had written a book about him. He spoke with disapproval. I was sitting next to Korzhakov, and I jokingly asked him: "Will you ever write about us, Alexander Vasilyevich?"

His wife Irina immediately said: "Never. Sashka is like one of your family – he could never do such a thing!" He could. Incredibly, too, he sent a signed copy to our post-office box – but neither I nor Boris took it home. It was too offensive.

# At a Patient's Bedside

One day in June 1996, when Boris returned home, I could see that he wasn't feeling well. He came in and sat down heavily in an armchair, grabbing at his heart. I ran to fetch the doctor – he always had to be nearby, and he came quickly. He did an electro-cardiogram and discovered that Boris had suffered a heart attack.

Boris flatly refused to be hospitalized. The doctor didn't insist – he said there was no urgent need for it. Boris could stay at home, he said, but should rest in bed. Our bedroom was on the first floor, but Boris couldn't climb the stairs, so we moved the bed into the living room. An IV drip was also installed. There was more fresh air in the living room than in the bedroom, so it was easier for him to breathe too.

Of course, it wasn't long before he violated the order of resting in bed. General Alexander Lebed was on his way to Barvikha. I was opposed to this. Boris said he couldn't cancel the meeting – and, besides, "I didn't invite him."

The results of the first round had Lebed in third place, after Boris and Zyuganov. He had received a fair number of votes – about fifteen per cent. He had been made Secretary of the Security Council between the first and second round, and when he pulled out of the elections, he called on his voters to support Boris in the next round.

When Lebed came into the room, Boris was already sitting in an armchair. The doctors had forbidden him to stand up, but he got to his feet all the same to meet the general, and shook his hand. The conversation went well, and, despite all our worries, everything was fine.

The last days of the campaign turned out to be very difficult for Boris – and for the rest of us too, for that matter. His trips were cancelled, he couldn't go to hustings and wasn't able to appear in public at all. We realized that this could lose him the election, and he knew then that all the effort put into the campaign would turn out to be a pointless waste. Zyuganov's chances of winning had increased. The situation appeared to be critical.

Boris refused to cast his vote from the residence – he and I argued a lot about this, but in the end we found a compromise: we could go to the nearby polling station at the Barvikha health spa.

He taped a television address in the hall there. There were few journalists in Barvikha, so everything took place calmly.

Before we knew it, it was the night of 3rd July, when votes were to be counted. None of us slept that night: we sat in front of the TV – although Boris was lying down, as directed. When the results came in, everyone but Boris drank the traditional glass of champagne to celebrate his victory.

People have since spread a lot of lies about the 1996 election. I have heard some say that the results were rigged. Everyone who had anything to do with the election know that's not true – one only has to look at the votes in the so-called "red belt": in the regions where the Communists held control and previously had a majority, Zyuganov won – in both the first and second round. What could have been manipulated there?

The victory cost Boris dearly – he paid for it with his health. But he did everything he could to stop power falling back into the hands of the Communists, who wanted to turn back the clock.

Straight after the election, Boris was told that he had to be operated on – and the doctors didn't hide the fact that it could cost him his life. "And if I don't have the operation?" he asked. The prognosis was bad: he would gradually lose the ability to work; heart attacks would increase in frequency, and the worst could happen at any moment. He decided to have it.

When the coronary angiography was done, it turned out that the degree of vascular stenosis was critical, which meant he had to have a quintuple bypass. No one gave him any guarantees of success. The doctors said: there is a 50–50 chance, a 40–60 chance. It was terrible, but he had no choice.

On 9th August 1996, the inauguration took place. Of course, it was hugely worrying for us – only a month and a half had passed since his heart attack, and Boris was still extremely weak. The ceremony was made as short as possible: it lasted only twenty-five minutes. We didn't have a new suit made for the occasion: we bought one off the peg. It was black with greenish pinstripes, and Boris didn't try it on first. As a result, it turned out to be a bit too big – but there was no time to make any alterations.

My memory of this solemn ceremony is fairly hazy, as I only had one thought on my mind: will he have enough strength?

Viktor Chernomyrdin, head of the government, was on the stage, as were Yegor Stroyev and Gennadiy Seleznyov, chairmen of the two houses of the Federal Assembly, His Holiness Alexy II and Nikolai Ryabov, head of the Central Elections Committee. Boris had a large golden chain put over his neck, which was the emblem of the Russian Federation President – the symbol of Russian statehood. When he recited the oath I could see how excited he was. He placed his hand on the Constitution, and he was given a copy of the text to read, but he remembered the oath by heart.

When it was all over, Tanya and I – and perhaps others, I don't remember – ran up onto the stage. Boris was completely drained, and sank into a chair. There was still the gala banquet after that. I was very worried – but he managed to find the strength. He looked lively, and even gave a toast – I still have no idea how he managed.

We hosted no inauguration party that time – Boris needed to rest. He had to get ready for the operation.

After each heart attack, he recovered much faster than most people would. After a couple of weeks he would be back to the same frenzied pace of life. This time, however, the recovery had to be longer: he had to face open-heart surgery, and we all knew it was extremely serious.

The doctors advised him to go to Zavidovo, to get his strength up before the operation, but we noticed that Boris had suddenly started to deteriorate. He was eating next to nothing, and he looked haggard and had grown weak. It turned out that his haemoglobin levels had fallen. The operation had to be postponed.

I also had to have an operation in August, but it wasn't very successful. The wound wouldn't heal, and my bandages had to be changed very often. A month and a half later, I needed another operation – so in the end Boris and I were in hospital at the same time. He was there before his procedure, and I was there after mine. He was on the first floor, and I was on the second floor – although I spent almost all my time in his room.

Our fortieth wedding anniversary was on 28th September 1996. Of course, we forgot all about it.

Our children remembered, however, and they and their husbands came to see us in hospital with a huge bouquet of flowers, which Boris loved, and a little saucer with two rings on it. Mine had diamonds, Boris's was a simple narrow gold band. We didn't even realize what was going on at first. "It's forty years since you got married!" they cried.

I saw that Lena and Tanya were welling up. Boris was sitting there in his unbuttoned gown, and I won't even mention my state… Neither he nor I was allowed to raise a glass of champagne.

I have never taken off that ring ever since; Boris didn't wear his for long – he wasn't used to it.

Boris didn't understand how people could get divorced. He had a friend who remarried when his wife died. This is a common thing – but for a long time Boris refused to call him or invite him to our house. I couldn't understand it at all. After a while they smoothed everything over and began to talk again, and I said to Boris: "I'm glad you finally accepted it." He replied: "I didn't accept it – I reconciled myself to it. I still can't understand how he could do it."

"What if I were to die first?" I asked.

"We must die on the same day – I can't live without you. You and I are one body, and we have one soul."

He repeated this a number of times, even though he didn't like to speak about feelings. Once, when we were watching a film, I suddenly remembered some of the other girls he liked at the Institute. But he cut me off, saying: "I can't even remember their names – there's only you."

Gradually, Boris's condition began to improve, and he went back to work. Sometimes, if he didn't feel well, he stayed in Barvikha. On those days, documents were delivered to him there. Members of the government and administrative officials all came to us – everyone who was needed, in fact.

Before the operation, the question of whether it should be announced publicly arose. I had my doubts – although I realized that it couldn't be otherwise: if he was going into hospital, the thing couldn't remain under wraps for long. The doctors couldn't guarantee a positive outcome – the country had to know. Boris himself had introduced openness in politics, after all.

But Boris was against it. So far, only a very small circle knew about the forthcoming operation – our family, the Prime Minister, the head of the administration, the head of Protocol and two or three others...

His team was convinced that he must go public, but he was immovable. But then someone remembered President Ronald Reagan's letter to the citizens of the USA, in which he disclosed details of his Alzheimer's diagnosis. Sergei Yastrzhembsky, Boris's press secretary, showed Boris the letter in which Reagan admitted that his mind was already fading, and that he would no longer appear in public – this is how he bade his country farewell. It must have been hard for Boris to read.

He was not happy – he felt as though he was being pushed into doing it. I didn't interfere, seeing that he was struggling with it. Finally, he decided he had to tell the people. Everyone sighed with relief. A television crew came to our house, and started scoping out locations – they opted for the winter garden. Naturally, a suit wasn't appropriate, so Boris put on his favourite wool jumper. When he spoke about the impending operation, his voice shook a little.

Although I was in favour of announcing the operation in principle, I still had my doubts about whether it was necessary – not in terms of political prudence, but because it would take a toll on him. But when the interview was shown on TV, I finally understood: yes, it was right.

Boris spent the last few days before his operation at the health spa. The doctors had advised him to go on a diet, and he had lost a lot of weight. The operation was scheduled for 5th November. He was unusually composed in the interim period, and told us that everything would be fine – and we could see he believed that.

He had decided, however, to have the operation in Russia, not abroad. I was against this.

*Questions on the Margins*

"You didn't trust Russian doctors?"

"That wasn't the issue. It just seemed to me that Russian doctors would be very aware that they were operating on such an illustrious patient, and that might get in the way of their work. For foreign doctors, the president of another country would just be a patient, I thought."

"Did you try to change his mind?"

"Yes – but in vain. The doctors, however, reassured me that a good surgeon thinks only about the job in hand as soon as the operation begins."

Renat Akchurin was chosen to perform the operation, and on 5th November, at 6 a.m., Boris went to the cardiology centre, with Lena, Tanya and me in tow. The operation was scheduled for 8 a.m., but there was already a team of doctors in the foyer, and Boris immediately began joking around with them. Prime Minister Viktor Chernomyrdin was there, as was Sergei Yastrzhembsky – who had to keep journalists up to date – and officers with the nuclear briefcase. A decree on the temporary transfer of powers to Chernomyrdin had to be made, and that took place at the cardio centre.

Boris was put on a stretcher, and the atmosphere became solemn – but then Boris asked Sergei Pavlovich Mironov, head of the medical centre, "Got a knife with you?" and the tension dissipated. He was taken to the operating room.

They offered to let us watch the operation on monitors, but we declined – I couldn't have endured it. My daughters and I were given a room; journalists were waiting for us as we went to and from the room, and they asked some questions – I answered them, but I don't remember either their questions or my answers, such was the state I was in.

*Questions on the Margins*

"Do you remember what you said to your husband when he was taken away for the operation?"

"I think it was, 'God be with you.'"

"And when he regained consciousness?"

"No. All I remember about that moment is that I was with my daughters and we cried with joy."

We sat in the room for six hours while the doctors were operating. Michael DeBakey, a world-famous American cardiac surgeon who had come to Moscow at the invitation of our specialists, watched on a monitor.

Waiting was torture, although doctors kept coming in to give us updates: they'd put him under anaesthetic; they'd opened up his ribcage; the surgery was under way; they'd attached the blood-circulation machine... in fact, that was the most worrying moment, as I suddenly thought: what if that machine breaks down? Tanya, Lena and I paced the room.

One question in particular tormented us – would his heart start beating again? But finally the doctor came in and said: "His heart started on the first try." "Is it working?" I asked – and, in my excitement, I didn't hear the answer. I asked again. The doctor patiently repeated: "It's working, of course, it's working." It took them some time to sew him up and put in metal staples. At this point, the tension had decreased somewhat – tears were flowing, but we tried to hold ourselves together. I don't remember the following hours at all, apart from a few snatches.

When Boris woke from the anaesthetic, we had to wait a long time before they let us see him. He lay there pale, almost white. We were only allowed to stroke him. He signed a decree returning the powers to himself straight away. This happened when I wasn't there – I know that only from stories. The nuclear briefcase was next to him in the hospital room. A day after the operation, Boris was put back on his feet. The shunts were taken out of the veins in his legs. His legs were bandaged, and it was very hard for him to stand up. I thought it would be better for him to stay in bed a little longer, but I kept silent. On 8th November, he moved from the cardiology centre to the Central Clinical Hospital, to which he was more accustomed. After such an operation, psychology has an enormous significance: if the patient is depressed, they will recuperate very slowly; if they believe they will get well, they will, and quickly. It was just so in this case.

For the first few days, Boris was bothered by coughing – which was very painful for him. Only then did I realize why they gave Boris a white heart-shaped pillow before the operation. In the intensive-care ward, it lay on his chest, and as soon as a coughing fit started, the little pillow could be pressed down – you couldn't just put a hand on his chest, as it was too painful.

A week later, a package arrived from America, and in it was a little pillow just like this – a present from an association of people who have survived heart operations. It was crimson-coloured.

It wasn't long until Boris said, "It's easier to breathe." The pain went away along with the torturous feeling that he couldn't get enough air.

When we were allowed outside for the first time, there was a light frost. Boris breathed deeply, filling his lungs. This was happiness. We have a photograph of Boris, Tanya, Masha and me walking in the hospital courtyard – our faces are shining with joy.

After his operation, Boris's character changed – he became softer, and he smiled more often. Masha even told him it was as if he had grown younger. The pain receded completely, and his breathing became free. This internal lightness seemed to fill him with joy, and we were delighted too. Even his tastes changed – he suddenly loved ice cream, which he didn't eat at all before. Gradually, he returned to ordinary life – of course, he wasn't able to take the trip he had planned to Portugal, so he sent Viktor Chernomyrdin in his place.

Of course, as expected, he didn't stick to the recuperation schedule set by the doctors – he believed himself ready for work.

We celebrated the New Year in a new home in 1997 – we had to move out of Barvikha, which was in very poor condition by that time, and required serious repairs.

Everyone was in a good mood – we believed we had left the worst behind. The new home in Gorki-9 was old, white and spacious, and it had columns, an open veranda and a large park. Its large windows made it bright in all weather, but unfortunately it was very cold – the window frames had dried out and didn't keep in the warmth. No one had lived there for several years, and before our arrival only cosmetic renovation had been carried out. There were such draughts from the windows and doors that we had to block them with pillows and blankets. On the whole, though, this house was in slightly better condition than Barvikha. When we moved again four years later, the ceiling fell in over the bed in Gleb's room. I went in to pick up a few things and saw huge chunks of plaster lying there. It was a miracle that Gleb wasn't in bed when it happened.

A wide wooden staircase led to the first floor. There was wood everywhere in the house, which I liked, although it was always creaking – sometimes it was the old parquet floor and sometimes it was the stairs. Thirteen-year-old Masha's room was set apart from the others, and my granddaughter complained that she was frightened by the creaking at night.

Our bedroom and Boris's office were both on the first floor, which was no longer a problem, as he could climb stairs easily again. On the doctors' advice, boards were put on his bed: after the operation he wasn't supposed to sleep on a soft mattress.

We discovered that the house had been built in the 1930s by political prisoners. When the leaky roof was repaired, a list of names was found in the attic – the workers had been sentenced under Article 58 ("Counter-Revolutionary Activity").

On New Year's Eve, Boris went to warm up in the banya, which was next to our house – he wanted to feel healthy again. It seems that the banya wasn't sufficiently warmed, though – it was my fault, as I hadn't seen to it. This, added to the cold of the house, made Boris fall ill. Renat Akchurin had warned us: "During the recovery period, the main thing is not to catch cold…" So it turned out we hadn't taken enough care.

At first he suffered from a light cough, but then it gradually grew worse. The diagnosis was pneumonia – and that soon became acute. A little later, he started to feel a sharp pain between his ribs. The doctors believed a nerve had become pinched as a consequence of the operation. The pain kept coming back in the same place, and was so sharp that only strong medication could relieve it. He sometimes had to have injections during meetings or official receptions – the pain went away for a time, but came back again and again. He suffered terribly. We went to an institute in Germany, and were told that such a complication after an operation is not frequent, but does happen. The pain never left him.

# By the President's Side Once Again

Gradually, our lives went back to the usual routine. Despite the fact that health problems remained, Boris's overall condition improved: he began to move more easily, he was in a good mood and his heart worked without serious problems. He gradually returned to his usual work regimen. When Sergei Yastrzhembsky, Boris's press secretary, reported that the President was working on documents again, sarcastic comments started to appear in the press – but Boris was really working. His capacity to work actually increased after the operation: he no longer got easily tired, and managed to get a lot done.

After the presidential campaign, Boris asked Tanya to stay on and work for him. He appointed her his advisor. She took part in all his meetings, accompanied him on trips and helped him to prepare his weekly radio addresses.

In March 1997, Boris gave his traditional address to the Federal Assembly. It was his first big public speech after the operation. His political opponents wanted to test his resolve. Not long before the address was due to begin, the Communists, who were forever trying to use Boris's health to score political points, introduced a draft resolution in the Duma to remove President Yeltsin from power due to his poor state of health. They knew the resolution wouldn't pass, but they continued trying to wrong-foot the President. When Boris went up to the podium, there was hostile heckling from the Communist Party rows. Speaking over them, Boris began his speech – he was on good form again and could take it. The Communists had miscalculated in thinking that he was now too weak to stand up to them.

In March 1997, Boris decided to strengthen Chernomyrdin's government by introducing fresh blood. He brought in two new vice premiers – Anatoly Chubais and Boris Nemtsov. As an experienced manager, Viktor Stepanovich Chernomyrdin, in Boris's opinion, needed the support of younger politicians with different expertise and knowledge. Boris Nemtsov didn't want to go into government – he was Governor of the Nizhny Novgorod region, and felt that that was his only calling. People tried to talk him into it, but he resisted – then Tanya went to see him in Nizhny Novgorod. Nemtsov later mentioned how effective her words were when she said: "Boris, when you needed help, Papa always helped you – now he needs your help, and you're refusing." They spoke well into the night, and Nemtsov finally agreed to come to Moscow.

In 1997, the economy had slightly recovered, but the social problems remained very serious. Boris very much believed in a new economic programme that had been prepared by Chubais and Nemtsov's team. The gist of the plan was to give back pay to state employees, help socially vulnerable people, raise domestic industry a little and try to resolve the rural areas' problems. Boris hoped the revitalized government would be able to accomplish these difficult tasks.

* * *

In March, Boris went to Helsinki to a bilateral Russian-American summit, on his first official international visit after his illness. After this, the schedule was relentless: in April, he went to Germany, in May to France, in June to the USA, and then to France again for the October summit of the Council of Europe, and after that to China and to Sweden… All of this was on top of trips around Russia and the neighbouring countries – as well as his usual schedule in the Kremlin, of course.

The last trip to Paris turned out to be a sad one, as it came not long after Bulat Okudzhava died in June in the French capital. Rema Ivanovna, the wife of our ambassador in France, Yury Alekseyevich Ryzhov, said: "Let's go to see Olya, Bulat's wife." Olga was holding up courageously, and she took us around the places Bulat loved to spend time in. Ever since, we have remained good friends, and we meet and phone each other when we can. Olga set up the Okudzhava Museum in Peredelkino, and she was its director for many years. In the week following Bulat's death, Boris had set about finding a way to commemorate the poet's life, and started working on plans to erect a monument in a prominent position on the Arbat – in the end, the monument was unveiled only after Boris's resignation, in 2002.

In 1997, there was another addition to our family: on 28th October, our fifth grandchild was born, Vanya. Lena was already forty years old, so of course I was very worried for her – not least because I was supposed to join Boris on a trip abroad, and I was afraid my grandchild would be born in our absence. When he arrived, Lena and Valera were overjoyed, as were Boris and I. Vanya was baptized in the Kremlin. By that time, next to the President's Kremlin apartment, a little chapel had been created.

Katya was already seventeen by now. She had graduated from high school, and was planning to study History at Moscow State University. Borya, who was in eighth grade, was sent to a British public school. I was opposed to this move, as I always wanted to have our children and grandchildren nearby, but Tanya insisted – she believed that it would be very difficult for a young boy named Boris Yeltsin to study in Moscow at such a politicized time. She was probably right – but Borya, of course, was very homesick.

Raising Gleb required a lot of effort on Tanya's part. Children with Down's syndrome can be amazingly gifted if their abilities are developed with care and love. Tanya did everything she possibly could for Gleb – as did we, of course.

\* \* \*

By early 1998, the political situation began to heat up again. Boris Berezovsky and Vladimir Gusinsky, who controlled Russia's two popular television channels, fell out with the "young reformers", as they dubbed Chubais and Nemtsov, and they waged a media war against the government. They believed that the Kremlin's policies was harming their interests. In the meantime, the new economic programme was stalling because of the opposition.

After much wrangling, the Duma didn't pass the Land Code, a piece of legislation which would have established private property on land. Without this, serious reform in the rural areas was impossible. The Tax Code was also rejected, and housing and utilities reforms were halted. Boris tried to use his authority to support the young reformers, as he had done in 1992. He even offered to meet the opposition halfway – to this end, he agreed to the creation of a *Parlamentskaya gazeta* (*Parliamentary Gazette*) – but the situation grew more and more complicated, and the Duma rejected the budget proposals time and time again.

I think that, by the beginning of 1998, Boris realized that the model of government he had chosen – the experienced Chernomyrdin plus the young reformers – was no longer working, and it looked as though there was a split in the Cabinet of Ministers. I even sensed that Viktor Stepanovich was uncomfortable with Nemtsov and Chubais – in the end, Boris was forced to consider replacing the Prime Minister. This was a very difficult decision for him – for many years, Viktor Stepanovich had been his right-hand man, and Boris trusted him implicitly; they were close in terms of both background experience and views.

Although they had known each other for a long time, long before Boris became President, I only met Viktor Stepanovich when he became head of the government. That was when I saw his wife, Valentina Fyodorovna, for the first time too – I think it was at our home in Zavidovo, and Boris had invited them for the weekend. I liked Chernomyrdin immediately – especially when I learnt that he was, like me, a native of the Orenburg region. Viktor Stepanovich and Valentina Fyodorovna were very warm people – easy to talk to, and with a good sense of humour. Valentina Fyodorovna was a wonderful singer and dancer – I still remember her Gypsy dance. We gradually became close friends; they came to our house and we went to theirs. Viktor Stepanovich was an avid hunter, and this pastime brought him closer to Boris.

Viktor Stepanovich and I formed a very trusting relationship. Boris, as I have already said, avoided political conversations, but I could discuss such things with Viktor Stepanovich.

When it became clear that Viktor Stepanovich had to step down from his role as chairman of the government, I was very upset, of course – but I knew that Boris would have thought a lot before making such a decision, although he didn't speak to me about it directly. I tried to reassure myself with the knowledge that Viktor Stepanovich, like Boris, always put the interests of the cause above his own, and that he would therefore understand and accept the President's decision – and that is what happened, although, of course, he wasn't entirely happy about it. I was very glad, however, that we managed to maintain our friendship for many years. After Boris's resignation, we met Viktor Stepanovich a number of times on holiday in the Crimea; often he and Valentina Fyodorovna still came to our home, and sometimes Valentina Fyodorovna came alone – when Viktor Stepanovich became ambassador to Ukraine, she did not go with him. If ever we were having a hard time and Valentina Fyodorovna found out about it, she always called us and said, "Let me come over – I'll sing and dance!" She and Boris sang together beautifully – she sang the lead, and Boris sang the harmony. Boris would joke: "Valentina Fyodorovna and I could earn quite a living with our singing."

One day in March, Boris took the unexpected step of appointing, as the new head of government, the thirty-two-year-old Sergei Kiriyenko – a man who had not been in Moscow for long, since he had only been transferred there recently at the recommendation of Boris Nemtsov. I think the President hoped that, unburdened by Moscow ties, the young, energetic Kiriyenko, relying on a team as young as himself, could implement the economic transformation that was needed. To some extent, this was an attempt to repeat the Gaidar experience.

Unfortunately, Kiriyenko's government was also unsuccessful, and in August 1998 the country suffered a bank default, which was a big blow for Boris. He was forced to dismiss the government under which the default had occurred. In the midst of the crisis, Viktor Chernomyrdin agreed to head the government once again, and from 23rd August he became Acting Prime Minister. The Duma, however, refused to confirm him for the post twice. Boris was forced to make a compromise, and nominated Yevgeny Maksimovich Primakov, a candidate supported by the Communists. People should give Yevgeny Maksimovich his due: he did not start by destroying what had been done before, as many had feared.

## Questions on the Margins

"Was Boris Nikolayevich close to Primakov?"
  "They were businesslike in their dealings."
  "Did you ever go to his house?"
  "No – our families weren't on friendly terms. I knew his wife, of course, but we didn't have the kind of warm relationship we had had with the Chernomyrdins."

1998 brought with it a discussion about the reinterment of the remains of the Tsar's family. This had special significance for Boris: when he was working as First Secretary of the Sverdlovsk Regional Party Committee, he was forced by the Politburo to tear down Ipatiev House in Yekaterinburg, where the Tsar and his family were executed. It is now known that the order came from the KGB – more specifically, from Yury Andropov, the head of the KGB – so the house would have been razed anyway, no matter whether Boris objected or not. At any rate, he couldn't get into a conflict with the Politburo or the KGB then, but years later he felt a great responsibility for the tearing down of the building – I think it tormented him.

  On 17th July 1998, we went to St Petersburg for the burial ceremony, which took place at the Peter and Paul Cathedral. Before the burial, a careful forensic analysis of the remains had been carried out, under the direction of a government commission headed by Vice Premier Boris Nemtsov. The specialists' conclusion was unambiguous: these were the remains of Nicholas II and the members of the his family. Even so, they decided to have the results corroborated by foreign scientists – who confirmed that there was no doubt as to the authenticity of the remains. The Church, however, was against the reinterment until the very last moment.

When I entered the cathedral, I felt as though the Romanovs' assassination was a tragedy in my own family. On that terrible day, the parents must have realized that their children were going to be killed along with them – I couldn't help thinking about that.

In 1992, the foundation stone for the Church of All Saints had been laid in Yekaterinburg on the very spot where the Tsar's family was executed at Ipatiev House. The construction couldn't be completed in the 1990s, however, as the economy was in too parlous a state, and the church was only completed in 2003. Boris and I went there to pay our respects once again to those innocents who had been killed. I think that visit to the Church of All Saints was very important to him.

We were forever meeting with reminders of the country's past – there was so much past which hadn't been fully understood, and which still caused pain to so many.

Until a certain age, I didn't think that the fact that Lenin's unburied body was still exposed in the centre of Moscow was anything out of the ordinary. The first time I saw the body in the Mausoleum was when I was a student, and I was interning in Moscow. It was hard to get in – you had to stand in a long queue. I returned to the Mausoleum as an adult, with colleagues, while I was living in Moscow. I became very uncomfortable, and I noticed that Lenin's face had an unnatural colour. I later read in an article that the body had been treated with chemical substances in a special laboratory, and the upkeep cost the government a lot of money.

Now I have no doubt that Lenin's body should be committed to the earth: no matter who he was, nobody should be treated like that. No one asked him if he wanted to lie in the Mausoleum after his death, and if they had asked him, I don't think he would have agreed to it. I totally understand why the Communists are still against the burial of their great leader. Gennady Andreyevich Zyuganov calls himself a follower of the Russian Orthodox culture, which means he should be troubled that the leader of his party hasn't been buried. He should be calling for the urgent reinterment of Lenin, according to Russian Orthodox custom.

At a Kremlin reception once, I went up to Gennadiy Seleznyov, Chairman of the State Duma, who had been elected by the Communists, in order to discuss Lenin's reinterment with him. He reluctantly answered my questions, and his wife said, "Let it be thirty years from now." I couldn't help asking, "Would you like to be treated like that when you die?" They both remained silent.

I met Lenin's grand-niece once at a function, and I asked her, "Perhaps it would be better to bury Vladimir Ilyich next to his mother at Volkovo Cemetery?" "And what about us?" she said unexpectedly. It was a very strange reaction.

I also spoke about Lenin's possible reinterment with His Holiness, Patriarch Alexy II, and, later, with Patriarch Kirill, when we met in St Petersburg at the opening of the Boris Yeltsin Presidential Library. Kirill said that he also considered the burial necessary. I don't know if the Church can initiate the procedure. The Communists' resistance has always been too great, so perhaps it would be right that it comes from the Church.

Red Square is connected with our recent history in another way too – I first thought about this when I was with Boris on the government podium, and in the square before us was a parade and a display, songs and loud music from speakers. Behind us, however, were graves. That was the first time it felt wrong. Now, it's not only parades that take place in Red Square, but concerts and fairs as well, and in winter there is even an ice-skating rink. But it is essentially a cemetery: there are human remains in the Kremlin Wall and near it. If Red Square is to be used as a setting for festivals and entertainment, I really think these remains should be moved to a cemetery, or perhaps the square itself should be turned into a memorial – although that, of course, would put an end to having any form of entertainment there.

# Simply Being

Boris's work was so intense that there never seemed to be any time for anything else. Of course, it wasn't quite like that in reality – there was definitely time for the little joys of life: talking to our grandchildren, meeting friends, spending time with the family... I remember certain precious moments from our life which, against the backdrop of public events, might seem trivial – but they're no less valuable to me for that.

Boris once showed me a plot in Gorki-10 – it was on a bend of the Moscow river, and beyond it was a field, with a forest in the distance; it was very pretty. "Let's buy this piece of land and build a house here," he said. We decided to do so. Boris commissioned the design, and my daughters and I gave feedback on it – we asked to make some tweaks, adding a wooden veranda. Some time later, however, he suddenly said, "We're not doing it!" No meant no. I didn't argue.

A little later I saw a photograph in *Moskovsky Komsomolets*: it was our plot, and behind the fence one could see a roof. The photo was captioned "THE PRESIDENT'S DACHA IN GORKI-10" – it was a rare case of the newspapers writing something true about us.

It turned out that Boris, after all, had begun to build the house – apparently, he wanted to make it a surprise. His book had met with worldwide success, with big print runs, and there was enough money for the construction.

"The President's family cannot have two dachas," we decided at a family council. "We'll have to say goodbye to the dacha outside Zelenograd." Tanya, who had put a lot of effort into building the home and laying out the garden there, was terribly upset – but we had to do it.

When the home in Gorki-10 was built, we didn't go there very often – as a rule, only on Sundays. We planted a kitchen garden, with raspberries, blackcurrants and other garden trees – not just apple and pear trees, but even a cherry tree. I went to Gorki-10 more than the others – especially in the summer – for the cucumbers and the raspberries. I even spent New Year's Day at Gorki-10 by the outside Russian stove.

I remember that night well. It was freezing, and huge flakes of snow were falling; the pines towered above... It was romantic, and later that day we gathered together as a family, and it was very cheerful. In general, however, the dacha was empty. For the few years after he resigned as the head of the presidential administration in 2003, Alexander Stalyevich Voloshin lived here – Boris thought it would be easier for him there, so offered him the house for some time.

We sometimes spent our weekends at the presidential residence in Zavidovo, and took short holidays to Valdai, or, during the second term, to Shuyskaya Chupa in Karelia. The residences had everything Boris needed to work – he couldn't tear himself away from his affairs.

Once, when we were at the residence in Valdai, I learnt that Eldar Alexandrovich Ryazanov and his wife Nina were staying at the health spa next door – we invited them over, and we spent the evening together. They were a remarkable couple. We agreed to go the next day to look at a plot he had bought to build a dacha. In the end, Boris was busy – someone had turned up on a business errand – so he couldn't come with me to the Ryazanovs. The plot turned out to be far away from the residence. When we arrived there, we saw a goat tied to a stake; it immediately lowered its horns and charged at us. Laughing, we moved the stake farther away and sat down on the overgrown meadow. I had bought a bottle of champagne and some sweets; we drank from glasses I had brought from home, and made plans of where the house could be built.

Time passed, and the Ryazanovs did build the dacha. The next time we went to Valdai, they invited us to their house-warming party. I noticed a champagne cork on top of a lampshade – it turned out to be from the bottle I'd drunk with them years before. Unfortunately, Nina died not long after the house was built. Some time later, Eldar was married again, to a woman called Emma, who was from my region – and we also became friends. I'm told that the cork remains in its old place.

We fell in love with the Shuyskaya Chupa residence in Karelia during Boris's second term. It was wonderful there, and we both really liked it.

It was in Karelia that I first saw cloudberries growing. The head of the local administration – a charming woman – once offered to show me some berry patches. When we met up, she had brought a treat with her – she had baked some sort of pirozhki with rice and potatoes which are called *kalitki* in Karelia. They smelt so good in the car that we ate them all on the way back. I had three, and the driver and our security guard had two each.

When we got there, there were clouds of mosquitoes, so we had to put on mosquito nets. We walked along the meadow from north to south. Bright berries were scattered among the silvery moss – as we walked along the meadow, they turned from an unripe rose-yellow colour to a ripe bright yellow. We picked a little bucketful, until we couldn't stand the mosquitoes any more. We made to leave when we bumped into a farmer with a large bucket full of berries. We persuaded him to sell them to us, and we brought them home and put them in a warm place. We noticed they had started leaking. We sprinkled sugar over them, and then separated them into two containers: over one we poured drinking alcohol, over the other vodka. We wanted to make an experiment.

We put them in jars and took them back to Moscow, stored them in a cool room and forgot about them. Just before New Year's Day, we remembered about them. The cook squeezed the berries and put them through a sieve and made a sort of cloudberry liqueur – the aroma was magnificent, but the taste turned out to be so-so.

There were also a lot of mushrooms in Karelia – I never saw them so big and clean anywhere else. I love mushrooms, but I only eat them if I have prepared them myself.

*Questions on the Margins*

"You seem to remember in detail the food you made and when you cooked it. Did food occupy a special place in your family life?"

"It's not that it was special, but it somehow united the family. Boris and I usually discussed the menu before we had guests – he loved doing that. Sometimes he set the table himself, and if there wasn't enough time before the guests came, he would at least check to see if the table was in order. In Sverdlovsk, the whole family prepared the *pelmeni* – it was a kind of ritual. But what made me happiest of all was to feed my family something tasty – it always seemed to me, and still does, that the atmosphere in a home depends on that, to some extent."

"You never saw cooking as a burden?"

"No. I often worried that there wasn't enough time for it. I dreamt of the day when I'd retire and life would become quieter, so that I could cook with no hurry and to my heart's content. But the quiet life never came."

# By the Ex-President's Side

As early as a year and a half before the presidential elections, newspapers and TV programmes began to talk more and more frequently about possible successors to Boris. The question had come up before, especially when Boris had brought it up: once, during a meeting with Bill Clinton, he introduced Boris Nemtsov as his successor; another time he wrote that Viktor Stepanovich Chernomyrdin might be the next President; at one point, he named both Nikolai Aksenenko and Sergei Stepashin as his successors. It sounded as though Boris planned to bestow the title on someone, but of course that couldn't happen – the second president of Russia had to win an election, just like the first president had done – there was no other option.

This, however, did not mean that Boris couldn't think about who could take his place – and of course he did. He felt it was important that the next president continue down the path the country had chosen in 1991 – one of a free-market economy, democracy and a state based on the rule of law; at the same time, he also knew his successor had to gain the support of the people. By 1999, it was clear that none of those who had been connected with the reforms of the early 1990s were electable.

Boris considered a great number of candidates for the role, including, as I mentioned before, Sergei Stepashin, who became Prime Minister in 1991 – but he soon came to realize, I think, that Sergei Vadimovich wasn't suitable. Boris appreciated his erudition and intelligence, as I understood, but I think he was bothered by the fact that he lacked certain qualities needed in a president – although Boris never discussed this with me. In August 1999, he dismissed Stepashin and appointed Vladimir Putin as head of the government.

I am always surprised when people say that Putin "came from nowhere" – it's just not true. Boris had long had his eye on

Vladimir Vladimirovich – from his days as Vice Mayor of St Petersburg under Mayor Anatoly Sobchak. First Boris made him head of the Presidential Control Directorate, then First Deputy Head of the administration and then Director of the FSB.

Boris considered Vladimir Vladimirovich not only a smart and competent leader, but also a profoundly honest person. He very much admired his tenacity and his strong-willed nature. For the several months that Vladimir Vladimirovich was the head of the government, Boris became more and more convinced that he had not been mistaken: Vladimir Putin had everything that was needed to be a worthy leader of the country.

Boris didn't discuss his choice of Putin with anyone – it was his personal decision.

After Boris's death, a rumour circulated, saying that Putin gave our family some sort of guarantees of immunity – needless to say, it's total nonsense. Boris wouldn't even think of negotiating such behind-the-scenes agreements.

There was only one thing he asked of Putin: take care of Russia – and these words were heard by everyone.

On the night of 30th December 1999, Boris slept poorly. He tossed and turned in his bed, and eventually got up. I brought him a cup of tea – it was clear that something was worrying him. He got up earlier than usual – at about six – and we had breakfast before he began to get ready for work.

He took a long time choosing his suit, which wasn't like him. He called in Tanya and me. "Which one should I wear?" he asked. "The dark-blue one," Tanya said. "Let's change the tie – I don't like the knot, and the colour…" he said. I didn't argue, I just brought him another, but I didn't understand why he was paying so much attention to his suit and tie – after all, the New Year's address had already been taped. After he put on his coat, Boris said, "Naya, I've decided to retire."

I threw myself at him – I hugged and kissed him, with tears of joy in my eyes. "Careful, you'll crease my suit!" he said, to lighten the mood.

*Questions on the Margins*

"People say that Tatyana and Valentin Yumashev knew about Boris Nikolayevich's decision two days before. Why didn't he tell you earlier?"

"He knew I would be overwhelmed with emotion. Of course, I wouldn't have told anyone, so in that sense he could rest assured – but it would have been written on my face: I'd be glowing. He could keep his feelings to himself – I couldn't."

"Were you desperate to share the news with someone?"

"Of course – but I couldn't. As he left, Boris warned me: 'No one must know about this,' and he pressed his finger to his lips."

Boris and Tanya left, and were gone for about eight hours. I was left alone. I didn't know what to do to keep myself busy – I couldn't focus on anything. I picked up first one thing, then another, to no avail. Then I began to wonder – how would Boris announce his decision? And when? Not in his New Year's address? That would mean leaving before the New Year… but people were already preparing for the holiday – buying presents, going away – and the news would signal a huge upheaval. It would be better if Boris didn't make the announcement before the New Year. I called his secretary, but was told, "Boris Nikolayevich is busy – he can't talk now." I called Tanya, but she didn't answer either. When I finally got through I said: "Tanya, don't do it today – wait for a few days, at least. Talk to Papa." Tanya began to reassure me: "Don't worry – everything will be fine. Make sure you have the television on at twelve o'clock."

*Questions on the Margins*

"At noon, Moscow time, you turned on the television and watched Boris Nikolayevich begin his speech. Do you remember your initial reaction?"

"I cried."

"How did you feel about the fact that Boris Nikolayevich asked his fellow citizens for forgiveness on that day?"

"He did the right thing. Life had been very difficult for them, and he had been partly responsible for that: he couldn't finish some of his projects – he didn't live up to some people's hopes… But he did everything he could."

I spent the last day of 1999 filled with joy and, at the same time, anxiety. What would happen to the country? How would Boris feel during this difficult time? Could we help him? Then Lena came over, and things became calmer. We waited for his return together.

Boris came home early – it was still light out. He didn't return to his Kremlin office after that – not once.

When he came home, he said from the doorway, "Bill Clinton called me in the car, and I didn't talk to him – I promised to call him back. I can allow myself that – I'm no longer President." Almost all the leaders with whom Boris had worked called him.

Our family always remember the great feeling of relief we were filled with on that day – we joked, saying that a huge burden had been lifted from our shoulders. Tanya later said: "That was the best New Year's of my life." In all the years we spent in Moscow, I don't recall such a light mood during New Year's. Raising a wine glass, Boris said, looking at me, "My priorities have changed. Work is no longer at the top: now that spot is for you and the family – all the rest comes later."

Boris loved New Year's Eve – the whole family did. He usually played the role of Father Frost himself – we had once bought him a red robe, hat, staff and beard and moustache. The little grandchildren didn't recognize him. We always put trees up – both in our home and outside. At midnight, we raised glasses of champagne and then went out in the snow, under the stars. We celebrated it twice – once on Sverdlovsk time, and once on Moscow time. That was how we passed New Year's Eve 1999 too. When morning came, Boris got up very late – at about ten – which was surprising, as he usually got up very early. We had all been a little afraid of that morning – marking the beginning of a new life. But that day, the 1st of January, passed easily.

We all supported Boris, and didn't leave him alone: the children, the grandchildren – everyone – surrounded him. We understood that it would be difficult for him: he had been immersed in work his whole life – now he had to adjust to a new way of life. How? What would he do to keep busy? Would he be able to fill his free time – which, for the first time in his life, he would have in abundance? But we had worried in vain: he could keep himself busy. He began to read a lot, watched sports programmes, and we went to see volleyball and tennis games. We also went to the theatre and saw friends more often.

Boris and his assistant, Vladimir Nikolayevich Shevchenko, put together some holiday plans. Now we could travel with the whole family – with the children and the grandchildren. This became a tradition after Boris's resignation. Every year, at the end of the year, he and Shevchenko planned our holidays – and we went around the country and the world.

Our first trip, in January 2000, was to Israel. The trip had been on the cards for a long time – he had been invited to a ceremony in honour of two thousand years of Christianity in Jerusalem. Despite his having resigned, it was decided that he should represent Russia. The acting heads of state and patriarchs of the Church were also there, and the solemn ceremony took place in the Church of the Holy Sepulchre. This was my first visit to the Holy Land.

On 1st February, we celebrated Boris's birthday at home, as usual. In the morning, Patriarch Alexy II came to see him, and later Acting President Vladimir Putin, as well as the heads of the Commonwealth of Independent States. Everyone sat at one table: Leonid Kuchma, Alexander Lukashenko, Eduard Shevardnadze, Askar Akayev, Nursultan Nazarbayev, Heydar Aliev, Islam Karimov, Emomali Rahmon and Robert Kocharyan. The only absent leader was the President of Turkmenistan, who was unable to come. We only had such a birthday party once.

We didn't order food in – everything was prepared in our kitchen. We served duck that Boris had shot in the autumn – they had been smoked and frozen. I had to spend quite a bit of time in the kitchen preparing the desserts – I baked them myself.

The heads of state pronounced a toast in Boris's honour, and they stayed for a rather long time – there was no lull in the conversation. For the leaders of the post-Soviet countries, it was important to see that everything was peaceful in Russia, despite the resignation of the President.

Boris greatly appreciated the friendly relationship he had with the heads of the states in the Commonwealth. He was on particularly good terms with Leonid Kuchma, Nursultan Nazarbayev and Askar Akayev, and our families were also on friendly terms. We remained friends with the Akayevs when they moved to Moscow. We also went to Minsk to visit Alexander Lukashenko.

We often entertained high-ranking politicians in our house, especially in the first few years after Boris retired. There were ministers and officials from the administration with whom he had worked – we had foreign guests too: Helmut Kohl, Bill Clinton, Brian Mulroney, Ryutaro Hashimoto and Jiang Zemin, among others.

Vladimir Putin also visited – both before and after he became President. I don't know what was discussed – Boris didn't tell me, and I didn't ask. The meetings became gradually fewer and fewer – although he and his wife Ludmila Alexandrovna always came to wish Boris a happy birthday.

I was pleased that Vladimir Vladimirovich didn't forget my birthdays, either. He proposed that we celebrate two round numbers – which we did without Boris – my 80th and 85th birthdays. I was very touched, of course – although I don't particularly like official events – and I invited the wider family, our friends and Boris's colleagues. We managed to make the atmosphere festive and warm – there was no formality.

For my 85th birthday, the President awarded me the Order of St Catherine the Great Martyr. I hadn't expected to receive such a high award, and in all honesty felt conflicted about accepting it. On the one hand, I was filled with gratitude. On the other hand, this award, which is given above all for charity work, presupposes actions on a scale that is almost impossible for one person to achieve, and I could not ascribe to myself the merits the President spoke of. I felt as though the thanks should go to Boris for what he did, and to the Yeltsin Center for what is now done in his name.

*Questions on the Margins*

"After Boris Nikolayevich's resignation, did you discuss politics at home more often?"

"Boris didn't think it was appropriate to discuss what his successor did – that was a hard-and-fast rule. If he had any questions, Boris passed them on to Vladimir Vladimirovich when he came to visit."

"The new president restored the Soviet national anthem. As far as I recall, Boris Nikolayevich was opposed to this. Did this come up in your discussions at home?"

"Yes, that we did discuss. I was also opposed to the change – I liked Glinka's anthem a lot."

In the year 2000, we moved back to Barvikha – by this time, the house had been renovated. Some partitions were taken away, the windows were enlarged and the balconies turned into bay windows. A second floor was built to make the house look more complete – this was where the grandchildren's rooms were – and a lift was installed. Boris now had his office in what had been a large dining room – before, the whole family had lunch and dinner in this room, and when there were only two or three of us, we still had to use an enormous table, which wasn't very convenient. During the renovation, a little dining room was also built, which had floor-to-ceiling windows – it was lovely and light. We put a little round table in there, and it was quite cosy – Boris and I loved it.

We also added a glassed-in veranda looking out towards the Moscow River, which Boris liked very much. In the warm weather, he spent a lot of time there, reading and resting, and sometimes we had lunch there. We even received guests there occasionally.

It was the first time that we had moved into a renovated, well-built residence – and this only came after Boris's resignation – and I fell in love with the house.

The grounds were transformed. I had spent many happy hours gardening – I grew herbs, potatoes and vegetables. I also planted peas, strawberries and currants in the orchard, as well as apple and pear trees. In the first summer after Boris's resignation, I discovered a new appreciation of the beauty of the surrounding world, and I began to set the alarm clock so that I could watch the sun rise – it was amazing in Barvikha. I always watched the sunset, too, even when the weather was grey. During the last half-hour before sunset, I would run out of the house several times to see the light change. I got carried away in the garden: for the previous ten years, I had to steal time for gardening – life was so intense that there was no time for nature.

In Barvikha, I learnt how to drive an Electrocar – it was the only form of transport I wasn't afraid of. When the Chinese President Jiang Zemin came to visit, I drove him around the grounds in it myself – I hadn't expected four of his bodyguards to flank us and run alongside. I kept glancing at them, worried I would leave them behind, and I ran onto the side of the road. Luckily, this provoked laughter rather than fright.

In 2001, Tanya married again, to Valentin Yumashev, whom she had known since 1989. I was very upset – I just couldn't reconcile myself to the thought that Tanya was leaving Lyosha Dyachenko. Lyosha and his mother Nina Alexandrovna had become like family – and Gleb was only five years old. I was absolutely tormented by this – and I tormented Tanya. In some ways I am quite old-fashioned – I just can't imagine how someone can divorce a person they have lived with for so many years.

Boris didn't support me in this – he had always believed that we shouldn't interfere in our children's lives. As always, he was right – Tanya and Valya were happy together, as was their daughter, Masha, who grew up with them. Their relationship is very special, I came to realize. Valya has become like family – and I look at the world quite differently nowadays. With the passing of time, I have come to realize that life goes by quickly, and each person has the right to live happily. One can't sacrifice one's feelings to the dictates of custom.

Lyosha Dyachenko remarried soon afterwards, and had another child. We are still in touch with him and his mother, and Tanya and Valya visit Gleb, which we are all glad about.

Even in retirement, Boris kept a routine, and stuck to his habit of getting up early. He had breakfast, lunch and dinner at certain times, and in between he took walks, looked through a huge amount of informative material and read.

During the first few weeks following his resignation, Boris was uplifted and happy – but there was a turning point. I saw the change in him, and decided to talk to him about it, and perhaps tell him how I had felt after leaving my job when we moved to Moscow. I sat him down in the living room; the conversation was gloomy, but the day was very sunny. "I feel empty inside – I don't know how to fill that void," he said. I wanted to remind him that he had endured worse – in 1987, for instance, when, after the October Plenary, he was isolated from everyone, and he couldn't see the next step – but then I realized that this wasn't worth bringing up. Instead, I simply reassured him: "Your friends will visit; we can travel together – we'll finally be able to take our grandchildren with us." "Yes, I understand that," he said, "but something important has gone."

He found a way to cope with this state of mind – not straight away, but before too long he felt better. Books were crucial to this process – he read an incredible number of books, and we acquired a library. He didn't usually reread books – as I said before, he had a brilliant memory, so he remembered everything for ever.

The only books he sometimes returned to were those by Pushkin and Chekhov. He read all of Pushkin's works, one after another: his prose, poetry, plays, articles and letters. When the complete works were published in one thick volume, on onion-skin paper, he immediately bought it. I even scolded him, saying, "Why ruin your eyes reading such tiny type?" We took a lot of books with us on trips, too. I remember once asking him: "Why are you dragging around such a load?" "You're not the one dragging it!" he said, laughing.

Tanya brought him two or three boxes of books a week. The sales assistants at the House of Books on the Arbat and the Moskva bookshop on Tverskaya helped her to choose them. Tanya asked her friend to make recommendation lists for Boris – and he demanded more and more. "I've already finished those," he would say to her. "Bring some new ones!"

It was like a ritual. Boris would stack the new books on the table and divide them into three piles: the first pile was the books he wanted to read first; the second was those to be read "later"; the third was those he wasn't interested in. He loved historical literature, memoirs, both Russian and foreign contemporary fiction and art books. He was indifferent towards fantasy and detective stories.

Boris now had the time to watch sports programmes too – his favourites were tennis and volleyball – and he created his own cinema at home with the television, leaving the light switched off. It was at that time that NTV Plus appeared, which offered a series of sports channels covering tennis, volleyball, soccer, hockey and athletics.

Sometimes, due to the time difference, he watched broadcasts at night – tennis tournaments in New York or Melbourne, for example.

We also watched films in this home cinema. Tanya brought us DVDs to watch – these were mainly action movies, which he loved (and I didn't), but there were some serious films, too. Sometimes, we rewatched old Soviet films – *My Beloved*, *Moscow Does Not Believe in Tears*, *White Sun of the Desert*. While he was still President, Boris had learnt that *White Sun of the Desert* hadn't won a single award, and he had issued a decree awarding the whole creative team behind it the State Prize of the Russian Federation. After this, Boris met Vladimir Motyl, the director of the film, a number of times.

I was watching many of these films for the second time, but Boris had missed many of them the first time they had appeared, due to work. We also listened to CDs of concert recordings – both popular and jazz music. Boris loved good music.

When our grandchildren visited, they liked to sit with their grandfather in the home cinema. Boris loved talking to them and hearing their news – he was genuinely interested, and they could sense it. He was so pleased to have time for them at last. If I went to visit the grandchildren or great-grandchildren on my own, he grumbled. Tanya and Lena were on my side, and they would tell him, "When Mama is with the grandchildren, her mood is entirely different." He just frowned in reply, and said: "And doesn't she care how I feel?" He wouldn't let me leave his side – he liked it when I sat with him while he watched television, read a book or listened to music. He just wanted me near him.

In 2002, Tanya gave birth to Masha, our youngest grandchild. Boris loved her very much – but at first she was afraid of him, and ran away from him – he seemed too big to her. Soon, however, she grew very attached to him, and now regrets she didn't spend enough time with him.

Tanya and Lena and their families visited us almost every day, and Boris looked forward to it. "Who's coming to see us?" he would ask me. If the children were late, he began to worry. At some point, they started to bring the grandchildren and the great-grandchildren to see him more regularly – they loved hovering around him and climbing up on his lap. He didn't get tired of them – on the contrary: he grew visibly younger.

Tanya tried to get Boris interested in playing golf. She thought that would be a good substitute for tennis, which he had to give up after his operation. She brought him books about golf, tapes of games, even clubs, but he said: "Tanya, that's not for me."

*Questions on the Margins*

"What's the most important thing about the family to you?"
   "The family itself."
   "But family means something different to everyone – to some it means emotional security, to others welfare, to others routine. What about you?"
   "Atmosphere – that was the most important thing to me – an atmosphere that draws everyone to the house. I tried my best to establish that in our home."

Boris didn't really like to have what is known as a "social life" – but he often went to the theatre, and took great pleasure in visiting friends. He loved the theatre; in Sverdlovsk, he tried not to miss a single performance. We went to the Theatre of Musical Comedy, the opera and – less often – to see plays. When we were in Moscow on business, we made time to go to the Taganka Theatre – we saw Vladimir Vysotsky in *Hamlet*; that production made a strong impression on us.
   We befriended the artistic directors of some theatres – after performances at the Sovremennik or the Moscow State Theatre (Lenkom), we always went to see Galya Volchek and Mark Zakharov to have a chat, drink some tea and discuss the premiere. Boris talked openly to Mark Anatolyevich about life and politics; Zakharov never hid his point of view – in that sense they were similar. He introduced us to many Lenkom actors too – including Nikolai Karachentsov, Oleg Yankovsky, Alexander Abdulov, Alexander Zbruyev and Inna Churikova. Boris was very warm towards them.
   We didn't miss a premiere at the Sovremennik, and we knew all of the stars – Marina Neyolova, Valentin Gaft, Sergei Garmash, Yelena Yakovleva and Chulpan Khamatova.
   We also went to the Mayakovsky Theatre often, and went backstage to meet Alexander Lazarev and Svetlana Nemolyayeva, Natalya Gundareva and Mikhail Filippov; they were wonderful actors and remarkable people.

We loved to go to concerts – especially those of Vladimir Spivakov, Yury Bashmet and Valery Gergiev, who gradually became our friends.

I was always amazed to see how much at ease Boris was in this milieu – almost from the first moment he made contact with new people. He knew a lot about literature and art, and talking to the performers was a real pleasure for him. I usually kept silent and listened in.

In early 2001, Boris fell ill with pneumonia. Once again, for quite some time he resisted our efforts to persuade him to get medical treatment – he had hoped that he'd get better by simply resting in bed. Instead, he grew worse and worse. When he finally did as he was told, even the Central Clinical Hospital course of therapy wasn't having any effect. His condition became critical, and he was put on a ventilator. Tanya, Lena and I took turns to sit with him on the ward.

One day, one of the consultants took me aside, held one of my hands and said, "Naina Iosifovna, you must prepare the girls – Boris Nikolayevich has three days to live." I can't even describe how I felt. I could not understand a thing. I simply couldn't believe it.

When the consultants left, I asked the doctor on duty, Nikolai Oktavianovich Malkov: "Is there really nothing that can be done?" It was he who told me about Doctor Binh from Vietnam. I would have done anything. The next day, Nikolai Oktavianovich brought Doctor Binh to the Central Clinical Hospital. Boris was still on the ventilator, and couldn't speak. The Vietnamese doctor held his finger on Boris's pulse for a long time – that was how he made the diagnosis.

Doctor Binh's initial instructions were that the temperature in the hospital room should be maintained above body temperature, the level of humidity should be raised and Boris should be undressed so that his skin could breathe. That, in his opinion, could compensate for some of the oxygen that normally comes through healthy lungs. We brought in heaters from home and put wet towels on them. The doctors went around the room dripping with sweat. Boris lay undressed, lightly covered with a cotton gown. The doctors at the Central Clinical Hospital probably found it hard to watch what was going on in the ward, but they showed understanding, because they couldn't help.

Doctor Binh gave Boris several injections. He promised to send an infusion that evening, made from Vietnamese grasses, which was to be administered by tube. He also told us we needed to buy a black bear's gall bladder – he had heard one could find them in Moscow. Apparently, nearly every Vietnamese family keeps a black bear's gall bladder, in case of illness – it is an expensive item, but the Vietnamese economize on other things, considering this very important.

Tanya managed to find the gall bladder in Moscow – it turned out to be expensive in Moscow too – the equivalent of about $1,000. The doctor cut open the bladder, rubbed the gall with his fingers, tested it on his tongue and concluded that although it was a bit dry, it could still be used. He made an infusion with vodka and showed us where it had to be rubbed on the body. Several days later, Sergei Shoygu, Minister of Emergency Situations – an avid hunter – gave us a black bear's gall bladder he had found in Altai. In the doctor's opinion, this was much better. The treatment continued.

Doctor Binh visited Boris every day, and we did everything he told us to do. Soon Boris's condition began to improve.

We learnt a lot about Doctor Binh while he was looking after Boris. It turned out that his father had treated the Vietnamese leader Ho Chi Minh. "During the war," he told us, "Vietnamese doctors didn't have the equipment we needed for testing, or the medicines we need. We were forced to fall back on our ancestors' techniques." He recalled how he had learnt to make a diagnosis from a pulse, and how to do a blood test by rubbing a few drops of blood with his fingers. Later, we tried an experiment – Doctor Binh examined a blood sample in his way, and the Central Clinical Hospital doctors did their usual test on it: the results coincided.

When the respirator stopped being effective, the doctors performed a tracheotomy on Boris, after which he had to breathe through a tube. That day, Doctor Binh warned us: "There's internal damage." So the doctors wheeled in an X-ray machine and took a picture – and that was indeed the case.

Boris gradually regained the ability to breathe naturally. To start with, they let him breathe without a tube for one or two minutes at a time. He then asked to be allowed to increase the length of time, so that he could get rid of the tube as quickly as possible.

Doctor Binh warned Boris that the wound wouldn't heal over: he had to learn to live with it. For example, while talking, he would have to cover it with his hand. But Boris refused to believe him. "It will heal over!" he said. The doctor merely nodded his head, but to me he repeated: "Such wounds do not heal over." Doctor Binh went away for a week, and when he returned, he discovered that the opening had started to heal over. Boris was talking freely. The doctor was amazed. Thank God, we were past the worst of it.

In July that year, when Boris was stronger, we went to stay with Jiang Zemin at his residence on the Yellow Sea. Jiang offered Boris some expert Chinese doctors. He gently declined. Nevertheless, doctors were sent for. They were a funny pair: one was very tall, the other was quite small. Boris refused to see them – I tried to persuade him, saying: "They will only check your pulse and make a few recommendations." Vladimir Nikolayevich Shevchenko, who was with us at the time, backed me up. "If someone has to see them, you see them!" said Boris. There was nothing for it – Vladimir Nikolayevich and I went off to see the doctors, and Boris went off to the banya in his robe, with a towel thrown over his shoulder. We apologized to the doctors for his absence, and asked them to examine us instead. The Chinese doctors assessed our condition, also by pulse. They asked what our complaints were. I spoke of my allergies – Vladimir Nikolayevich mentioned his problems. We were both prescribed Chinese medicines, which took the form of large brown balls. The medicines looked identical, but their effect was, of course, different. The balls had to be chewed, and had an unpleasant taste. Both Vladimir Nikolayevich and I found relief from them. Later, I went to a private Chinese clinic in Moscow and ordered the same medicine.

Jiang Zemin's residence was located in a very beautiful place. Every day, we took Electrocars to the ocean, took a swim and basked in the sun. We rode in a speedboat and explored the coast. We liked everything – our mood was great. In the dining room, we were served twelve to fifteen dishes in very small portions – two or three kinds of edible mollusc, as many shrimps and something that we had never seen before. At first it was all interesting – some things were tasty, some not so nice. Boris was the first to get tired of the food, and he asked for meat patties with potatoes. I remember how our cook, Yura, peeked into the kitchen – he desperately wanted to go in and sort things out. Muttering excuses about how he wanted to learn from the Chinese cooks, he went in and mopped the worktop. Boris was happy to return to the cuisine he was accustomed to, but Vladimir Nikolayevich and I didn't refuse the Chinese food – we liked to try new things.

We managed to travel around China – I still remember the trip with pleasure. Boris returned to Moscow in better shape, rejuvenated and cheerful. Rumours flew around: Yeltsin had been treated by Chinese doctors.

\* \* \*

Boris had always loved fishing, and after he resigned he could do it to his heart's content. He found it more and more difficult to go hunting, although he still went, sometimes – he had always been a good shot, and in Sverdlovsk he hunted elk, red deer and other kinds of deer. We were always well stocked with venison – in the winter we preserved it on the balcony, or in a box on the dacha's veranda. When Boris was President, he usually travelled to Zavidovo to hunt; one of his favourite pastimes was duck-shooting, and he often went boar-hunting. I went with him once, in the Baltics – for the first and last time. I felt too sorry for the boars – it just wasn't for me.

I loved cooking venison, however, and still do, even though to a lesser extent. My favourite delicacies are moose lips and bear paws. I love moose lips in aspic: they have a unique taste. I only eat them if I make them myself, though – I don't trust the cook – and Boris always liked them served hot. We made bear paws in aspic, too – we served them on a special plate shaped like a paw.

Once, when we were in America, I tried bison meat for the first time. We were treated to steaks – we were told it was tenderloin, the tenderest cut. We liked it a lot: the meat just melted in your mouth. We brought some back to Moscow as a treat for our children and grandchildren.

Unlike his hunting trips, I always joined Boris when he went fishing. He was very good at catching fish – both angling and fly-fishing – and he was fond of ice-fishing, too. I love fishing, and I'm a dab hand at it too. We often caught fish together at the Ivankovsky reservoir. Boris always took a long time to choose a spot – and once he had done that, he would sit down and settle in comfortably. I usually fish standing up. In spring or early summer, there were shoals of perch. We once made a bet over who would catch more, and fished on different boats. I caught fifty perch and won the bet, so I got a bottle of champagne from Boris.

We sometimes caught fish in Zavidovo, in the pond next to our house, which was stocked with trout, but I didn't enjoy that: trout grab the piece of meat on your hook straight away – it's embarrassing to be proud of such skill-less fishing.

Both Boris and I loved to cook *ukha* on a campfire – you throw several types of fish into a pot with onions, then add tomatoes, cut in half, and slosh over 100 or 150 ml of vodka – about half a glass. Finally, you drop red-hot embers into the bucket for a few seconds so that the *ukha* smells of the campfire.

After Boris retired, we often planned our trips around fishing, and we fished around much of the country, and abroad as well.

In 2004, we went to Norway – Boris, Lena, Valera, Vanya and I. A fishing trip on the open ocean was organized for us. We went out on a fishing schooner – it was a very pretty boat, perhaps a hundred years old or more. On the fjords it was quiet and absolutely still, and on the open sea it was also calm, at first. We caught pollock with rods. Suddenly, the wind picked up and high waves appeared. Lena lay down near the mast – she couldn't bear the pitching. The Norwegian security guard and translator also lay down – they were seasick too. But Valera, Vanya and I stood with our fishing rods, alongside Boris, at the boat's side.

When Boris spoke to the captain, the translator stood up for a few minutes, translated, and then lay back down. But Boris was happy – he had six hooks on his rod, and there was a fish on each; the weight was enormous. The schooner rocked so hard that water splashed in from the side. At one point, Boris's feet were clear of the deck, and he was about to fall overboard. An assistant hurled himself at him in horror, trying to hold him back. But Boris was shouting, "Don't touch me – grab the fish! It's getting away!"

After that I didn't feel like fishing any more, and I lay down on the deck next to Lena out of fear. But Boris kept fishing, and I could hear him laughing. The rest of us were happy to return to the safety of the fjords, where *ukha* was waiting for us. We took a few fish back to Moscow for our friends.

That same year, Valera convinced us to go to Ireland. Once again, we went in a large group – we took my sister's granddaughter, Yulya. We stayed in a castle, and went fishing on a lake. Once Boris, Valera and Vanya went deep-sea fishing – they dreamt of catching a shark, but didn't.

While we were there, we decided to try golf. I couldn't get to grips with it. Lena struck at the ball three times, and missed three times. We quickly abandoned that sport, but had great fun trying archery.

In 2005, we went fishing on the Kola Peninsula. There are dozens of shallow little rivers there, which flow into the Umba River, and where salmon spawn. When the fish reach a certain age, they swim up the Umba to the ocean. They spend several years swimming to the shores of Canada, and then they spawn and return to the same river in which they were born. In order to catch salmon, we had to purchase a licence, and were only allowed to catch a certain amount of fish. We were taken to an empty shore, where there were just a few fishermen's huts. I was lucky – I caught the first fish – but Boris caught more in the end. We divided up our catch on shore and ate it with wasabi – it was a bit like sashimi.

Later that year, we flew to Alaska. This trip, like the others, had been planned by Boris and Vladimir Nikolayevich Shevchenko at the start of the year. We chose the warmest month – July. It was raining in Moscow, but the weather was marvellous in Alaska. We were expecting quite a barren landscape, but we discovered that it is paradise: the nature was astounding, and the towns were small and clean, well kept and well organized.

In Anchorage, the Governor met us – he held a reception in Boris's honour. It was quite an event – before us, no Russian or Soviet leader had visited Alaska. The Governor spoke with gratitude about Alexander II, who sold Alaska to America – it was hard for us to agree with him. When we were alone, I said to Boris, "How nice it would be if this still belonged to Russia!" He laughed and said, "It wouldn't be as well kept."

The next day, we went to a Russian Orthodox church and to a Russian shop. We were glad to see Russian culture and traditions preserved in Alaska.

We sailed along the coast, the four of us – Boris and I, Vladimir Nikolayevich Shevchenko and our son-in-law, Oleg – on a yacht, sometimes stopping at harbours. We had a small helicopter at our disposal, and we went up over the mountains in it, two at a time. Looking down on the blooming mountainsides, the soaring crags, the tiny little lake so high above the ocean – it was all so wonderful. The helicopter landed on a small mountain field – it seemed to me to be very dangerous. Boris, as ever, was absolutely calm, while I worried away – although I soon found out there was nothing to worry about.

Of course, a fishing trip was also organized. We sailed through canyons and caught salmon and halibut, fishing from the yacht. I caught a halibut that weighed forty-three kilos, and Boris caught one that weighed thirty-seven. "I think they mixed up the rods," joked Boris. We had enormous difficulty pulling out the fish, but when we managed, we cooked them straight away. It was delicious. Unfortunately we couldn't take any home – it's illegal to take fish out of Alaska.

One day, we went out on speedboats to a glacier, from which streams of water were pouring under the glare of the sun.

We watched dolphins play around us, and we saw a colony of sea lions lying on a sparkling iceberg – there were such amazing sights all around us.

In front of the glacier was an iceberg as tall as a four-storey building. Boris wanted to get closer to see it more clearly. The guide warned us that icebergs are dangerous, because they melt in the sun and tip over – but could anyone stop Boris? We sailed closer. We admired the iceberg for a while – and then, before our very eyes, it flipped over and swept the boat away on a powerful wave. We were soaked from head to foot. But Boris was calm. "Let's sail right up to the glacier – we're already wet now." We were very lucky – we survived the trip and got to see a glacier. To convey in words the beauty and might we experienced is impossible.

*Questions on the Margins*

"If you could chose any place to live, where would you go?"

"Wherever my family is. I'm the kind of person who can't live alone – I'm always on a leash, tied to my family – I prefer it that way. I have never chosen where we lived – it was always Boris who made the decision. But I must say, I can't imagine living outside Russia."

"What if your children or grandchildren moved to another country?"

"It's their life – I wouldn't try to impose my choice on them. But, of course, I'd prefer them to make their home in Russia – and fortunately they have."

The next trip after our Alaska holiday was in Sardinia, where some friends had invited us to stay. On the third day of our holiday, a tennis tournament was starting in Melbourne. Boris and I watched the nail-biting game between Elena Dementieva and Maria Sharapova on TV – it ended at 5 a.m. We sat and watched in the dark, as usual; the light from the bedroom lit the room very slightly, but we were still in semi-darkness. After the match, Boris got up straight away and went through the dining room to the bedroom. I had a bad leg then, so I got up slowly before going after him.

The villa we were staying in was split across two levels, and the living room where we had been watching the match was on the lower level. It was open-plan, and the rooms were divided by pillars, with steps in between. Boris slipped on the steps: trying to recover his footing, he reached out for a pillar, but lost his balance and fell on his side. As soon as the doctor examined him, he said: "He's fractured his hip."

An ambulance was called. The driver tried to get as close as possible, and got stuck on the lawn – we had to pull the ambulance out with our car. Boris was brought out on a stretcher and taken to the hospital, where the diagnosis was confirmed. They recommended operating straight away, but Boris insisted on being taken to Moscow – so in the morning we flew out, and went to the hospital on Michurinsky Highway, just near the airport. Vladimir Petrovich Abeltsev, an extremely skilful surgeon, did the operation, which was successful.

Boris recovered quickly, and we were soon able to get out and about again. We went to all the tennis championships in Moscow and to volleyball tournaments (the Yekaterinburg team Uralochka had just emerged at about that time). It was hard for Boris to sit in the stands for long periods of time, but he endured it – he was an avid fan. He knew all the members of the Russian volleyball team by name, knew their individual skills and their careers – especially those on the women's team. He often called the chief trainer, Nikolai Karpol, who was from the same area as us, and they would have a "post-mortem" of the match. Sometimes this took place in the dead of night, but that didn't stop Boris, and he discussed the nuances of the game in detail. I once asked Karpol if he wasn't exhausted by these conversations. He was surprised. "Of course not!" he said. "It's for a good cause."

His conversations with Shamil Tarpishchev were just as long. Boris knew all our tennis stars – Zhenya Kafelnikov, Marat Safin, Lena Dementieva, Svetlana Kuznetsova, Nastya Myskina, Dinara Safina and Vera Zvonareva, among others. We entertained many of them at our home, and Boris always congratulated them on the phone after they won. He knew dozens of young players who were just making a name for themselves, and he took an interest in their careers and latest results. Sometimes Shamil asked him: "Who's that?" Boris knew many of the young players better than their coach did.

Boris had done a lot for tennis as President: the Kremlin Cup was begun under him, and many amateur tournaments were organized – sometimes in Moscow, sometimes in Sochi. Boris always took part in them – and sometimes he won, playing the double with Shamil Tarpishchev. At one point, a Presidential Tennis Club was organized on Sparrow Hills, and Nikolai Karachentsov, Gennady Khazanov and Mark Zakharov came. For them, as for Boris, tennis wasn't a burden, but a "solace".

When he retired, Boris could finally go to see Wimbledon and the Roland-Garros, something he had always dreamt of doing. I went with him, of course. I remember Wimbledon well – the sun was scorching, and we were given straw hats. Boris didn't look like himself in that straw hat and dark glasses. Some of the players signed their autographs on the hat later on.

We went to the Davis Cup finals in Paris at the invitation of Jacques Chirac, taking Tanya and Valya with us. Boris sat next to Jacques Chirac at the stadium, and each rooted for his player. Boris was terribly worried – and with good reason! In the deciding rubber, Misha Youzhny was trailing 2-5 in the fourth set, but he managed to push the match to a decider – and then the Davis

Cup was ours! I couldn't stop Boris – he charged onto the court, throwing himself at everyone, hugging and congratulating them. After the tournament, Jacques Chirac received us at Élysée Palace.

Boris loved France. We went several times with our children and grandchildren, and even the youngest, Masha, once came with us. On one of these trips, we took Lena's family with us, and Jacques Chirac gave little Vanya a remote-controlled car. He played with it at the residence.

Another time, we were taken to the famous perfume factory, Galimard, in Grasse. At the end of the tour, we were invited to experiment and create our own fragrance. Boris branded his creation "Urals Taiga", and someone helped him select the ingredients. I asked for some light, flowery fragrances, and I hesitated for a long time, struggling to think of a name. But Boris said: "Just call it 'Naina'." We took two bottles of our fragrances home as souvenirs.

When the museum was created, someone happened on a French newspaper with a story about this trip, and she called me. We got in touch with Galimard and asked if they could make a batch for the museum shop – fortunately, they still had our perfume formulas.

Now both perfumes – Urals Taiga and Naina – can be bought at the Yeltsin Center, and our original bottles are part of the exhibition.

Boris kept up his friendships with world leaders even after he retired. Everyone always had such respect for him, and conversation was always warm. These were sincere relationships. The closest relationship he had was probably with Helmut Kohl – he and Boris trusted one another very much.

Whenever Boris went for a heart check-up at a German clinic, we always met Kohl in Berlin. He once even cancelled a long-planned trip so he could meet with us. Kohl came to Barvikha and to Zavidovo, and, when he retired, we flew with him to Baikal twice. He and Boris went to the banya, and then dove into cold water – about 8°C, no more. Kohl was delighted, and said: "We don't have anything like this in Germany." We sailed together, visited leisure centres, and were glad that things seemed to be looking up.

In a restaurant once we were given some cake made from cherry flour for dessert – before that, I didn't even know there was such a thing. I really liked it, and I bought all the flour that I could find in the shop – about ten kilos of it. Ever since, when people visit, they bring me cherry flour and I bake cakes with it. Now there is a dessert made to my recipe at the museum café at the Yeltsin Center, which I hear is in great demand.

In the year 2000, Bill Clinton came to visit us at Barvikha with an official delegation. Although he was still in office at the time, he suggested forming a club of retired world leaders, to formalize these meetings and make them a regular occurrence – sadly, the idea never got past the talking stage.

In early 2007, the future seemed bright. On 25th March, Boris and I went to Jordan – we wanted to see the holy sites, and to visit the Dead Sea. From the airport, we were taken through the desert to our hotel – through endless sand dunes – and suddenly we were in an oasis, where everything was absolutely drowning in green. Our hotel was right on the shore of the Dead Sea, on the very edge of this oasis.

The Dead Sea amazed me. It was impossible to swim – the water pushed you to the surface. There were several pools of fresh water on the shore, where you could wash off the salt. I rubbed myself with curative mud, and my skin became silky-smooth. The water was cold, but I dipped in, and took some holy water with me – I'm not sure why.

When we got home, Boris started to suffer from health problems again. His legs began to swell up, so they decided to remove excess liquid from his blood in a procedure called plasmapheresis. He had to stay at the Central Clinical Hospital for a week, where they were going to give him five treatments before allowing him to go home. Everything was going according to plan.

On the Saturday, I talked on the phone to Tanya, who was away and, knowing that Boris was in hospital, wanted to come home earlier than planned. I reassured her: "Papa feels better, and he's coming out of hospital on Monday." On Sunday, I spent the whole day on the hospital ward, which I was used to, and I only went home at about midnight, with Boris hurrying me out: "You have to rest – it's late, and I'll be home tomorrow!" I kissed him before leaving, and he said goodbye to me more warmly than usual – pressing my hand to his cheek. I went away in tears, and scolded myself for getting so emotional.

The following morning, on 23rd April, just after 7 a.m., Boris's assistant called to ask which shoes he had. It was a cool day, and I hadn't checked the night before to see if he had taken his warm boots with him. While I had the assistant on the phone I asked, "How did the night go?"

"Not very well," came the answer. I wasn't worried, though – I was used to the ups and downs, and he had also said that Boris had woken up, and was sitting up and planning to shave. I went to get a jumper, and then the phone rang again – Boris Nikolayevich was feeling worse. For some reason, I ran to get the holy water from Jordan.

I hurried to the hospital and ran into Boris's room – but no one was there. I was taken to the intensive-care unit, where I saw Boris. His face had changed dramatically – it seemed flat, as if all the air had been let out of him. He was unconscious. He didn't speak again. I took a handkerchief and began to wipe the holy water on his brow. I called Tanya, and told her: "Papa is worse – he's in intensive care." We started thinking about how to break it to Lena – she was a much more emotional person. We decided we just had to tell her – she would never forgive us if we hid it from her. When she heard the news, she immediately rushed over to see him, and we asked her to stop at a church on her way and light a candle.

I was standing outside Boris's room, watching through the glass, and I watched them wheel in an X-ray machine. Just at that moment, Lena arrived – I ran to meet her. When I got back, Boris could no longer be seen. Upon enquiry, I discovered that they had found blood in his abdomen, and had to perform an emergency operation. He never returned from the operating room.

The doctor came out of surgery and said something like "Boris Nikolayevich is gone" – or that he could not save him – I don't remember his exact words. Time stopped for me. It was good that there was a wall nearby – I felt behind me, and I leant back against it.

Only after Boris was gone did I remember that the doctor who had operated on his heart had guaranteed him five years of life. He lived twice as long.

We bid farewell to Boris at the Cathedral of Christ the Saviour, in a ceremony which lasted two days – people even kept vigil at night. Many of Boris's former colleagues came. I was in a daze, and can't remember what happened very well. I remember raising my eyes to the cupola and asking God for the strength to go on – my death would be too much for Lena and Tanya.

*Questions on the Margins*

"Did you and Boris Nikolayevich ever speak about death?"

"He said a few times that we had to die on the same day. I always answered that that sort of thing didn't happen – not unless there was some kind of disaster... 'I won't live without you, anyway,' he would say. But I go on living – the memory of our life together helps."

"You didn't try to turn these conversations into a joke?"

"No – I reminded him that we had children, and the one who remained must live for the other. I said that then, and now that's what I'm doing."

At Boris's farewell service at the Cathedral of Christ the Saviour, Helmut Kohl, Bill Clinton, George Bush Senr and Leonid Kuchma – as well as many other people I knew or didn't know – came up to me and said kind words. I just about managed to keep myself together.

Then we went to the Novodevichy Cemetery, where there was a military salute. Vladimir Vladimirovich Putin said some official words of farewell. I only recall a few fragments of that difficult day – I remember taking a handful of sand and throwing it on the grave, and I remember noticing that the grave was lined with a flag.

For a long time afterwards, I couldn't go to funerals – it was just too hard. I went for the memorial service, but I couldn't go to the bit at the cemetery – I just didn't have the strength. The only exception to this was the funeral of Slava Rostropovich, who died four days after Boris.

At the beginning, I went to the Novodevichy cemetery every day. I began to wonder what sort of gravestone there should be – a stone bust? I couldn't think of anything. Lena and Tanya couldn't either. The sculptor, Georgy Frangulyan – the artist who made the monument to Okudzhava – proposed a sculpture resembling a rippling Russian flag. At first he made a scale model to show us – we had our doubts, but we thought about it and discussed it, and then we decided: it was just right.

For a year, a simple cross marked the grave, and the mound was covered with artificial grass and wreaths. I didn't see the sculpture before its grand unveiling. When it was put in place, it was covered with white silk; during the ceremony, soldiers removed the drape. It took me a long time to get used to the monument – at first, I couldn't shake the feeling that the massive mound of stone was crushing Boris. I had become accustomed to my husband's new home over the last year – the simple mound and cross. I didn't expect it to be so hard to get used to the change – of course, in time I did, and now I can't imagine a more suitable monument.

Oddly enough, I never thought to ask Tanya and Lena whether they had felt the same way.

*Questions on the Margins*

"Do you still dream about Boris Nikolayevich?"

"Yes, often at times. Then for quite some time I don't dream of him. And then he comes back again."

"It must be hard for you."

"No – I'm glad I have these dreams, and I even talk to him in my dreams – I ask him things, and he answers. I don't believe in paranormal encounters. But I can't claim that they do not exist, either. At least for now."

# Without Boris

They say that time heals – it doesn't. One just adapts to a new way of life, while feeling empty inside. Boris occupied such a large place my life that it's impossible to return to a normal existence without him. I try to, but for me, it will also be a different life.

The Yeltsin Foundation was created with money from private donations, and Tanya keeps it running smoothly as its director. The Foundation established Yeltsin bursaries for the Urals University, and each year I go to Yekaterinburg to hand them out. Some of the Yeltsin bursaries are awarded in Bishkek – to students of the "B.N. Yeltsin" Kyrgyz-Russian Slavic University. Some of the bursaries are also awarded to young tennis players. A tradition has developed: they come to visit me in Gorki, and we sit and drink tea and talk. There is a volleyball tournament in Yekaterinburg each year, where the teams vie for the Cup of the First President of Russia – and of course in Kazan there's the Yeltsin Cup, a large international youth-tennis tournament.

The foundation also helps physically impaired athletes and sick children. Once every two years, in memory of Vera Lotar-Shevchenko, who spent ten years in Stalin's labour camps, the foundation organizes a competition for pianists. The foundation also funds research – most notably into "The History of Stalinism".

In 2008, a law was passed which obliges every president, when leaving his post, to create a legacy centre which tells the story of his presidency. The first created was the Yeltsin Center. At first I was opposed to the idea – the country has so little money and so many problems: should funds really be spent on presidential centres? But then I realized that this was quite right: it's important to collect documents, testimonies, photographs, newsreels which

tell the whole story of Russia's recent history. It is customary
nowadays to see the 1990s in a negative light – but it wasn't all
like that. Yes, we lived through a difficult time – but how could it
have been otherwise, given that the era witnessed the collapse of
a huge country and the construction of a new one in its place?
It's very important to me that discourse on our recent history is
honest – without embellishment, but also without exaggerating
its negativity.

We decided the centre should be built in Yekaterinburg. Although
Boris was born in Butka, he always thought of Sverdlovsk as his
native town. After all, it was here that he studied at the Institute,
it was here that he met me and worked for the greater part of
his life. The venue was chosen – a building which had recently
been erected on the Iset River Embankment. The Moscow-based
architect Boris Bernaskoni took on the modernization of the
building – it turned out to be quite complicated to adapt it
into a museum. Tanya and Valya flew to the construction site
almost every week – it was exhausting for them. Tanya said
she remembered what it had been like working with Papa – the
experience came in handy. A large team of historians, archivists
and writers created the museum, and the space was organized
based on a suggestion by the film director Pavel Lungin. The
American company Ralph Appelbaum Associates, one of the
leading museum-design companies, also played a part in the
project.

I visited the centre several times while the construction work
was in progress, but I couldn't imagine how those cement walls
could be turned into a museum. I only saw the completed centre
a day before the official opening. Tanya asked everyone to leave
us alone in the museum, and she and I went through all the
rooms – reliving those years together. I had tears in my eyes,
but I kept composed – it was only in Boris's office, when I heard
his voice on the tape of his farewell address, that I broke down,
and it took a while for Tanya to calm me down. I sat there for a
while, and when I regained my composure I went into the Hall of

Freedom – an enormous, bright space with panoramic windows and a painting by Erik Bulatov taking up the entire wall. I hugged Tanya. "Aren't you and Valya great? You did all this!" I said. "It wasn't us – there was a whole team," said Tanya, and she led me through to meet the colleagues with whom she had worked on the museum. I shook everyone's hand heartily. I had been so impressed that words failed me.

The Yeltsin Center is alive and well. It has become a favourite spot for many city residents – I sense that each time I visit. There are so many interesting things there, and the exhibitions change regularly, so my only regret is not having enough time to see everything. Since the museum opened, hundreds of thousands of people have come to visit – we never expected that there would be so many. Lectures are held in the Educational Centre, always fully attended; public discussions are held in the Cinema-Conference Hall, as well as film premieres, interviews with directors and other events... the hall is always buzzing. There is also the wonderful Piotrovsky bookshop, the Newton Park for children, which also has a science section, a children's café, the 1991 Café and the BarBoris restaurant – which has two of my desserts on its menu.

Most of all, I am glad that the Yeltsin Center didn't become a formal memorial – it's a very lively place. The museum itself, with its honest approach to our history, sparks a sincere dialogue about things which are important to everyone. I think Boris would have liked it.

Our whole family went to the grand opening. We still live in Moscow – none of us have left – although there has been much speculation about this in the press. Our youngest granddaughter, Masha, studies in London, and our grandson Vanya goes to the University of Chicago – but even their home is here, in Russia.

My eldest granddaughter, Katya, has three children. Her sister, Masha, has two. Tanya's eldest, Borya, is already a grown man. He doesn't have a family yet. He is in the movie business, and several years ago he opened a nursery school in Moscow with some friends.

Gleb has met with amazing success in sports. In April 2015, he won the IPC Swimming World Championships for Russia, as well as a silver medal at the Special Olympics World Summer Games in Los Angeles. Here in Moscow, he trains young swimmers with Down's syndrome. He is good at drawing, and can make himself understood in English. He knows many pieces of classical music by heart – Bach, Tchaikovsky, Mozart, Beethoven – and plays some shorter pieces himself. He does yoga and acts in an amateur theatre.

Even while Boris was still alive, our home in Gorki-10 needed some repairs – but it turned out that the basement was flooded and the foundations had been damaged, so we needed more than simple cosmetic repairs. The house had to be rebuilt from scratch. I was only able to move back in 2012.

*Questions on the Margins*

"Did you get used to your new home easily?"

"No – and I didn't expect it to be so difficult, although apparently my doctor, Natalya Nikolayevna Nekrasova, warned my daughters the move wouldn't be easy for me. After Boris's death, while the house was being rebuilt, I lived in Barvikha for five years. I was used to everything there – it was our place. But in the new house, I didn't feel at home, although we took all our furniture there. For about a month I had to keep reminding myself that this place had been chosen by Boris for the two of us. He liked the view over the river; the apple trees we planted when he was alive were still there – I tried to talk myself into liking it."

"And did you end up liking it?"

"There was a definite turning point. I have the Virgin of Vladimir icon in the bedroom, and I went up to it one day and started thinking. I don't know how long I stood before it – but I suddenly felt a sense of relief, and my tension dissipated. When I came out of the bedroom, everything felt like home."

The house is spacious – there are three rooms for the grandchildren and the great-grandchildren, and a great hall on the first floor full of bookcases – part of the library which Boris began to collect back in Sverdlovsk. This is where I keep his memoirs, in various editions: *Against the Grain*, *Midnight Diaries* and *The Struggle for Russia*.

My favourite spot in the house is the little dining room with floor-to-ceiling windows – just like the one we had in Barvikha. Of course, we can't fit the whole family in, but when there are just a few guests I receive them there, and it is there that I have lunch, watch the TV and read newspapers – I even worked on my book there sometimes.

The only thing I regret is that this house doesn't have a wooden veranda, something I have always loved in other houses.

The property grounds are covered with pine, fir and birch trees. I must say, I don't like it when trees block out the light, and I sometimes feel they weigh down on me – I'm more a steppe-dweller than a forest lover – so I made sure there were lots of open spaces around the house, with just bushes and flowers. From early spring until late autumn, there is always something in bloom – the crocuses appear first, before the snow has even melted, then tulips and narcissi, then peonies, roses, daisies and petunias. And by the autumn, the white clusters of hydrangeas become dark pink, and remain so until the snow falls. In the autumn, we cut them and put them in vases around the house. I really love arranging flowers; I make the bouquets for the house myself.

I love to work in the orchard and in the garden. We grow our own cucumbers, tomatoes, herbs, apples and berries, and since we have greenhouses, there are fresh tulips all year round, enough for the entire family. My daughters find it funny – I even grow potatoes.

There are many kinds of tree in the grounds. I don't like birches very much – I read somewhere that they shouldn't be planted near a house, and I think that's right. When Tanya planted some young trees near the house, she and I argued about it. Of course, we laughed about it later.

*Questions on the Margins*

"What do you do in your spare time besides gardening?"

"I spend a lot of time reworking old clothes. I don't do it myself, of course – I take them to a seamstress – but I think of what I want done to them. Sometimes I ask for the sleeves to be shortened, the shoulders to be removed or the colour changed. Fashions change, but the fabric is still good. My daughters tell me: 'Stop it – let's buy something new!' But I don't want to – each dress brings back some memories, many of which are of Boris. Besides, I'm used to them, and it is very hard to part with them. That applies to the furniture and the tableware too. Old things give me comfort."

My daughters keep an eye on me, of course. They make sure I don't overstrain myself – I have a fair number of engagements at the Yeltsin Center. They often bring things to cheer me up – but I scold them. What do I need another pair of shoes or a blouse for? But I understand that they enjoy doing this. And I try to help them out, too – sometimes I look after the great-grandchildren at my house, or prepare a meal I know the family loves and pack it in baskets and send it to them.

I have been ill very rarely in my life, but problems have begun to appear with age. I don't like to speak of my ailments – I try to endure them. Even while Boris was still alive, I had troubles with my legs, and at one point I was barely able to walk. The doctors' prognosis was not very reassuring: "There's nothing to be done – you'll need a wheelchair in a few years." But then we went on holiday to Kislovodsk, and Boris's masseur examined me and suggested massages, which helped a lot. Then, back in Moscow, I found a doctor who gave me the correct diagnosis: the treatment yielded results, and I literally began to run.

At a certain point, Valya and Tanya became enthusiastic about yoga. I tried it at their recommendation, and I worked with a trainer for several years. This was also of great help.

I rarely watch television now – instead I read. I love memoirs, and I have recently become addicted to audiobooks. When I go for a walk, I usually listen to music – either my favourite popular songs or classical music.

We still get together as a family for Sunday dinners. The family has grown very large – including the grandchildren and the great-grandchildren, there are seventeen of us now. When it's warm, we eat outside by the Russian stove, and inside when it's cold. We eat the food my daughters, their husbands, the grandchildren and the great-grandchildren like.

We try to spend holidays together, too – and we all get together for my birthday. They always give me some treat – they make arrangements well in advance, thinking up unexpected presents. When I turned eighty-four, Tanya bought me a thousand pink roses, which had an amazing fragrance, and put them in glass vases all over the house. It was like stepping inside a fairy tale.

*Questions on the Margins*

"Do you ever feel the need to be alone?"

"I've never thought about it. When I'm alone, I don't have time to think about whether I like it or not – I look through papers, leaf through photo albums… there are so many unfinished projects, and I won't live for ever. There are still boxes to be sorted, folders of papers I have yet to get round to filing – only I can do it, and it keeps me busy. I also have my great-grandchildren, and I try to spend as much spare time with them as I can."

There are always so many things to do, and there isn't enough time. Very often in recent years I've planned to watch the sun rise over the river in the summer, as I used to do in Barvikha, but I always remember when it is autumn already.

Sometimes I wake up at night with a sense of alarm, and can't fall asleep again. I get up and try to distract myself, and start doing the laundry. A blouse, scarves – whatever comes to hand.

This calms me. I even put up a washing line on the balcony, which is the best way to hang out clothes to dry.

I don't know what depression is – it's not a state I'm familiar with, perhaps because I've never had time to think about myself, and I've always had a lot of people close to me who needed my help. I hope it will remain this way.

The weather doesn't affect my mood. I like to walk, even in the rain – if it's snowing, I feel good; if there's no snow, I feel good too. I like spring best of all, but each season has its charm. Joy can be found in everything. I think I know how to find it, and I know how to be happy.

– Yekaterinburg, 2013–17